THE TREKKING CHEF

W9-CSH-308

THE TREKKING CHEF

Claudine Martin

Illustrations by
Karen Jacobsen

Lyons & Burford
Publishers

Copyright © 1989 by Claudine Martin

ALL RIGHTS RESERVED. No part of this book may be reproduced in any manner without the express written consent of the publisher, except in the case of brief excerpts in critical reviews and articles. All inquiries should be addressed to Lyons & Burford, 31 West 21 Street, New York, NY 10010.

Designed by Mary McBride

Printed in the United States of America

10 9 8 7 6 5 4 3 2 1

Library of Congress Cataloging-in-Publication Data

Martin, Claudine.
    The trekking chef / Claudine Martin.
        p.   cm.
    Includes index.
      ISBN 1-55821-005-9 : $11.95
      1. Outdoor cookery.   I. Title.
    TX823.M298   1989
    641.5′78—dc20   89-12345
                                                              CIP

Contents

	INTRODUCTION	vii
1	HUT-TO-HUT SKIING	1
2	A HELICOPTER SKIING PICNIC	46
3	SNOW CAMPING	56
4	SEA KAYAKING	84
5	BACKPACKING	123
6	LLAMA TREKKING	154
7	NEW YEAR'S EVE IN A YURT	182
	INDEX	198

Introduction

It was the full moon before Easter. Around the kitchen table of a rustic ski ranch outside Sun Valley, Idaho, a rowdy group was celebrating the ranch's closing night. I happened to sit next to Bob Jonas. In the general brouhaha I could barely perceive what he was talking about: A dream of his was becoming real; he talked about guiding people into the wilderness areas of the world; on foot, on skis, in kayaks.... He would call his company "Sun Valley Trekking"; in the mountains nothing was hidden from him, and he would share this secret with others....

The dream fascinated me. I had never thought the mountains could become a familiar place, I had never traveled on foot, or on skis, or by kayak; I had never carried a backpack. But if anyone could follow him into the wilderness, so could I....

"How do you feed people on a long trek?" I asked. "You need a chef. Let me be your chef!"

So, in a cry from the heart, *The Trekking Chef* was born.

A large section of our society has developed a fascination for FITNESS. This is due, in part, to our new concepts of beauty. Our ancestors achieved physical beauty with tight corsets, wigs, perfume, lace, and ruffles. We are content, nowadays, only if the body is naturally beautiful with strong muscles and a lean, flexible structure.

These new criteria for beauty, some cravings for physical challenges, and maybe a congenital reaction to too much comfort manifest themselves in the numerous activities that have become part of our lives—indoors, with various forms of exercise from the ancient yoga and martial arts to the modern aerobics; outdoors, with as many variations as the human mind can conceive to master water, rock, and air.

A fast-growing number of people now choose a back-country adventure for their recreation needs. The "pension-hotel-with-view-on-the-beach" or the campground accessible by car does not satisfy them anymore. Indeed, our modern technology has the ability to fulfill one escapade dream after another; man-made fabrics keep us warm and dry, new materials allow strong, lightweight equipment for shelters and gear.

On the collective level, nations conquer space; on the individual level, we are given means to become "explorers," "adventurers." Fewer than a hundred years ago, such a person, one in a million, was regarded as an eccentric, sometimes with respect if his venture was supported by science or politics, many more times with disdain, if he was just an ordinary citizen. No wonder they were so very few: they were confronting an unknown, often hostile world, with the most inadequate equipment. Imagine walking on glaciers with army boots, portaging heavy, wet canvas tents, surviving on bacon and crackers . . .

It is quite ironical, though, that our civilization, with its technology, gives us means to unveil the secrets of this planet, reach its most inaccessible spots, explore its hidden treasures; and yet, with the same technology, we pollute its air and water, endanger its animal and plant species, and harm our physical and mental health with unnatural food and stress. I cannot help but see, in our common drive toward oceans, deserts, and mountaintops, an urge to escape the pollution and stress of the cities, maybe a desire to see the quiet and serene places while they still exist . . . Thank goodness, if man's ingenuity almost destroyed our beloved planet, it still allows him to discover so much of its charm, grandeur and exquisiteness that a new consciousness has risen to save it.

The same story is true for the way we have been feeding ourselves. Our ancestors, either peasants and fishermen in villages or hunters and foragers of nomadic tribes ate natural foods and preserved them in natural ways for the times when no fresh food was available. Their lives were made precarious by the many risks taken to find the food and the many dangers of their environment—tribal fights, wars, invasions, natural disasters, and epidemics. Nowadays, we have eliminated many of these dangers; there is less risk involved in selecting food in a supermarket than in hunting or fishing, but the greatest threat to our health is the food that our scientific ingenuity has created for us.

It makes sense to want to "preserve" our food, to give it a long shelf life, to grow fat animals in no time, to protect crops from diseases and pests. We thought we could do it with chemicals and hormones; we are finding out that we are creating a nation of sick people. The medical research is discovering that our new calamities such as cancer and heart disease are related to our nutrition. We learn the lesson: Now we have "health food stores," unheard of years ago; doctors emphasize the importance of prevention; many of us rediscover the knowledge of the past with natural ways and remedies.

When, with my desire for new adventures and my love for the mountains, I volunteered to become the cook for an outfitting enterprise, I knew very little of the challenge this new life was to offer me. With my faith in and admiration for the technology that provides us with clothing and equipment, I could not find any satisfactory "expedition food." I would read well-intentioned literature advising backpackers to take salami, bacon, processed cheese, instant soups, canned foods, chocolate candy, and beverages, etc., on the premise that these items contain not only many calories but also preservatives that will make them last without refrigeration; that their artificial flavor enhancers would guarantee optimum taste in spite of the processing. I even saw people follow their advice.

In our time, when so many people are changing their eating habits for health reasons, eating more natural foods, vegetables, fruits, and fish, and fewer processed and chemically treated and fatty and refined products, why, as they sojourn in a wilderness area, should they use the foods they avoid at home? Why should they accumulate garbage in their intestines and arteries as they escape the pollution of the civilized world, "cleanse their spirit," in John Muir's words?

My first task as a backcountry chef was made easy by the circumstances: short hut-to-hut skiing trips. I could plan excellent meals, using fresh and natural ingredients. Preservation was not a problem; we were moving in a naturally refrigerated environment. Many times, though, it is a freezing environment! I learned to adjust to this by blanching and freezing fresh vegetables ahead of time, by tucking a box of fresh herbs or other delicate ingredients inside my sleeping bag to insulate them. Weight was not a problem, either, within limits, thanks to our sleds pulled by strong guides who use skins under their skis for a better grip. I learned then to reduce weight by trimming all nonedible excess from vegetables and bones from meats. I reduced the weight of soups by cooking them ahead of time with only a small amount of the water needed. Each became a thick purée that could be contained in a quart bottle and would turn into a soup for twelve at the campsite by adding water and warming it up.

The real challenge came when I was faced with the task of packing the food for a ten-day snow-camping expedition of ten members. I asked technology for the answer: I tried freeze-dried food. I found this solution less than satisfactory! Those dishes with wonderful names like Cordon Bleu, Stroganoff, à la king, have lost all flavor, unless a flavor enhancer is used. Besides, with a little investigation and my personal experience I realized that the human body is not able to use the nutrients of a product that has been so radically treated. So, I remembered our heritage, that we are children of nomadic or agrarian societies that have survived for centuries without our modern luxuries, and did not suffer from stress, pollution, or starvation. I studied how they treated their foods for preservation and transportation purposes. Their natural methods of dehydrating vegetables and fruits, smoking meat and fish, fermenting raw milk and clarifying butter, did not produce tribes and, later, nations of sick people. On the contrary, they bred strong, healthy men and women, some living to be 120, 140 years old in some regions of the world before technology touched them with its magic wand.

In this book, I intend to share the results of my experiences in order to provide the adventurous amateur with a guide to proper nutrition in the backcountry, ways to prepare ingredients for the trail that eliminate weight and spoilage, and the enjoyment of an easy meal-preparation routine.

PROPER NUTRITION

It is becoming more evident every day that proper nutrition is essential to a healthy life. I believe that in the backcountry it is even more necessary in order to assure a constant level of energy. Junk foods, candy bars, refined foods, don't do that! Plain sugar rushes to the blood and gives the illusion of high energy for a short time only to drop it later. Refined foods, called "empty calorie foods," do not provide nourishment for the body, and worst of all, use its energy to be digested. You want food that gives you lasting energy without its being wasted. Only natural whole foods will give you this kind of fuel: whole grains, legumes, and nuts. In addition, vegetables and fruits provide the supplemental vitamins and minerals that assure proper bodily functions. This diet will also build up your resistance to the environment, its climate and terrain. It will enhance the body's capacity to heal rapidly many ailments that can affect you. Actually many of the herbs and spices that are in my kitchen kit are excellent remedies for colds, indigestion, burns, sprains, etc. For example, cayenne pepper has been known to stop a heart attack in fifteen seconds. It is also nonacidic, the only kind of pepper used as a contact healer. My first-aid kit is in my pantry.

FOOD-DRYING

Almost any food can be dehydrated. Only fats are the exception. Vegetables, fruits, lean meat and seafood, cooked grains, legumes, and eggs can submit to this method. The same method can be used to make healthy snacks: fruit leather and bars, chips, bean snacks. The recipes are given throughout the book.

Dehydration is a simple process in which moisture is removed. Its advantages are numerous:

1. Since most of the weight in foods is water, it is eliminated.
2. Bacteria that cause spoilage cannot develop without water, so dehydrated foods can keep for months, even years, and recover their original freshness as soon as water is added.
3. The food is not cooked, so the life force is preserved. You can plant a seed from a dried tomato slice and a plant will grow! However, it is indispensable that the food be dried

naturally, without blanching or using chemicals, at a low temperature: 110°F to 120°F, to avoid cooking it.

4. The natural flavors are enhanced; and if flavor is already an important source of pleasure in normal life, it becomes a supreme enjoyment on the trail.

5. Drying is incredibly easy. The steps are:

- Wash the food, eliminate any spoiled parts;
- slice, dice, shred, purée it;
- place it on trays;
- put the trays into the dehydrator for any length of time, varying with the type of food and its preparation;
- when the food is dry, remove from the trays, and place it in paper, plastic bags, jars, whatever;
- store it in a cool, dark, dry place.

If you want to know more about food-drying, I recommend my favorite book on this subject: *Food-Drying at Home, the Natural Way*, by Bee Beyer, published by J. P. Tarcher, Inc., Los Angeles.

THE ENJOYMENT OF A SPECIAL TIME IN THE FIELD

I was reared in France, in a society where meals are a joyful time shared by the family in preparation, in the delectation of a succession of dishes, during which the conversation flows and bonds are renewed. A similar ambiance is re-created in the preparation of the Trekking Chef's meals: the way the food is packed in several bags, the instructions that everyone can share to rehydrate the food, cook some of the ingredients, add the rest.... It becomes a ceremony where simplicity and camaraderie reinforce the pleasure of an adventure shared together. Even if you are traveling alone, the daily routine of taking the time to prepare a tasty meal turns it into a meaningful ceremony. One doesn't get this kind of pleasure out of emptying a bag of freeze-dried food into a pot with some water and warming it up—especially if the result is tasteless.

Of course, the Trekking Chef's type of preparation is not for every kind of adventure. There are times when a quick preparation has its validity: for climbers at a high elevation, for expedition assaults, a one-day rapid ascent, a kayak rapid descent ... for any backcountry endeavor where food is secondary and its appreciation compromised for the sake of speed.

EQUIPMENT
Two simple tools are necessary for the preparation of the trail food at home:

A HOME FOOD DEHYDRATOR
It is important to possess a good-quality food-dehydrator that circulates the drying air evenly and is equipped with a thermostat. As we have said before, it is essential to be able to regulate the temperature to an even and steady 110°F to 120°F. Below this temperature, the food will spoil before it is dried; above, it will burn, scorch, and cook.

A SEAL-A-MEAL MACHINE
Sealing the meals' ingredients in one or several plastic pouches, expelling as much air as possible, ensures that they will remain fresh and unspoiled. Sometimes the ingredient is liquid, like Tamari sauce, another reason for the bag to be sealed.

Some other items are of great help when packaging expedition food:

PLASTIC BAGS WITH HERMETIC CLOSURES
I will use these when the food that is to be contained is not used up all at once. Seal-a-meal bags, once opened, cannot be used again. Certain ingredients, like soy-milk powder, turbinado sugar, tea bags, must be in bags you can open and close many times. I like these bags because they do not need a twister or tag that can be dropped and trash the place. It is advisable to double-bag them to prevent them from bursting open inside a stuffed sack under pressure.

DUCT TAPE
My favorite tool, I would not go anywhere without duct tape. It repairs, holds, seals anything. I seal food containers by running the tape all around the closures. Nothing has ever leaked sealed in this manner.

On the trail, no other equipment than the standard camping gear is required.

A GOOD STOVE

My preference is for a stove that burns liquid fuel: white gas, kerosene, or the like. These fuels perform better at high altitudes and give a hotter fire. MSR's Whisperlite International stove burns all fuels, weighs less than twelve ounces, and the flame can be adjusted from high to low.

A SET OF STAINLESS STEEL POTS AND PANS

Even though aluminum is a better metal for distributing the heat evenly, I don't like the way it poisons our food with its oxide. Stainless steel is safe and easy to clean. Its cooking performance has been improved by Coleman, who paints the bottom of the pot with copper. MSR sells a heat exchanger: a piece of corrugated brass that can be adjusted to fit around any pot and increases the cooking ability by 25 percent.

A lot of The Trekking Chef's recipes call for a "deep skillet." For my own use, I bought in a hardware store a cheap lightweight nonstick ten-inch skillet; I removed the handle (make sure you buy one with a screwed-on handle) to make it easier to pack. When I cook in it, I use a pot gripper to hold it.

If I have enough space in my pack I take along one of my favorite cooking tools—a mini wok that was given to me by a friend and that comes totally apart. It is equipped with all the paraphernalia: ring, grills, lid, spatula, and spoons, all very lightweight. It has a nonstick inside coating.

For dinnerware I favor metal above plastic. I use a Frontier enamel plate, shaped like a pie plate. It can be used while you are cooking to keep food warm near or above the campfire. The best mug is REI's stainless Thermo Mug, with an insulating space sandwiched inside a double wall.

SPECIAL INGREDIENTS

BULGUR

This is a fine cracked wheat that has been steamed and dried. Just like dehydrated precooked grains, it is ready in a very short time in the field.

CLARIFIED BUTTER
Or butterfat, it is produced by removing all the water, curd, and whey from the milk. It needs no refrigeration, no preservative, and has a twelve-month shelf life, guaranteed. An Idaho company, Odell's, packages it in easy-to-carry ¾-ounce pouches.

COUSCOUS
France's occupation of the North-African territories for many years enriched the culinary French tradition with many ethnic dishes. Couscous, the staple food of Morocco, Algeria, and Tunisia, is one of them. The traditional Arabic preparation of couscous is a lengthy labor of love, by which the only ingredient, wheat flour, is hand-rubbed with water to form tiny grains that are steamed, rubbed again, steamed again, and so on. The couscous we buy nowadays is precooked and dried. All we have to do is bring to a boil a liquid—salty water, milk, or stock, with a little butter, stir in the couscous, cover the pot, and let it stand five minutes—perfect for the backcountry! I use it for breakfasts and dinners, and also in salads. For dinner in our yurts, I like to use a method as close to the traditional Arabic one as possible. This method is described in Chapter 1.

FREEZE-DRIED EGGS
Even though I see no value in freeze-dried food, I do use freeze-dried eggs for convenience. I use eggs in so many recipes that I could not dehydrate at home all that I need. Moreover, eggs spoil so easily that I am afraid that if they were not perfectly dehydrated, it could result in some spoilage, and you know the unpleasant smell! I use Backpacker's Pantry scrambled eggs mix.

HEINZ INSTANT BABY FOOD
Heinz company makes little cans of dehydrated baby food: vegetables, fruits, puddings. They are totally natural and re-constitute instantly. Whenever I want some apple sauce, or banana cream, or puréed berries, I open a few cans, transfer their contents to a plastic pouch, and pack it with the rest.

HONEY FLAKES
Honey can be dehydrated and comes then in dry flakes. It is a lot less messy in a pack, and lighter, too. It does not recon-

stitute very well if you want to sweeten a drink, but it works well when cooked in the morning cereal. I get it from a health food local wholesaler.

INSTANT PROTEIN POWDER

Many health food stores sell protein powder mixes that you can use as a substitute for breakfast or lunch, or as extra energy food for athletes. Choose a kind you like and add it to your favorite recipes as I do.

INSTANT VEGETABLE-STOCK POWDER

Health food stores sell vegetable and spice powder mixes to use as salt substitutes. I choose a kind that also makes delicious stock base; I use it as a soup base and wherever salt is needed.

KASHA

Kasha is the Russian name for toasted buckwheat groats. It is not a grain but a fruit, and one of the best-known nutritional foods. For the backcountry, I precook and dehydrate it to use for breakfasts and dinners.

KOREAN SOUP

Chinese and Korean shops have a lot of treasures for back-packers; they provide many dried foods: shrimp, mushrooms, soups, even anchovies. The Korean soup I use in Chapter 3 has no food enhancer or chemicals. It is made of noodles and seaweed in a spicy fish stock.

POTATO FLAKES

Whenever I need potatoes in casseroles or soups or to make hot cakes I use a natural instant mashed-potato mix.

PRESSED BARLEY

I found pressed barley for the first time in a Korean shop. It cooks as fast as quick-cooking oats. It saves me from cooking and dehydrating pearl barley.

RICE-BRAN SYRUP

Nutritionally, rice-bran syrup is a "good" kind of sweetener. I buy a product that is a mixture of rice-bran extract, wheat-germ extract and malt extract. It tastes a lot like molasses.

SOY-MILK POWDER
Nutritionists say that dairy products really are not good for adults. Indeed, no wild animals drink milk after weaning. The only kind of milk I use to drink or in recipes is soy milk, a nondairy product. Many varieties of soy milk taste too sweet for me, but I have found a good kind that tastes just like milk.

STEVIA
This is a very sweet-tasting plant with many healing properties, and it contains no sugar. Much research has been done in Japan, and Stevia is likely to become the natural non-sugar sweetener of the future. It can be found in powder form in good health food stores.

SUGAR—TURBINADO
If I really have to use sugar, then I use turbinado, which is not as refined as white sugar.

CHEESE
I choose to buy sliced cheese: Swiss, Monterey, and mozzarella. This cheese is commercially sealed in plastic, in six-ounce packages. This is the right amount for each lunch, with the convenience of not having to pack each portion myself. Also, trying to slice frozen cheese on the trail with a pocket knife always results in a mess.

1

Hut-to-Hut Skiing

Among all the forms of expeditions for which I have had to prepare the food, hut-to-hut skiing remains my favorite.

Such trips have helped my companion Bob Jonas create a successful business, guiding small groups for trips of several days' length into the spectacular Sawtooth Range outside Sun Valley, Idaho. So many factors help minimize all the challenges that outdoor adventures present: The winter climate there creates an immense refrigerator in which, nine days out of ten, we can move comfortably with the right clothing in the warmth of a brilliant sun. It is an immense refrigerator in which food cannot spoil and which sustains Bob's perfectly equipped operation with a group of strong guides for whom pulling a two-hundred-pound sled is almost easy.

The rewards have always surpassed the efforts: the pleasure of our customers' renewing their bonds with the natural world, a world made more magical in the winter season with the whites and blues of ice and snow; and their applause at discovering that fun skiing, comfort, and good food are all part of their experience.

Hut-to-hut skiing is one of the easiest and most enjoyable forms of backcountry adventure. Besides the fact that there are no bugs around, the climate is usually to our advantage. The only challenge in this regard is to prevent food spoilage by freezing. For example, I can't imagine cooking without herbs, and I usually use them fresh unless I have dehydrated them myself; I have no use for commercially dehydrated herbs. The best way to transport fresh herbs on the winter trail (herbs such as the coriander for day number three) is to place them in a small box, tucked in the middle of my sleeping bag inside my pack. I have been known to sleep with them, too. If I want to serve fresh green vegetables like the green beans for day number four, instead of losing them because they have frozen on the trail in their raw state, I blanch and freeze them at home before departure.

I also pre-freeze all fresh meat: lamb, veal, chicken— trimmed, boned, and cut as required by the instructions. This reduces the amount of work at the campsite and, more importantly, avoids any excess weight. The meat is often still frozen when I am ready to use it, or is in the process of slow thawing, which is perfect.

Many other foods, like the soups, breads, cakes, and crêpes, can be frozen ahead of time. Foods that should not freeze, like the eggs or the lentil salad, are wrapped in several layers of newspaper, which can always be used to start the fire in the huts. Actually, the food will rarely freeze on the trail during the day, with the Idaho sun constantly brightening our days. At night we place all of it in the hut inside a "cooler," mis-named in this case since its purpose is to keep the food from getting too cold.

Freezing also helps preserve fragile pastries on a rough trail. The sleds allow me many luxuries—fresh food, wine, boxes instead of bags; but even if the guides and some of our guests don't mind pulling the extra weight, they cannot guar-antee a smooth journey. The sled is often tossed about, some-times tipped over in irregular terrain. But I can still serve intact "Turkish Birds' Nests" and "Chicken Boreks" if I have prefrozen them and packed them in a box (cardboard or plastic) with a lot of waxed paper.

Most of the food served on this sort of trip is cooked ahead of time: the baked items—breads, cakes, pastries, snackbars—the pâtés, salads, relishes, and spreads, and the sauces such as fruit sauces, pesto, coriander butter. The soups are made ahead, too, but with a difference: I put into them just the amount of water necessary to cook, cutting it down to a half or quarter of the total amount. Actually, I prepare a thick purée with less weight and less volume than the regular soup. Remember, water is the heavy ingredient in all foods. I have been able to pack soup for twelve people in a plastic quart bottle by just adding two more quarts of water to it at the campsite.

Does all this appear to you as a lot of preparation work before a trip? Indeed, it is! A five-day trip keeps me in the kitchen for three full days. But if you cannot afford three such days, with more planning you will be able to cook one evening here, one weekend there, in the month ahead, freezing the stuff as you go along. I believe that this type of planning and work ahead of time helps every aspect of the trip by avoiding spoilage and extra weight and by making the cook's respon-sibility much lighter: less work, no worry, and more time to go out and play with the rest of the group.

MENUS

DAY 1
◆
LUNCH

*Spinach pâté sandwiches with
mustard mayonnaise and mini Italian loaves
Pickled carrots, cheese slices
Crisp apples* and apricot bars*

DINNER

*Green pea soup
Garlic pita toasts
Moroccan lamb tagine with apricots
Steamed couscous
Turkish birds' nests*

DAY 2
◆
BREAKFAST

*Crêpes with gooseberry sauce
Chicken Boreks in shredded phyllo dough*

LUNCH

*Cream cheese-Parmesan spread with pumpernickel bread
Toasted soybeans and stuffed litchi nuts
Tofu cream bars*

DINNER

*Herbed tomato soup
Italian country bread, sweet butter
Lemon tarragon veal*

*Citrus fruits are excellent frozen and thawed, but fruits that
are high in water content freeze very easily and spoil. I therefore serve apples on the first day only.

Zucchini and spaghetti with pesto
St. James carob cake

DAY 3
◆
BREAKFAST

Orange slices
Cast-iron egg and cheese puff
Idaho potato braided bread
Sweet butter and preserves

LUNCH

Smoked fish spread with dried vegetable slices: tomato, beet, zucchini, celery root
Shrimp rolls
Mixed nuts and protein bars

DINNER

Stilton cauliflower soup, melba toasts
Grilled chicken breasts with coriander-lime butter
Brown rice with herbs
Date-walnut cake, rice-bran syrup glaze

DAY 4
◆
BREAKFAST

Orange slices
Oatmeal cream with fruit sauce
Sugarless gingerbread
Sweet butter and orange marmalade

LUNCH

Orange red lentil salad with Finland country bread
Feta cheese-red pepper spread with blue corn chips
Nutty-rye bars

DINNER

Almond soup, pita bread
Tofuburgers with red pepper sauce
Steamed green beans
Orange raisin cake

DAY 5
◆
BREAKFAST

Blueberry buttermilk pancakes
Blueberry-honey sauce, poached pears

LUNCH

Backcountry minestrone
Crusty bread and provolone cheese
Dried figs and papaya

BEVERAGES
◆

On the trail, water is a must. In cold weather, dehydration can be a very devious yet more serious danger than in warm weather. I like to put slices of lemon into the water, or use a good instant lemonade mix rich in vitamin C.

At the hut there are always two steaming pots on the stove: one with water for various herbal teas and instant hot chocolate, the other with coffee. White wine stays cold outside, stuck in the snow; the red wine is well "chambré" (brought to yurt temperature) near the wood stove.

SANDWICHES

SPINACH PÂTÉ

Number of servings: 8

PREPARATION:

Location: Must be prepared at home before the trip. Can be stored frozen.

Equipment: Electric blender or food processor. 8½ -by-4½ -inch loaf pan, waxed paper, and foil.

Time: 20 minutes preparation, 1 hour baking.

*I use only red pepper or cayenne in cooking. Black or white pepper is too acid. Red pepper is soothing, can heal stomach ulcers, and has been reputed to stop a heart attack in fifteen seconds.

INSTRUCTIONS:

Preheat the oven to 375°F.

Grease the loaf pan with soft butter. Line the bottom with waxed paper. Grease the paper, too.

Heat 1 cup of water with a pinch of salt in a medium-size saucepan. When water boils add the frozen spinach, cover the pot, and let it simmer over low heat until the spinach is completely thawed. Drain the spinach in a colander, rinse it with cold water, drain again, and with your hands squeeze all the moisture out. Reserve.

In the food processor, mix together cream, eggs, tuna, scallions, anchovies drained out of the milk, lemon juice, salt and pepper, and any other flavorings of your choice. Process the mixture until it looks like a smooth cream. Turn it into a mixing bowl. Add the bread crumbs and the spinach. Stir to mix well. Pour into the loaf pan. Cover tightly with a piece of foil. Place inside a larger baking pan, filled 2 inches high with boiling water. Place the whole thing in the preheated oven and bake for at least an hour, or until an inserted tooth-

INGREDIENTS:

20 ounces frozen chopped spinach (2 boxes)

¾ cup heavy cream

3 large eggs

4 ounces canned tuna in spring water

½ cup minced scallion (1 bunch)

10 anchovy fillets (1 can), soaked 10 minutes in milk

2 tablespoons lemon juice

⅓ cup soft bread crumbs

1 teaspoon salt, ⅛ teaspoon red pepper*

Optional: Dried thyme, mace, minced garlic, capers, chopped olives to taste

pick comes out clean and wet. Cool to room temperature.

To store the pâté, unmold it, peel off the waxed paper, pat with paper towels to absorb excess moisture, then wrap in a plastic film. The pâté will keep 2 or 3 days in the refrigerator. Freeze it for longer storage. The day before your trip, transfer it to the refrigerator to start thawing. Transport it in a plastic box sealed with duct tape.

SPINACH PÂTÉ SANDWICHES

The sandwiches are made at the picnic or campsite.

INSTRUCTIONS:
Open the loaves horizontally and spread some mustard mayonnaise on each half of bread. Slice a thick slice of spinach pâté and make a sandwich with the two halves of bread. Repeat with the other loaves. You may add a slice of ham inside each sandwich.

INGREDIENTS:
FOR 8 SANDWICHES
Spinach pâté (see recipe)
Mustard mayonnaise: Mix 1 cup of a good brand natural mayonnaise with 2 tablespoons of Dijon mustard before departure for the trip, and pack it in a small plastic box.
8 individual Italian bread loaves (recipe follows)

CREAM CHEESE-PARMESAN SPREAD

Makes about 1½ cups.

INSTRUCTIONS:
Process all the ingredients together in a food processor. The mixture has a nice pale-green color. I also call it green cheese.

INGREDIENTS:
10 ounces cream cheese
3 ounces freshly grated Parmesan cheese

Transfer it to a plastic container. Refrigerated, it will keep for as long as 5 or 6 days.

2 large cloves of garlic, peeled and chopped
¼ cup packed fresh coriander leaves, chopped
¼ cup packed fresh basil leaves, chopped
Sea salt and cayenne pepper to taste

SMOKED FISH SPREAD

Makes enough spread for 8 sandwiches.

PREPARATION:

Make the spread at home before the trip. It will keep 3 or more days in a plastic container. Cover the surface of the spread with a plastic film to make it airtight, and seal the box with duct tape. It doesn't matter if the spread freezes, but do not let it get warm until the day you use it.

INSTRUCTIONS:

Beat the cheese, horseradish, and lemon juice together. Mash the smoked trout on a plate, removing all skin and bones. Add the smoked fish to the cheese mixture, stirring to blend it well. Add the seasoning and taste to adjust the amount.

SMOKED FISH SPREAD SANDWICHES

To make eight sandwiches, use 8 ounces smoked trout and 16 slices rye bread.

If you want to assemble the sandwiches in the morning, in the hut, where it is warm, before going on a day's tour, and then travel light, each person carrying a sandwich, some snacks, a water bottle, and some personal items, it is a good idea. But the sandwiches may get soggy with the spread. The trick is

INGREDIENTS:
8 ounces smoked trout
8 ounces plain kefir cheese (cheese made from yogurt)
2 tablespoons prepared horseradish
1 tablespoon fresh lemon juice, or more to taste
1 teaspoon kelp, or a little salt; watch if you use salt—the smoked fish is already salty
⅛ teaspoon cayenne pepper

to spread a thin layer of butter on the bread before spreading the smoked trout mixture. Divide the extra smoked fish equally among all the sandwiches, wrap them tightly in a plastic film, and enjoy a day's tour in the white wilderness!

FETA CHEESE-RED PEPPER SPREAD

Makes one cup spread.

PREPARATION:

Make the spread at home and keep it in a plastic box or bag in the cooler. Assemble the sandwiches just before eating.

INSTRUCTIONS:

Blend the Feta, red pepper, and thyme in a food processor until puréed smoothly. With the motor running, add the olive oil in a fine steady stream and blend until smooth. Store the spread in a box and refrigerate it until ready to pack for the trip. The spread will keep up to one week.

INGREDIENTS:
6 ounces Feta cheese, crumbled
1/3 cup chopped red pepper
2 tablespoons olive oil
1 teaspoon crumbled dried thyme leaves.

RELISHES, SNACKS

PICKLED CARROTS

Makes 2 cups.

PREPARATION:

Location: must be prepared at home, one or several days before the trip.
Equipment: 2 saucepans, cheesecloth, and string.

INGREDIENTS:
6 medium carrots
3/4 cup sugar
3/4 cup apple-cider vinegar
3/4 cup water

Time: 20 minutes.

INSTRUCTIONS:

Scrape the carrots. Cut them into 3-inch lengths and each length into thin sticks. Simmer them in a small amount of boiling water for 5 minutes. Drain and rinse them under cold water. Tie all the spices in a piece of cheesecloth with a string and combine the spice bag with all the remaining ingredients in another saucepan. Bring the mixture to a boil and let it simmer for 10 minutes. Pour it over the carrots. Let it cool completely. Transfer the carrots with the liquid to a plastic container with a well-fitted lid. Refrigerate until departure time. Seal the container with duct tape for transportation. To serve, drain the carrot sticks out of the liquid.

1 tablespoon yellow mustard seeds
2½ inches stick cinnamon broken into pieces
3 whole cloves
3 inches fresh orange peel
½ teaspoon ginger
⅛ teaspoon cayenne pepper

STUFFED LITCHI NUTS

Makes 8 servings of 3 stuffed litchi nuts each.

PREPARATION:

You can stuff and store the litchi nuts 2 to 3 days ahead of time. Place them in tight layers in a plastic box with a plastic film or waxed paper between each layer. If there is an empty space between the last layer and the lid, fill it up with crushed waxed paper to secure the contents during transportation.

INSTRUCTIONS:

Drain the canned litchi nuts and reserve.

Mix together, thoroughly, the cream cheese, chopped nuts, minced crystallized ginger, and lemon juice. Fill the cavities of each litchi nut with the cheese mixture, and top each one with a piece of crystallized ginger.

INGREDIENTS:
2 cans of litchi nuts (11-ounce can)
½ pound cream cheese
¼ cup chopped toasted pine nuts or almonds
¼ cup minced crystallized ginger
24 larger pieces of ginger to top the litchi nuts
1 tablespoon fresh lemon juice

TOASTED SOYBEANS

Makes one pound.

PREPARATION:

The soybeans can be toasted several weeks ahead of time and stored in a plastic bag in the refrigerator or freezer.

INSTRUCTIONS:

Soak the beans overnight. Preheat the oven to 350°F.

Drain the beans and toss them with the olive oil. Spread them on a baking sheet. Toast them in the oven for 1 hour or more until golden brown. While still hot, transfer them to a bowl and toss them with the tamari sauce and the spices. Let them cool to room temperature, stirring occasionally to flavor them evenly with the tamari sauce.

INGREDIENTS:
 1 pound whole dried
 soybeans
 2 tablespoons olive oil
 2 tablespoons tamari sauce
 1 tablespoon dry mustard
 1 tablespoon ground cumin
 ¾ teaspoon cayenne pepper

SOUPS

Many soups for the backcountry are precooked at home, using as little water as possible. The result is a thick purée, providing much less volume or weight for the trail. The purée can be frozen in portions of 2 or 4 servings or more. All you have to do at the campsite is reheat the "soup concentrate" with the amount of water necessary to bring it back to normal consistency.

GREEN PEA SOUP WITH MINT

Number of servings: 8.

Equipment: An electric blender or a food mill.

Time: About half an hour at home to cook the peas, purée, and freeze them. Then 10 to 15 minutes at the campsite.

INGREDIENTS:
 8 cups of shelled peas, fresh
 or frozen
 3 or 4 sprigs of fresh mint
 plus ½ cup chopped

INSTRUCTIONS:
Cook the peas in 2 cups of water with the sprigs of fresh mint and the vegetable-stock powder, until they are very tender— about 15 minutes for fresh peas, 7 or 8 minutes for frozen peas. Purée them with the cooking liquid in the electric blender, with the sour cream. Adjust the seasoning with salt and cayenne pepper to taste. Pack the purée in plastic containers with well-fitted lids in quarters (2 servings) or halves (4 servings).

At the campsite, reheat the purée with water: 1½ cups per 2 servings. Stir in 1 tablespoon of chopped fresh mint per serving, and serve piping hot.

fresh mint at the campsite
4 teaspoons vegetable-stock powder
2 cups sour cream

HERBED TOMATO SOUP

Makes 8 servings.

INSTRUCTIONS:
Melt the butter in a heavy-bottom casserole, add the leeks, onion, and garlic; press a buttered foil on the vegetables with the buttered side against them, cover the casserole with a lid, turn the heat down to low, and let the vegetable mixture "sweat" in its own juices for ten minutes.

Uncover the pot, remove the foil, and add the stock powder, the potatoes, tomatoes, and 1 cup of water or tomato juice from the can. Cover the pot again and let its contents simmer over low heat until the potatoes are tender—15 minutes or more. You may have to add a little more water or juice if it gets too dry.

When the potatoes are cooked, add the herbs, salt, and

INGREDIENTS:
6 tablespoons butter
3 medium leeks (white part only), chopped coarsely, then washed thoroughly and drained
1 medium onion, chopped
3 cloves of garlic, chopped
4 teaspoons of instant vegetable-stock powder
2 medium-size potatoes, peeled and cubed; you should have 3 cups

cayenne pepper to taste, and the sugar if necessary, and simmer the mixture 10 more minutes. Purée with a blender or food processor and let the purée cool to room temperature. Store and freeze in plastic boxes as instructed above.

At the campsite, reheat the amount of purée needed, adding ¾ cup of water per 2 servings. When the soup is hot, add ½ cup of buttermilk per 2 servings. The buttermilk may be reconstituted from powder: ¼ cup powder per cup of water.

6 large ripe tomatoes, peeled, seeded, and chopped or 1 large can (1 lb., 12 oz.) whole tomatoes; drain and chop them and use the juice instead of water to dilute the soup concentrate

2 cups chopped fresh herbs, chef's choice: parsley, chives, basil, tarragon, thyme, marjoram, chervil...

1 pinch of sugar if the tomatoes are too acid

2 cups buttermilk, or ½ cup buttermilk powder

Salt and cayenne pepper to taste

STILTON CAULIFLOWER SOUP

Makes 8 servings.

PREPARATION:

Like most of the soups I prepare for backcountry trips, this one is precooked at home with very little liquid, and the result is a thick purée that weighs less for transportation. The "soup concentrate" can be kept frozen in portions of 2, 4, or more servings. This Stilton cauliflower purée can also be used without adding water—which is the procedure to reconstitute the soup—as a dip for vegetables or crackers.

INSTRUCTIONS:

Melt the butter in a heavy-bottom casserole, add the onion, leek, and cauliflowerets, stir them to mix with the butter;

INGREDIENTS:

1 large onion, finely chopped

3 or 4 leeks, white only, chopped

1 pound cauliflowerets (1 medium head cauliflower)

6 tablespoons butter (¾ stick)

2 cups plus ¼ cup soy milk made from powder

1 sprig fresh thyme, or 1 teaspoon dried leaves

lower the heat, cover the vegetables with a buttered foil, buttered side against the vegetables. Cover the casserole with a tight-fitting lid and let the vegetables "sweat" for 10 minutes. Uncover the pot, remove the foil, add the 2 cups of soy milk with the thyme, bay leaf, sage, salt, mace, and cayenne pepper. Bring the mixture to a boil, stirring on high heat; lower the heat and let it simmer, covered, for 25 minutes. The cauliflowerets should be very soft.

Purée the mixture in a food processor, return it to the pan, and adjust the seasoning with pepper; do not add any salt yet because the Stilton cheese is salty. Dissolve the cornstarch in the ¼ cup soy milk, add it to the purée; bring it to a boil again, stirring, and simmer it 2 minutes.

Stir in the Stilton and simmer the soup, whisking, until the cheese is melted—about 1 minute—and the purée is smooth. Let it cool to room temperature, and transfer to one or several plastic containers for storage and transportation. Make sure the containers are securely sealed around the lid with duct tape for transportation.

At the campsite, to make soup, reheat the purée with ½ cup of water added per serving. Bring it to a boil, add ¼ cup buttermilk per serving, reheat, and serve with melba toasts.

Or, to use as a dip, let the purée come back to room temperature, stir in the buttermilk, and serve with toasts, crackers, and vegetables.

1 bay leaf
1 teaspoon rubbed sage
¼ teaspoon each, sea salt, mace
⅛ teaspoon cayenne pepper
2 tablespoons cornstarch
½ pound Stilton cheese, crumbled
1 cup buttermilk, fresh or made from powder

ALMOND SOUP

Makes 8 servings.

PREPARATION:
This soup can be made from scratch at the campsite, using mostly powdered ingredients.

INSTRUCTIONS:
Heat 6 cups of water in a large saucepan. Add the vegetable-stock powder and stir to dissolve. Melt the butter and mix it

INGREDIENTS:
2 tablespoons vegetable-stock powder
¼ cup butter (2 ounces)
2 tablespoons millet meal
2 cups almond meal
¼ teaspoon each ground clove and nutmeg

with the millet. Add the butter mixture to the stock with the almond meal, clove, nutmeg, thyme, garlic, coriander, and cumin. Bring to a boil and keep simmering until just before serving. Stir the cayenne pepper and sherry into the yogurt, and blend into the soup. Reheat and serve.

¼ teaspoon each ground thyme and garlic powder
½ teaspoon each ground coriander and cumin
⅛ teaspoon cayenne pepper
2 cups plain yogurt
¼ cup dry sherry

BACKCOUNTRY MINESTRONE

Makes 8 servings.

PREPARATION:

This soup could be entirely made at the campsite, using fresh ingredients that have been cleaned ahead of time. But if there is a possibility that they might freeze on the trail, when the environmental temperature is below 20°F., you may want to cook the soup ahead of time, with a small amount of water, adding the extra water at the campsite when ready to reheat and serve it.

INSTRUCTIONS:

Bring two quarts of water to a boil in a large saucepan, and add the instant vegetable stock, cumin, rosemary, and oregano. If you are making the soup ahead of time use only 2 cups of water and cook only the vegetables in it. Add the macaroni at the campsite after reheating the soup with 6 cups of water.

Or else: when the broth is boiling, add the macaroni and the vegetables, except the chives, cover the pot, and simmer 30 minutes over low heat. Stir in the chives and ½ cup of grated Parmesan. Cover the pot and simmer the soup 15 minutes, until the vegetables are tender.

To serve, ladle the soup into warm bowls and sprinkle the remaining cheese on top.

INGREDIENTS:
3 tablespoons instant vegetable-stock powder
1 teaspoon ground cumin
2 tablespoons tamari sauce
1 tablespoon each chopped fresh rosemary and oregano leaves, or 1 teaspoon each if dried
1 cup elbow macaroni
1 large potato, peeled and diced
2 bell peppers, red, green, or yellow, seeded and chopped
1 large can of tomatoes (1 lb., 12 oz.)
½ cup each sliced celery and chives
¾ cup grated Parmesan

MEAT AND SEAFOOD DISHES

MOROCCAN LAMB TAGINE WITH APRICOTS

Number of servings: 8

PREPARATION:

Location: The entire dish can be prepared at the hut. The meat is first sautéed in a cast-iron or other heavy-duty casserole, then left to simmer on top of the wood stove, filling the hut with an appetizing aroma. It is important that the meat be trimmed and cubed ahead of time and then packed in a sealed plastic bag. If it is to be used more than a day later, freeze it.

Equipment: A heavy-bottom casserole or Dutch oven.

Time: 1 hour and 45 minutes after the meat has been thawed slowly near the wood stove, if it was transported frozen.

INSTRUCTIONS:

Heat the oil or butterfat in a large heavy casserole or Dutch oven and sauté the meat cubes, a few at a time, transferring them to a bowl when browned on all sides, until all are done.

Add the onion to the casserole and sauté it, stirring and scraping the bottom of the pan to release the meat scraps. When the onion is soft and lightly browned, place the meat back into the casserole with the coriander, cinnamon sticks broken, ginger, cayenne, instant vegetable stock, and 3 cups of water.

Bring the liquid to a boil, cover the pot and let it simmer on the wood stove for 45 minutes. Uncover the pot and let it simmer another 30 minutes, or until the lamb is tender.

Add the apricots, the lemon slices, and the honey. Stir to blend the sauce and cook the mixture for 15 more minutes

INGREDIENTS:

2 tablespoons olive oil or butterfat

2½ pounds boned, lean lamb shoulder, cubed

1 large yellow onion, chopped

1½ teaspoon ground coriander

1 stick cinnamon, 4 to 5 inches long

½ teaspoon ground ginger

¼ to ½ teaspoon cayenne pepper, according to taste

1 tablespoon instant vegetable stock

8 ounces unsulfured dried apricots

1 lemon, sliced

6 tablespoons raw honey

until the fruit is tender. Lift out the meat and fruit and transfer them to a platter, cover it with foil and keep the food warm near the stove.

Place the casserole back on a propane burner and boil the cooking juices over high heat to reduce them to a good consistency. Pour the sauce over the meat and fruit and serve.

CHICKEN BOREKS IN SHREDDED PHYLLO DOUGH

Makes 8 servings.

PREPARATION:

Since most huts do not have an oven, most pastries have to be baked at home, then frozen and warmed up before serving. These boreks are fairly flat and can be warmed up, wrapped in a foil individually, on top of the wood stove; be careful to turn them over frequently, to avoid scorching one side. You may also choose to warm them up like the crêpes on a hot griddle, but keep the heat low and cover them with a foil so that the inside can become hot before the outside is burnt. If you select the second method, it is advisable to undercook the pastries at home, and let them cook more on the griddle and let the shredded dough turn to a rich golden color and a crisp texture.

INSTRUCTIONS;

Mix together in a large saucepan the milk, herbs, and spices. Bring this mixture to a boil, add the chicken breast, and poach it in the simmering milk for 20 to 30 minutes, until cooked through. Lift the chicken breast out and mince it. Strain the milk and reserve it, discarding the solids.

Rinse the saucepan and return it to the stove; heat the

INGREDIENTS:

1 whole chicken breast, skinned and boned

1½ cups milk

1 thick slice of onion

1 sprig each of parsley and thyme

1 bay leaf

1 pinch of cayenne pepper, ¼ teaspoon mace, 2 whole cloves

2 tablespoons butter

2 tablespoons whole-wheat flour

½ teaspoon each salt and paprika

2 egg yolks

1 cup shredded, unsweetened coconut

½ cup raisins

¼ teaspoon each cinnamon and cardamom

pinch of cayenne

butter in it over medium-high heat. When the butter is bubbly, add the flour and stir it vigorously with a whisk for 30 seconds. Take the pan off the heat and pour some of the poaching milk on the flour-butter mixture, stirring rapidly and scraping the sides with the whisk until you have a smooth paste.

Add the rest of the liquid, always stirring and making sure there are no lumps in the sauce. Return it to the heat, bring it to a boil without stopping to stir, and cook for 1 minute. Season with salt and paprika. Beat the 2 egg yolks lightly in a small bowl to mix; add a little of the hot white sauce to the yolks and stir to blend, then pour this mixture into the white sauce and blend it in. Turn the heat off.

Stir the coconut, the raisins, the cinnamon, cardamom, and cayenne into the white sauce. Pour it over the minced chicken breast and mix it well. Reserve.

Preheat the oven to 375°F.

Tear off half of the shredded phyllo dough and place it in one even layer on the bottom of a 9-by-13-inch baking pan. Pour half the melted butter on it, spread the filling evenly on the dough, and top with a second layer of shredded dough. Brush the remaining butter on top and bake for 35 to 40 minutes until golden brown.

Cool slightly and cut into 8 equal pieces. Transfer them to a clean baking sheet and quick-freeze them. Wrap them individually in clear plastic film and keep them frozen.

To take the boreks to the backcountry, place them in a cardboard or plastic box with crushed waxed paper to cushion them. Remove the plastic wrap to reheat them as instructed above.

½ pound shredded phyllo
  dough
6 ounces melted butter

LEMON-TARRAGON VEAL

Makes 8 servings.

PREPARATION:
  Location: The day before the trip, place thin veal scalop-

INGREDIENTS:
8 veal scaloppine slices
4 lemons

pine slices in a plastic box with a simple marinade made of lemon, salt, and cayenne pepper. Lemon is a natural preservative and tenderizer. The veal is cooked at the campsite, and the marinade is used to make a sauce.

Time: The preparation at the campsite requires only 1 skillet and about 15 minutes.

Important point: Though you may use a good quality plastic box with a well-fitted lid for the meat and the marinade, even so, seal the entire length of the box lid with duct tape.

salt and cayenne pepper
3 to 4 sprigs of fresh tarragon, or 1 tablespoon dried
½ cup unsalted butter (1 stick)

INSTRUCTIONS:

The day before the trip, place the veal in a plastic box, add the juice of three lemons, the grated peel from one lemon, salt, and cayenne pepper to taste. Juice the fourth lemon and transfer the juice to a small plastic bottle with a screw lid. Seal the box as instructed above, and the bottle too.

At the campsite, drain the veal slices out of the marinade; reserve the marinade. Melt ⅓ of the butter in a skillet or rimmed griddle, and sauté the veal slices, about 5 minutes on each side, until cooked through. Transfer the veal to a warm platter and keep it warm, covered with a piece of foil on the wood stove. Pour the marinade into the skillet or griddle, add the juice of the fourth lemon, the tarragon leaves, chopped or crumbled if using dried herb. Stir, add all the remaining butter, cut in small pieces. Stir and cook until the sauce is hot and well blended. Adjust the seasoning; pour the sauce over the veal and serve.

SHRIMP ROLLS

Makes 8 servings.

PREPARATION:

Make the shrimp rolls at home anytime before the trip. Place them in a strong plastic or cardboard box with crushed waxed paper around each roll to protect them. Freeze them before departure. They will gradually thaw during the several days preceding the time when they are served.

INSTRUCTIONS:

Heat the olive oil in a large skillet. Add the shrimp, celery, mushrooms, red pepper, scallions, gingerroot, and cayenne to taste. The mixture should be quite spicy. Cook 3 to 4 minutes, until the shrimp turns pink. Transfer the mixture to a bowl. Add the rice, parsley, lemon juice, Dijon mustard, tamari sauce, and rice-bran syrup or brown sugar. Stir to blend well. Taste and add a little salt and more cayenne pepper if necessary. Let cool.

Place 1 egg-roll wrapper on the working surface with one point of the square facing toward you, in a diamond pattern. Place ⅓ cup shrimp mixture in a thick roll on the bottom half of the diamond, parallel to the front edge of the working surface. Fold up the bottom corner of the wrapper over the filling, then bring the side corners over to cover it completely and roll it to the end of the fourth corner to wrap it up. Transfer the roll to a plate and repeat until all 16 wrappers have been used.

Brush the shrimp rolls with the yolk-water mixture. Heat the peanut oil in a deep skillet until a drop of water sizzles in the oil. The oil should be hot but not smoky. Fry the shrimp rolls in the oil in batches, turning them over once, 5 to 8 minutes, until golden on all sides. Lift them out with tongs and place them to drain on paper towels. Repeat until all the rolls have been fried. Let them cool completely before storing them in a box as instructed above.

INGREDIENTS:

¼ cup olive oil

1 pound raw shrimp, shelled, deveined, and sliced

1 cup chopped celery stalks, about 2 stalks

1 cup chopped mushrooms (sprinkle ¼ cup lemon juice on the mushrooms to prevent discoloration)

⅔ cup chopped red pepper, about 1 pepper

½ cup chopped scallions with some of the green part, about 4 scallions

1 tablespoon minced gingerroot

Cayenne pepper to taste

3 cups cooked brown rice

¼ cup minced parsley

¼ cup freshly squeezed lemon juice

¼ cup Dijon mustard

¼ cup tamari sauce

1 tablespoon rice-bran syrup or brown sugar

16 egg-roll wrappers

1 egg yolk mixed with 2 tablespoons water

1 cup peanut oil

GRILLED CHICKEN BREASTS WITH CORIANDER-LIME BUTTER

Makes 8 servings.

PREPARATION:

The chicken is grilled at the campsite, but for the 3 days on the trail, it is preserved in a marinade, the main ingredient of which is lime juice, a natural preservative and a rich source of vitamin C. The coriander butter is prepared ahead of time and stored in a plastic container or bag. It can be frozen until you are ready to use it. If you want to garnish the dish with fresh sprigs of coriander, be sure the sprigs never freeze: a plastic bag or box filled with paper with the herb in the center will usually protect it. In subzero temperatures I keep the herbs with their container inside my sleeping bag!

INSTRUCTIONS:

Pound the chicken breasts flat between two pieces of waxed paper until they are half an inch thick. Place the meat in a plastic container or bag. Ziplock bags are a great favorite in the backcountry. Double-bagging, with one sealed bag inside another sealed bag, is very secure.

Mix the marinade ingredients together: grated peel and lime juice, ground coriander, coriander leaves, olive oil, salt, and pepper. Pour the marinade over the chicken and seal the bags or box with duct tape, covering all the seams.

To make the coriander butter, process all the coriander butter ingredients in the food processor with salt to taste. Transfer to a plastic bag or box, and seal.

At the campsite, oil a cast-iron griddle, let it get very hot over the stove; lift the chicken breasts out of the marinade

INGREDIENTS:
Juice of 2 limes, about ³/₈ cup
Grated peel of 1 lime, 2 teaspoons
1¹/₂ teaspoons ground coriander
¹/₂ cup minced coriander leaves
¹/₂ cup olive oil
Salt and cayenne pepper to taste
4 pounds chicken breasts, about 4 whole breasts

CORIANDER BUTTER:
¹/₂ cup unsalted butter, 4 ounces
2 tablespoons each minced coriander and parsley leaves
1 tablespoon Dijon mustard
2 teaspoons fresh lime juice, about ¹/₂ a lime
1 teaspoon grated lime peel, about ¹/₂ a lime
¹/₂ teaspoon ground coriander
¹/₈ teaspoon cayenne pepper

and grill them 10 to 12 minutes on each side, basting them occasionally with the marinade. Make 3 slashes on each half-breast serving; insert a thin slice of coriander butter in each slash and serve with the brown rice and additional coriander butter.

FOR GARNISH:
Lime slices and fresh coriander sprigs

GRAINS, LEGUMES, AND VEGETABLE DISHES

COUSCOUS

BASIC METHOD FOR STEAMING COUSCOUS

Let the couscous grain soak in water for 5 minutes, fluffing it once with the fingertips. Place it in a cheesecloth-lined colander. Place the colander over water or a stew. Wrap the lid with a dishcloth to prevent condensation and cover the colander.

Steam the couscous for 15 minutes and remove it to a large platter. Roll the grains between the palms of the hands with melted butter for a sweet couscous or with olive oil for stew couscous. Continue rubbing until the grains are completely coated and separated, about 5 minutes.

Return the couscous to the covered colander and steam it 15 minutes longer until it is tender and fluffy. Remove to the platter and toss with melted butter, using a fork to keep the grains well separated.

To serve it in the traditional Arabic way, you need deep plates like French soup plates. Metal pie plates are a perfect substitute in the backcountry. Spoon out a mound of couscous on a plate, make a well in the center and fill with a serving of stew, soaking the grain with the sauce.

For quantity, allow one cup of dry couscous per four servings.

ZUCCHINI AND SPAGHETTI WITH PESTO

Makes 8 servings.

PREPARATION:

Location: The pesto sauce is made at home. It will keep for 3 or 4 days in a well-sealed bottle. This bottle's lid should be sealed with duct tape for the transportation.

Because the fresh zucchini may freeze on the trail or at night, I clean, cut, blanch, and freeze it before the trip. Then it does not matter whether it thaws or stays frozen before being used. The recipe calls for roasted peppers; this too is easier made at home, as instructed below, and the peppers transported to the hut in a plastic bag, just like the zucchini. All the components for the dish are therefore bagged, boxed, or bottled separately and the whole dish is very easily assembled at the campsite.

INSTRUCTIONS:

One to several days before the trip,

MAKE THE SAUCE:

Grind the pistachios, pine nuts, and garlic to a paste in a food processor. Add the basil and continue to purée. With the motor still running, add the olive oil in a fine stream until all used up. Keep the processor running a few more seconds until the sauce is well emulsified. Transfer it to a plastic box or bottle and seal it.

PREPARE THE VEGETABLES:

Clean the zucchinis, trim off the ends. Halve them crosswise; slice each section lengthwise ¼-inch thick, and cut each slice lengthwise again into ¼-inch strips. Blanch the zucchini strips in salty boiling water for just 30 seconds; drain them immediately and refresh them under running cold water. Drain them again and pat them dry on several layers of paper towels. Transfer them to a plastic bag, expel most of the air out before

INGREDIENTS:

PESTO SAUCE:

⅓ cup shelled pistachio nuts

⅓ cup pine nuts

3 cloves of garlic, peeled

1 cup fresh basil leaves, packed

½ cup good Italian olive oil

ZUCCHINI AND SPAGHETTI DISH:

1 pound zucchini

1 pound thin spaghetti (thin, because it cooks faster)

1 large or 2 small red bell peppers

1 large or 2 small green bell peppers

1 tablespoon salt

3 tablespoons olive oil

½ cup freshly grated Parmesan cheese; it can be grated at home and carried in a box; a box is better than a bag to keep it from being pressed back to a solid block.

sealing it, and freeze.

Wash the peppers. Place them on a baking sheet and broil them under the broiler, 4 inches from the heat, to char their skins all over. Turn them frequently as they roast. This should take about 15 minutes. Wrap the peppers loosely in foil or a brown paper bag, and let them "sweat" for 20 minutes. Remove them from their wrapping, halve them lengthwise, discard the stems, seeds, and filaments. Peel the skin off, and cut the flesh in long strips. Transfer them to a plastic bag, seal it to expel the air, and refrigerate or freeze them.

AT THE CAMPSITE:
Heat plenty of water in a large pot with the salt and 1 tablespoon of the olive oil. When it boils, add the spaghetti and cook it, stirring occasionally until tender but still firm to the bite. Drain it and put it back into the pot, covered to keep warm, near the wood stove.

Heat the remaining olive oil in a large skillet, and sauté the zucchini strips for 2 minutes. Toss them with the spaghetti and mound the mixture on a warm platter. Top with the pesto sauce, toss well. Arrange the pepper strips alternating colors around the dish. Serve with the grated Parmesan.

BROWN RICE WITH HERBS

Makes 8 servings.

PREPARATION:
This dish is easily prepared at the campsite. We have equipped most of our huts with pressure cookers to cut down cooking time and save fuel.

INSTRUCTIONS:
Melt the butter in a heavy casserole equipped with a well-fitting lid, or a pressure cooker. Sauté the onion over medium high heat until limp but not brown; add the rice and sauté it with the onion until translucent, about 1 minute. Add the scallions with 4 cups of hot water, the vegetable-stock powder,

INGREDIENTS:
1 large onion, chopped
4 tablespoons butter
2 cups brown rice, washed and drained
1 bunch scallions, chopped
4 cups hot water
4 teaspoons instant vegetable-stock powder
½ teaspoon cardamom or coriander
⅛ teaspoon cayenne

the cardamom or coriander, and the cayenne.

IF USING A CASSEROLE:

Bring the liquid to a boil, turn the heat down to low, cover the pot with the lid and let it simmer for about 45 minutes. The rice should be tender but firm. If all the liquid has not been absorbed, boil the excess away. If the liquid is absorbed before the rice is cooked, add a little hot water and cook it a little longer. Let it stand for 10 minutes.

IF USING A PRESSURE COOKER:

Bring the liquid to a boil, turn the heat to low, and adjust the lid to close the cooker hermetically. As soon as the steam activates the valve, allow 15 minutes cooking time. Turn the heat off and let the pressure decrease until the steam stops activating the security valve. Remove the lid and check the rice, which should be firm-tender. If any liquid remains in the pot, boil it away over high heat.

½ cup chopped fresh herbs of your choice: parsley, cilantro, tarragon, basil, mint, chervil...

Optional: plain natural yogurt as a sauce

JUST BEFORE SERVING: *Fluff up the rice with a fork, being careful not to crush the grains as you stir the chopped herbs into the rice. Serve with the yogurt if desired.*

ORANGE RED LENTIL SALAD

Makes 8 servings.

PREPARATION:

This is a perfect salad for Day 4 in the backcountry because the flavor improves as it marinates. So make it the day before leaving home, transport it in a plastic box, well sealed with duct tape (make sure the tape covers the entire seam where the lid and the box join) and enjoy it several days later!

INSTRUCTIONS:

Place the lentils in a large saucepan, with water to cover by 2 inches. Add the orange pieces, onion, garlic cloves, bay leaves, and salt. Bring the liquid to a boil, lower the heat, and

INGREDIENTS:

2 cups red lentils (a small-size lentil grown in Idaho)

1 whole orange, quartered

1 large onion, halved and studded with 4 whole cloves

3 cloves of garlic, crushed but kept whole

2 bay leaves

1 tablespoon salt

let it simmer, covered, for 15 minutes, until the lentils are firm but tender. Drain them and discard the orange, onion, garlic, and bay leaves. Cool the lentils to room temperature and toss them with the red onion slices and the dressing. Refrigerate from 6 hours to 3 or 4 days.

DRESSING:

Mix in a bowl all ingredients except the olive oil. Add the olive oil in a fine stream, whipping the dressing constantly until emulsified.

1 medium red onion,
peeled and thinly sliced
DRESSING:
grated peel of 1 orange
2 tablespoons fresh orange
juice
2 tablespoons raspberry
vinegar
½ teaspoon ground cumin
½ teaspoon ground
cardamom
1 large clove of garlic,
minced
½ teaspoon salt
⅛ teaspoon cayenne pepper
½ cup olive oil

TOFUBURGERS WITH RED PEPPER SAUCE

Makes 8 servings.

PREPARATION:

The tofuburgers can be assembled and cooked at the campsite; the sauce should be made at home to be puréed to a smooth texture in a food processor. The sauce can be carried in a plastic box, well sealed on all seams with duct tape.

INSTRUCTIONS:

Heat the olive oil in a skillet, and sauté the onion until limp. Add the garlic and peppers, sauté until peppers are very soft, about 4 minutes.

In the meantime, pour boiling water over the bulgur and let it stand for 30 minutes.

In a large bowl, mash the tofu and beat it with a wire

INGREDIENTS:
1 cup chopped onion,
about 1 medium onion
2 cloves of garlic, chopped
2 small red or green
peppers, finely chopped
2 tablespoons olive oil
½ cup bulgur
1 pound firm tofu
¼ cup chopped fresh mint
4 large eggs, broken into a
plastic bottle; seal the
bottle with duct tape for
transportation

whisk until smooth. Shake the eggs in their bottle to blend and pour them over the tofu; add the mint, vegetable-stock powder, cumin, and cayenne pepper. Stir to blend. Add the cooled onion mixture. Drain the bulgur, pressing to remove all moisture, and add it to the tofu mixture. Stir to blend all the ingredients together.

Heat some olive oil on the griddle or in a skillet. Form eight equal balls with the tofu mixture. Place them on the hot griddle, flattening them to form patties; fry them like pancakes, turning them over once, 6 to 8 minutes on each side until browned. Serve them with the red pepper sauce. If using a skillet, cook 4 patties at a time.

RED PEPPER SAUCE

INSTRUCTIONS:

Heat 2 tablespoons of butter in a heavy-bottom saucepan; sauté the chopped onion until limp, add the garlic, and cook over low heat 4 more minutes. Cover the pan to keep the onion from drying out. In the meantime, heat the wine in a small saucepan to boiling and flame it to remove the alcohol. Toss the red peppers in the onion mixture, add the wine with the thyme, bay leaves, and cloves; reheat to boiling, lower the heat, and simmer for 20 minutes.

Purée the mixture in a food processor. Press the purée through a fine mesh sieve to remove the pulp. You should have about 3 cups of sauce. Return it to the saucepan, place it over medium heat. Knead to a paste the remaining two tablespoons butter with the flour. When the sauce is hot, add the butter-flour mixture in small pieces at a time, whisking after each addition to blend. Boil the sauce, uncovered, for 1 minute. Remove it from the heat, add the lemon juice, salt, cayenne, and basil. Let the sauce cool completely before pouring it into a plastic container. Seal all the seams carefully with duct tape for transportation. The sauce will keep for several **days** when refrigerated.

2 teaspoons instant
   vegetable-stock powder
1 teaspoon ground cumin
1/4 teaspoon cayenne pepper
Red pepper sauce, recipe
   follows

INGREDIENTS:

1 1/2 cups chicken or
   vegetable stock
4 tablespoons unsalted
   butter (1/2 stick)
1/4 cup chopped onion (1/2 a
   small onion)
1 teaspoon minced garlic
   (1 clove)
5 or 6 cups chopped red
   peppers (4 large ones)
1/2 cup dry white wine
3 or 4 sprigs fresh thyme,
   or 1 teaspoon dry
2 bay leaves
3 whole cloves
2 tablespoons whole-wheat
   flour
1 teaspoon salt (taste
   before adding, the stock
   may be salty already)
1 teaspoon lemon juice, or
   more to taste
1/4 teaspoon cayenne pepper
1/2 cup chopped fresh basil
   leaves; if no fresh basil is
   available, add 1
   tablespoon dry basil
   with the thyme and bay

BREAKFAST DISHES

CRÊPES WITH GOOSEBERRY SAUCE

THE CRÊPES

To make 16 crêpes, 8 two-crêpe servings:

PREPARATION:

Location: It may be fun to make the crêpes in the hut, asking each guest to flip his or her own just the way my mother used to do with us, little girl sisters. I still laugh at the remembrance of crêpes flying around the kitchen; some would land on top of the cupboards (they would bc retrieved months later on a spring-cleaning day), others would flop into my mother's apron held up in front of her. My option is to make them at home and freeze them ahead of time because I do not choose to feed the local pine martens with half-burnt crêpes that have landed on the woodpile.... To freeze and store crêpes for a length of time, just pile them with a piece of waxed paper between each, place the pile in a plastic bag, and freeze it. The crêpes can be transported frozen.

INGREDIENTS:

1 cup unbleached flour
1 teaspoon sugar, or more
*   for sweeter crêpes*
pinch of salt
3 large eggs
3 tablespoons melted butter
3 tablespoons orange
*   liqueur or cognac, or 1*
*   tablespoon orange*
*   extract*
1½ cups milk
¼ cup melted butter, or
*   more if necessary*

INSTRUCTIONS:

Mix together the flour, sugar, and salt. Add the eggs one at a time, beating well. Add the melted butter, the liqueur, or extract. Gradually add the milk, blending it well to obtain a very smooth batter. Let it rest at least 30 minutes.

To make the crêpes: Grease a 6½-to-7-inch, well-seasoned crêpe pan or nonstick frying pan. Let it get hot on the stove. Lift it up in your left hand; with the right hand pour in it about 3 tablespoons of batter as you create a circular motion with the left wrist to coat the bottom of the pan evenly. Bring it back to the burner and cook it on a medium-high setting until the edges of the crêpes begin to turn color. You can flip the crêpe in the air to turn it over, or lift it with a spatula and turn it around.

Cook the other side briefly until it is golden brown, and slide the crêpe onto a warm plate. Repeat until all the batter is used up.

INGREDIENTS:
2 quarts gooseberries
4 to 6 cups of honey, taste for sweetness to your taste
½ cup water

THE GOOSEBERRY SAUCE

PREPARATION:

Every Saturday in the summer a large truck called "The Berry Patch" comes to the valley with cases and cases of freshly picked berries from Oregon. What a joy! Raspberries, blueberries, huckleberries, and, for a short time only, gooseberries. The price is right, the fruit are beautiful, and during the week I am busy dehydrating or preserving. Making fruit leather is another way to use them with the idea of backcountry trips to come. Some recipes for fruit leather and bars are in Chapter 4. One summer I used all my gooseberries to make a sauce that I froze for the Sun Valley trekking season: Bob's hut-to-hut ski business. The following winter, the crêpes, topped with gooseberry sauce, were an exceptional treat for our guests.

INSTRUCTIONS:

Wash, top, and tail the gooseberries. Place them in a preserving pot with the water and cook them gently for 20 minutes. Heat the honey and pour it into the fruit. Bring the mixture to a boil, cook until it reaches the desired consistency—for 10 to 15 minutes. Let the sauce cool; transfer it to plastic boxes (2-to-4-cup sizes) and freeze them.

Four cups of sauce make 8 servings.

TO ASSEMBLE THE CRÊPES

Now it is early morning in the hut and the temperature inside may be 40 degrees. You think that you must get up and re-kindle the fire in the wood stove, but if you think about it long enough, somebody else does it for you. When the ambient temperature has become more clement, you slip outside your sleeping bag and reach inside the cooler to pull out the crêpes and the gooseberry sauce, which are probably still frozen. You place them near the wood stove to let them come back to room temperature. Then, with the friendly community, you prepare yourself for the day.

When everybody is ready for breakfast, after the first hot drinks, melt some butter on the griddle. Peel each crêpe from the waxed paper and warm it up in the hot butter. As each crêpe becomes very hot and soft, fold it in four, transfer it to a warm platter, cover it with foil, and keep it warm on the top or on the side of the wood stove. In the meantime, warm up the gooseberry sauce in a pot. When all the crêpes are hot, serve them topped with the hot sauce.

EGG AND CHEESE PUFF

Makes 6 to 8 servings.

PREPARATION:

Location: Here is an example of how a dish normally baked in the oven at home can be cooked on top of a wood stove, using a Dutch-oven method.

Equipment: My trick is to heat up two 9-inch cast-iron skillets on the stove; I pour the egg mixture in one, use the other as a lid, turned over, and keep the whole thing on a hot burning stove for the required time.

INSTRUCTIONS:

Pour the eggs into a mixing bowl. Beat them well with a wire whisk as for an omelet. Reconstitute the soy milk with 1 cup water. Grate the Gruyère and Parmesan cheeses. Melt the butter. Add the flour, soy milk, grated cheeses, melted butter, chopped scallions, salt, pepper, and nutmeg to the eggs and beat well.

Use the two-cast-iron-skillet method described above to

INGREDIENTS:

4 large eggs, broken into a plastic bottle; make sure the bottle is well sealed with duct tape for transportation

4 tablespoons whole-wheat flour

2 tablespoons soy-milk powder

4 ounces Gruyère cheese

2 ounces Parmesan cheese

2 scallions

1 tablespoon butter

½ teaspoon grated nutmeg

¼ teaspoon salt, ⅛ teaspoon cayenne pepper

cook the mixture on top of the wood stove for 20 minutes, until it is puffy and the edges are brown. Check the puff occasionally to ensure that the bottom doesn't cook too fast and start to burn. If it does, lower the fire or move the skillets to a cooler spot on the stove.

On the other hand, if the puff is still liquid in the center after 20 minutes, cook it longer—5, even 10 minutes—until it is done.

OATMEAL CREAM WITH FRUIT SAUCE

Makes 8 servings.

PREPARATION:

This easy breakfast can be prepared at the campsite; it is a delicious and different way to present oatmeal.

INSTRUCTIONS:

Heat 4 cups of water in a saucepan and turn the heat off. Dissolve the soy-milk powder in the water, add the oats, and let them soak for 30 minutes. Return the saucepan to the heat and bring the mixture to a boil, stirring. Turn the heat down and let the oats simmer 3 to 4 minutes.

Stir the eggs, lemon rind, juice, and honey into the oats and cook, stirring constantly, until the mixture thickens to the consistency of pudding. Serve immediately, topped with whipped cream if desired, and hot fruit sauce.

FRUIT SAUCE:

Heat the fruit spread with half a cup of water and the lemon juice until the mixture is well blended and almost boiling. Adjust the flavor with more lemon juice or honey. Spoon 3 to 4 tablespoonfuls on each serving.

INGREDIENTS:

¼ cup soy-milk powder
2 cups rolled oats
2 large eggs, broken into a plastic container and well sealed for transportation. Shake the container before opening it to blend the eggs together.
Grated rind and juice of 1 lemon
¼ cup honey
Optional: 1 cup heavy cream, whipped to soft shape

FRUIT SAUCE:

1½ cups natural fruit spread: a good commercial brand unsweetened or sweetened with honey— raspberry, blueberry, strawberry, apricot . . .
Juice of 1 lemon
More lemon juice or honey to taste

BLUEBERRY-BUTTERMILK PANCAKES

Makes 8 servings.

PREPARATION:

Making your own complete pancake mix is quite easy and much better than a store-bought one. You can use freeze-dried eggs and powdered soy milk or buttermilk. To go to a hut site, if you do not mind the extra weight, take some fresh eggs, broken into a plastic container, and fresh buttermilk or yogurt.

INSTRUCTIONS:

Soak the blueberries in very hot water to plump them up, if using dehydrated ones.

If using fresh ingredients, beat the eggs until frothy, and beat in the buttermilk. Add to the dry ingredients with the blueberries and stir quickly and lightly with a rubber spatula, just until the dry ingredients are moistened. Do not overmix.

If using powdered eggs and buttermilk, just add 3 cups of water and stir in the same manner as above for a thick batter. Add up to 1 more cup of water to obtain the desired consistency.

Melt 4 tablespoons of the butter, let it cool a little, and stir it into the batter.

Heat the griddle, melt a little butter on it. Pour small quantities of batter onto the griddle, about ¼ cup each, and cook until the tops are bubbly. Turn them over and cook the other sides until browned. Transfer the hot cakes to a warm platter, cover with a foil, and keep warm on or near the wood stove. Repeat until all the batter is used.

Serve the cakes hot, with extra butter and the blueberry-honey sauce.

INGREDIENTS:

PREMIX INTO A PLASTIC BAG:

2 cups unbleached white flour
1 cup whole-wheat flour
½ cup cornmeal
¼ cup raw sugar
2 teaspoons baking powder
1 teaspoon baking soda
¼ teaspoon salt
4 oz. freeze-dried eggs, or, if using fresh eggs, break 4 large eggs into a separate container
¾ cup powdered buttermilk, or, if using fresh buttermilk, 3 cups packed separately

PACK IN A SEPARATE BAG:

3 cups frozen blueberries or 1 cup dehydrated blueberries. I dehydrate blueberries in the summer. They look like currants or raisins, and can be used in the same manner. To use them in the pancakes, soak them first in some very hot water for 30 minutes.

ALSO PACK SEPARATELY:

1 stick unsalted butter, 4 ounces
2 cups blueberry-honey sauce, recipe follows

BLUEBERRY-HONEY SAUCE

INSTRUCTIONS:

Wash the blueberries and drain them. Place them in a large noncorrosive pot with water, the honey, and the cinnamon stick if desired. Bring the mixture to a boil, cook it until it reaches the desired consistency, about 15 minutes. Let the sauce cool, remove the cinnamon stick. Transfer the sauce to two-cup-size plastic containers. Cover them with well-fitted lids and freeze.

Makes about 10 cups sauce.

INGREDIENTS:

2 quarts blueberries
*About 4 cups of raw honey,
    taste for sweetness to
    your taste*
½ cup water
*Optional: 1 4-inch stick
    cinnamon*

BREADS, CAKES, AND FOOD BARS

ITALIAN COUNTRY BREAD

This recipe will make one large loaf or two smaller loaves or eight small individual loaves to stuff for lunches and picnics.

PREPARATION:

Location: Make the bread at home, anytime before the trip. It keeps very well frozen. Take the small picnic loaves out to thaw at room temperature one day before departure.

Equipment: A large mixing bowl or an electric mixer. Baking stones: I use red brick tiles and line baking sheets with them. They must be soaked before being placed in a cold oven.

Time: 1 hour to prepare the dough and let it rise, 1 hour baking (45 minutes for the small loaves).

INGREDIENTS:

¼ cup dry yeast
1 tablespoon sugar
2 to 3 cups unbleached white flour
4 to 5 cups whole-wheat flour
1 tablespoon salt
¼ cup cornmeal

INSTRUCTIONS:

Combine the yeast and the sugar with 2½ cups of warm water (100°F) in a large bowl. Let it stand 10 minutes until foamy. Blend in 2 cups of the white flour, 4 cups whole-wheat flour, and the salt. Add up to 1 cup each of both flours to the dough to make it workable. Turn it onto a floured surface and knead it for 10 minutes until it is smooth and elastic. Form a ball, dust it with flour. Clean and oil the mixing bowl. Transfer the dough to the bowl and turn it around so that it is oiled all over. Cover the bowl with a plastic film and let the dough rise in a warm place 40 to 45 minutes until it is doubled in bulk. Punch it down with a fist and let it stand 5 minutes before shaping the loaves. Shape 1 to 8 oblong or round loaves.

Drain the tiles out of the water. Line a large baking sheet with them. Sprinkle them with the cornmeal. Place the loaves on the tiles at least 1½ inches apart. Slash the top of each loaf with a razor blade and brush it with water. Place the loaves in the cold oven. Set the oven at 350°F and bake the bread until it is golden and makes a hollow sound when tapped. Transfer the loaves to racks. When they are completely cool wrap them tightly and individually in foil to be stored in the refrigerator or freezer.

IDAHO POTATO BRAIDED BREAD

Makes one large loaf.

PREPARATION:

Location: Breads can be baked at home any time before a trip, and kept frozen.

Equipment: For most yeasted breads, I use an electric blender and baking tiles (see Italian country bread instructions).

Time: Allow about 30 minutes to prepare the dough, if you already have cooked potatoes. The first rising time is 1½ to 2 hours long, the second one, 45 minutes. The baking time is 30 to 35 minutes.

INSTRUCTIONS:

Pour ¼ cup warm water (110°F) into the electric blender bowl. Sprinkle the yeast on top of the water with 1 tablespoon of the sugar; let it stand for 10 minutes, until foamy.

In the meantime, in another bowl, mix together the mashed potatoes, the soy milk, melted butter, and eggs. Stir this mixture with the remaining sugar and blend it well.

When the yeast mixture is ready, add the potato mixture and blend them together with the electric wire whisk at medium speed. Add 1½ cups of flour and beat 2 more minutes, scraping the bowl occasionally. Replace the whisk with the dough hook, add 1 cup of flour, and work the dough until well blended. Add the remaining flour and blend it in. Transfer the dough to a marble or wooden slab and knead it 5 to 8 minutes more by hand until the dough is smooth and easy to handle. You may have to add a little more flour.

Grease a large clean bowl. Form a ball with the dough and roll it inside the bowl to oil it all over. In a warm place, let the dough rise in the bowl covered with a plastic film until double in volume. Punch the dough down and divide it into equal thirds. Roll each third into a rope 14 inches long on the marble or wooden slab. Join the three ropes at one end and braid them together, tucking the ends underneath. Transfer the braided dough to baking tiles or a greased baking sheet.

INGREDIENTS:

1 tablespoon active dry yeast

3½ cups whole-wheat flour

¼ cup raw sugar

1½ teaspoons sea salt

1 cup cooked potatoes, mashed

⅔ cup soy milk made from powder

¼ cup melted butter; clarified butter is best

2 large eggs

1 egg wash made with 1 egg white and 1 teaspoon water

2 teaspoons poppy seeds

Cover it with a loose cloth, and let it rise until doubled in size, about 45 minutes.

If you are not using baking tiles, preheat the oven to 350°F. When the bread has risen, brush it with the egg wash and sprinkle the poppy seeds on top. If using baking tiles, place the bread in a cold oven, turn it on, and set the oven thermostat at 350°F. Otherwise, place the bread in the pre-heated oven. Bake it until it is golden and sounds hollow when tapped. Cool the bread on a wire rack.

FINLAND COUNTRY BREAD

Makes two 8-inch-round loaves.

PREPARATION:
Bake the bread at home, any length of time before a trip; it keeps very well wrapped airtight and frozen.

INSTRUCTIONS:
Pour ½ cup warm water (110°F.) into the electric mixer's bowl. Sprinkle the yeast on the water and let it stand for 5 to 10 minutes until foamy. Add the buttermilk, salt, whole-rye and whole-wheat flours, and the wheat germ. Stir with the wire whisk until well blended.

Change to the dough hook, and gradually beat in the white flour until a smooth dough is formed. Transfer it to a marble or wooden board. Cover it loosely and let it rest for 30 minutes.

Divide the dough into 2 equal pieces. Pat each one into a 6-inch round. Brush them with water and press wheat germ on top. Transfer them to a lightly greased baking sheet or to baking tiles (instructions on how to use baking tiles are given with the Italian country bread recipe). Let them rise 1 hour, until doubled in volume.

Using a very sharp knife or a razor blade, slash a crisscross pattern on top of each loaf. Bake them in a 400°F. preheated oven if you are not using baking tiles, or place them in the

INGREDIENTS:
1 tablespoon active dry
  yeast
2 cups buttermilk
1 teaspoon salt
1½ cups whole-rye flour
1½ cups whole-wheat flour
¼ cup wheat germ
2 cups unbleached white
  flour

cold oven if using tiles and turn the thermostat up to 400°.

Check the loaves after 30 minutes. If they sound hollow when tapped, transfer them to the wire rack to cool. Wrap them airtight in foil and freeze them for a long storage.

TOASTED PITA BREAD

Each pita round makes 8 toasts to serve 2 or 3 guests.

PREPARATION:
> Location: I prefer to make them at home and to pack them in a plastic bag.
> Equipment: I use seal-a-meal bags, sealing them with as much air as possible kept in the bag so that the toasts cannot be crushed during transportation. The toasts could be made at the campsite, grilled on a cast-iron griddle.
> **Time: This is a quick recipe; the time depends on the number of pita rounds used.**

INGREDIENTS:
> *For 4 rounds of pita bread,*
> *6 tablespoons of sweet butter*
> *2 cloves of garlic, minced*
> *Salt and cayenne pepper to taste*

INSTRUCTIONS:
Melt the butter over low heat and cook the garlic in the butter for 5 minutes. Remove the garlic butter from the heat. Cut each round of pita bread into 4 wedges, and separate each wedge into two triangles. Brush each triangle with the garlic butter; sprinkle salt and cayenne pepper on each to taste. Transfer the triangles to a baking sheet and broil them under the broiler in the oven until toasted, 3 to 4 minutes. Remove them and let them cool completely before packaging them.

SUGARLESS GINGERBREAD

Makes one 9-inch-round bread, or two small loaves.

PREPARATION:
> This bread could be made at the campsite using a Dutch-

oven method. I like to bake it at home, ahead of time, as the flavor improves the next day if it is wrapped airtight in a plastic film. It can also be kept frozen for longer storage.

INSTRUCTIONS:
In a saucepan, heat the molasses and the butter together, stirring until melted. Let it cool 10 minutes; add the buttermilk.

Sift together the flour, baking powder, salt, and spices. Stir the dry mixture into the molasses mixture, and combine them well.

DUTCH-OVEN METHOD:
Heat a 9-inch Dutch oven, or two skillets, until very hot. Melt some butter in the baking dish. Pour the batter into the Dutch oven or one skillet, top it with the lid or the second skillet, and keep it on the wood stove until done, 30 to 40 minutes.

REGULAR OVEN METHOD:
Preheat the oven to 400°F. Heat two 8½-by-4½-inch loaf pans in the oven. Melt some butter in them, divide the batter equally between the two pans, and bake for 30 to 35 minutes until a wooden pick inserted in the center comes out clean. Cool the breads in the pans for 10 minutes, invert them on a wire rack, and cool them completely.

INGREDIENTS:
1½ cups molasses
½ cup and 2 tablespoons unsalted butter
1 cup buttermilk, fresh if baking the bread at home, or made with ¼ cup buttermilk powder if making it at the hut
3 cups whole-wheat flour
2 teaspoons baking powder
1 tablespoon ginger
1 tablespoon cinnamon
½ teaspoon salt
½ teaspoon allspice
½ teaspoon clove

DATE-WALNUT CAKE WITH RICE-BRAN SYRUP GLAZE

Makes 1 8-by-8-inch square cake: 8 generous servings.

PREPARATION:
The cake can be baked at home and saved for a few days well wrapped in a plastic film. The flavor actually improves during these few days. It can also be frozen for a longer storage and will still remain moist and tasty.

INGREDIENTS:
3 cups chopped pitted dates, 1½ pounds
2 cups all-bran cereal
2 large eggs
½ cup molasses or rice-bran syrup

INSTRUCTIONS:
Preheat the oven to 350°F.

Combine the dates and cereal with 2 cups boiling water (use 2¼ cups if using rice-bran syrup). Let stand 30 minutes.

Beat the eggs until pale, add the molasses or rice-bran syrup in a stream, beating well until thick.

Combine the flour, baking powder, baking soda, and salt. Stir into the egg mixture, alternately with the date mixture, including the water.

Pour the batter into a well-greased 8-by-8-inch square cake pan. Stir the walnuts with the rice-bran syrup until well coated and spread them on top of the batter. Bake the cake for 40 to 45 minutes, until a wooden pick inserted in the center comes out clean.

Let the cake cool in the pan, and turn it out onto a wire rack to cool completely. Wrap it airtight in a plastic film and refrigerate or freeze.

2 cups whole-wheat flour
2 teaspoons baking powder
1 teaspoon baking soda
¼ teaspoon salt
1 cup chopped walnuts
⅜ cup rice-bran syrup

ST. JAMES CAROB CAKE

Makes 8 to 10 servings.

PREPARATION:

This is a great cake to bake at home and take on a trip, for the flavor improves when the cake is refrigerated for 2 to 3 days. I have adapted the Spanish recipe for a chocolate cake made in honor of Saint James of Compostella. Traditionally a rising-sun design, which is the symbol of that great saint, decorates the surface of the cake. This can be done at the campsite. In the recipe, I have substituted carob and honey for the chocolate and sugar.

INSTRUCTIONS:
Preheat the oven to 325°F.

Butter a 9-inch round cake pan. Line the bottom of the pan with a circle of waxed paper, and grease it too.

Cream the butter; add the honey and cream the mixture

INGREDIENTS:
1 cup (8 ounces) unsalted butter
1 cup raw creamed honey
5 large egg yolks
1 teaspoon almond extract
4 ounces carob powder
5 ounces blanched almonds, ground
5 egg whites
½ teaspoon cream of tartar

thoroughly. Beat the yolks into the creamed mixture, add the almond extract, and keep beating until light and fluffy. Add the carob powder and the ground almond, and stir the batter until very well combined. Reserve.

Using a clean bowl and clean beaters, beat the egg whites until foamy. Add the cream of tartar, and beat until the whites are stiff but not dry. Add a large spoonful of whites to the butter mixture, and stir gently with a metal spoon to loosen the batter. Fold in the remaining whites.

Turn the batter into the prepared pan, and bake it in the preheated oven until the edges of the cake shrink slightly from the pan, 40 to 45 minutes. The cake will still be soft in the center. Let it cool completely in the pan.

Cut a round of poster paper, the size of the cake; draw a rising-sun pattern on the round by drawing a half circle along the bottom edge with rays reaching from the half circle to the edge of the round. Cut out the pattern, making sure to keep the poster piece whole. Lay the pattern on top of the cake. Transport the cake to the campsite in the pan. When ready to serve, set aside the pattern, invert the cake onto a plate, and remove the waxed paper. If the cake seems oily, blot the excess oil with a paper towel. Place the rising-sun stencil on top of the cake, sprinkle powdered sugar over cake and stencil, and remove the stencil, revealing the rising-sun design on the cake.

TURKISH BIRDS' NESTS

Makes 8 nests.

PREPARATION:

Location: At home, anytime before the trip. For an easier transportation I quick-freeze them, that is, put them unwrapped on the baking sheet in the freezer; when they are frozen solid, I wrap them airtight in a plastic film and keep them in the freezer until ready to go.

INGREDIENTS:
6 ounces unsalted butter
*3 ounces each shelled
    pistachios and walnuts*
¼ cup raw turbinado sugar
*¼ to ½ teaspoon ground
    cinnamon*

For transportation, pack them in a cardboard box or a plastic box well padded with waxed paper.
Equipment: A food processor, a medium-size mixing bowl, a small saucepan with a pastry brush, a baking sheet.
Time: 30 minutes plus 15 to 20 minutes baking.

8 sheets phyllo dough ($^1/_3$ of a box)
2 tablespoons honey
1 tablespoon fresh lemon juice

INSTRUCTIONS:
Preheat the oven to 400°F.

Melt the butter in a small saucepan. Lay the sheets of phyllo dough on the work surface, place a piece of waxed paper on top of them and cover it with a dampened dishcloth, until ready to use.

Take one third of the nuts, mixed together, and coarsely chop them. Grind the other two thirds finely in a food processor. Transfer the ground nuts to a mixing bowl and blend in the sugar and cinnamon.

Uncover the phyllo dough, carefully lift one sheet and spread it on a marble or wooden board. Cover the remaining sheets again. Brush half the sheet with melted butter, using a pastry brush. Fold it in two and brush again with butter. Spread about 1½ tablespoons of ground-nut mixture on two-thirds, lengthwise, of the dough. Roll up the phyllo, starting at a long edge, around the filling until the one-third without filling is left. Shape the roll into a circle, tucking the loose pastry underneath to form a cup, or, better, a "nest." Transfer it to a greased baking sheet, and repeat the procedure with all remaining phyllo sheets.

Brush each pastry with the remaining melted butter, and bake them in the preheated oven until crisp and brown.

Fill the nests with the reserved chopped nuts. Melt the honey with the lemon juice and brush it over the warm pastries.

APRICOT BARS

Makes 32 3-by-1-inch bars.

PREPARATION:
Location: At home, days or weeks before a trip.

Equipment: Electric mixer, a 9-by-13-inch baking pan.
Time: 15 minutes preparation, 15–20 minutes baking.

INSTRUCTIONS:

Soak the apricots in boiling water for 5 minutes; drain them well. Preheat the oven to 350°F.

Cream the butter in the electric mixer. Add the sugar and beat the mixture until light and fluffy. Add the honey or rice-bran syrup and beat until creamy. Beat in the egg, the vanilla, and the orange peel until well combined.

Sift together the flour, salt, baking soda, and cinnamon into the creamy mixture. Add the apricots and oats; stir to blend well.

Spread the batter into a greased 9-by-13-inch baking pan. Use moistened fingers to pat it evenly. Bake it in the preheated oven for 15 to 20 minutes, until the edges are golden. Let it cool, and cut 32 3-by-1-inch bars and let them cool completely on baking racks. For the backcountry, wrap each bar individually in a clear plastic film.

The bars will keep several days in the refrigerator. You can freeze them for longer storage.

INGREDIENTS:

6 ounces unsulfured dried apricots, chopped fine
2/3 cup sweet butter at room temperature
1 cup turbinado sugar
1/4 cup honey or rice-bran syrup
1 large egg
1 teaspoon vanilla
1 tablespoon grated orange peel
1 1/4 cup whole-wheat flour
1/4 teaspoon salt
1/2 teaspoon baking soda
1/2 teaspoon cinnamon
2 cups old-fashioned rolled oats

PROTEIN BARS

Makes 32 bars.

PREPARATION:

All food bars can be baked at home at any time, and stored until the next trip. Wrapped individually in a plastic film, then placed in a bag with a label indicating the kind of bars and the date they were baked, they will keep in the freezer for several months. The protein bars are so called because they are made with instant protein powder. It can be found with various manufacturers' labels as a nutritious high-protein, low-carbohydrate, natural food supplement. I use it to make a food bar, enriched with essential vitamins and minerals, a complete meal in itself.

INSTRUCTIONS:

Preheat the oven to 350°F.

INGREDIENTS:

1 cup rye flour
1 cup quick-cooking oats
1/4 teaspoon salt
1 teaspoon baking powder
1/4 cup instant protein powder
1/4 cup vegetable oil
1 cup raw honey
2 large eggs
1 teaspoon vanilla extract
1 teaspoon cardamom
1 cup walnuts, lightly toasted and coarsely chopped

Mix together in one bowl the rye flour, oats, salt, baking powder, and instant protein powder.

In another bowl, beat together the oil, honey, and eggs.

Stir the dry ingredients into the oil mixture, add the flavorings and nuts. Stir to blend well.

Spread the batter onto a greased 13-by-9-inch baking pan. Bake in the preheated oven for 25 to 30 minutes, until a toothpick inserted in the center comes out clean. Cool on a rack to room temperature, and cut into 32 bars.

NUTTY-RYE BARS

Makes 32 bars.

PREPARATION:

The bars can be made any time before a trip, wrapped airtight individually in plastic film, and kept frozen for long storage.

INSTRUCTIONS:

Preheat the oven to 375°F.

Grease a 9-by-13-inch baking pan.

Place the almond butter, unsalted butter, honey, and almond extract in the electric blender's bowl. Using the wire whisk, beat at high speed until well blended. Mix the dry ingredients together in another bowl with the ground almonds. Add the dry ingredients to the butter mixture and beat at medium speed until a soft dough is formed. Transfer it to the prepared pan; pat it with wet fingers until it coats the bottom of the pan evenly. Bake 12 to 15 minutes. It should still be soft and will harden as it cools. Let it cool completely and cut into bars.

INGREDIENTS:
- ½ cup almond butter
- ½ cup unsalted butter, soft
- ½ cup raw honey
- ½ teaspoon almond extract
- 1½ cups whole-rye flour
- ¾ teaspoon baking soda
- ½ teaspoon baking powder
- ¼ teaspoon salt
- 6 tablespoons finely ground, blanched almonds

TOFU CREAM BARS

Makes 16 bars, 2 inches square.

PREPARATION:

Bake the tofu cream bars any time before the trip. In this

INGREDIENTS:
- a/ ¼ cup pure vegetable oil, sesame or safflower

case, as an "off the sled lunch dessert," they can be cut and stored airtight in a box; they will keep 4 to 5 days in a cold place. They can also be wrapped individually in a plastic film just after baking and stored in the freezer. They make great snacks to stick in a backpack or a kayak.

INSTRUCTIONS:

Preheat the oven to 350°F.

Mix together all the a/ ingredients, and stir them with a wooden spoon until well blended.

Spread the mixture evenly in a greased 8-inch-square pan. Bake it in the preheated oven for 12 minutes.

Mix all the b/ ingredients together in a food processor and process until well blended. When the crust comes out of the oven, spread the tofu cream over it and top with the sesame seeds. Return it to the oven and bake 25 minutes. Let it cool to room temperature and cut into bars.

¼ cup raw honey
1 cup whole-wheat flour
⅓ cup toasted sesame seeds
1 teaspoon fresh orange or lemon peel or ½ teaspoon dry
b/ *¼ cup raw honey*
8 ounces tofu
1 large egg
1 tablespoon soy-milk powder
1 tablespoon freshly grated lemon peel (or orange peel)
⅛ teaspoon ground cardamom
¼ teaspoon ground nutmeg
c/ *¼ cup sesame seeds*

ORANGE RAISIN CAKE

Makes a 9-by-5-inch loaf.

PREPARATION:

Make the cake at home, any time before the planned trip, and freeze it if prepared more than a week before serving. The cake could be baked in an 8-by-8-inch cake pan, but a more compact loaf, frozen, is less likely than a flat square to break during transportation.

INSTRUCTIONS:

Preheat the oven to 350°F.

Grind the raisins and orange in a food processor.

Cream the butter and sugar together. Add the eggs, one at a time, beating well. Mix together the dry ingredients in a small bowl and add them, a third at a time, to the butter mixture, alternating with the buttermilk, one half at a time, beating well after each addition.

Fold in the puréed fruit. Pour the batter into a greased 9-by-5-inch loaf pan. Bake 35 to 40 minutes.

INGREDIENTS:
½ cup raisins
½ medium orange, with the peel
¼ cup unsalted butter, 2 ounces
½ cup raw sugar
2 large eggs
½ teaspoon baking soda
1 cup whole-wheat flour
1 pinch of salt
½ cup buttermilk

2

A Helicopter Skiing Picnic

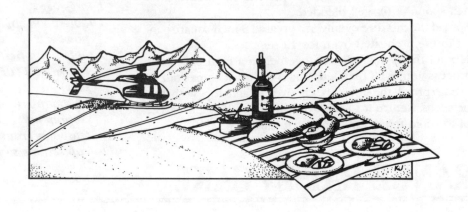

Flexibility! That's the key word for caterers.

One has to be willing and prepared to offer gourmet feasts in the most unusual situations. For whatever desires and fancies dreamt by the customer, the caterer acts as the Fairy Godmother to realize them. The magic of gourmet cooking regularly turns pumpkins into stagecoaches. The art of French cuisine transforms the loathsome snails and eels into delectable treats, repulsive tripes, brains, glands, into scrumptious temptations . . .

The art of a backcountry caterer is to materialize exquisite repasts in the most uncustomary locations. Consider a wedding ceremony in a remote mountain area: I remember Bob and me roasting several lambs on a spit over an open fire, next to a yurt covered with fresh roses; the mayor and the wedding cake, unharmed, reached the high plateau where the guests had already joined the bride and groom.

So, when I was asked to provide a special picnic for a helicopter skiing adventure, it sounded quite simple: How attractive to be able to plan a culinary affair without concerns about volume and weight; how marvelous to be able to prepare very hot food at home, and to have it airlifted by helicopter in insulated containers to the picnic site!

The lentil soup was still piping hot when it came to the picnic table, so pretty with its bright tablecloth and fresh flowers; the toasted pita bread and the spinach pies, wrapped in foil first, then in several layers of newspaper, then in dishcloths as soon as they came out of the oven, impeccable and hot on their serving platters.

As I was contemplating the charm of this adorned buffet table in this magnificent setting, I admitted to myself that an exceptional use of mechanized means has a lot to offer: Besides the attraction of a fine gourmet picnic, think of the promise of 30,000 vertical feet of powder downhill in a single day's skiing!

HELICOPTER SKIING PICNIC MENU

*Rillettes de saumon on croûtes**
Harira: Moroccan lamb and lentil soup
*Toasted pita bread****
Spinach, leek, tofu, and cheese pie
Marinated olives
Sun-dried tomato salad with fresh basil
French lemon pies
Rochers Congolais

*Croûtes are slices of French baguettes, brushed with olive oil and toasted. They may be flavored with garlic and herbs. The recipe follows the rillettes recipe.

**The recipe for toasted pita bread can be found in Chapter 1.

RECIPES

RILLETTES DE SAUMON

This French salmon spread improves with age. Keep it up to one week, refrigerated, under a layer of clarified butter. This recipe, given by Vanel, the celebrated French chef, to *Cuisine* magazine in 1981, is the best I have ever found. It makes 8 servings of ¼ cup each.

INSTRUCTIONS:

Sprinkle the fresh salmon with the ¼ teaspoon of salt. Let it stand at room temperature for 20 minutes.

Melt two tablespoons of the butter in a wide skillet equipped with a tight-fitting lid. Cook the shallot over medium-low heat in the butter until soft, about 4 minutes.

In the meantime heat the wine to boiling in a small saucepan and flame it to remove the alcohol. Add the wine and fresh salmon in one layer to the skillet. Cover the salmon with waxed paper, cover the skillet with the lid, and cook for 2 minutes. Uncover the salmon, turn it over, cover it again with the paper and the lid, and cook 2 more minutes, until the fish is opaque inside and flakes easily. Let it cool. Flake it with a fork, mixing it with the shallot and the cooking juices.

Cream the remaining butter in an electric blender. Blend in the cooked and smoked salmon. With the motor running, quickly add the oil, the yolk, the lemon juice, nutmeg, pepper. The texture should be grainy. Add more salt and/or lemon juice to taste.

Transfer the rillettes to small crocks. Heat the clarified butter to liquefy, and pour it on top of the rillettes. Refrigerate 2 to 3 days before serving. Keep it up to 1 week, or freeze it.

Serve the rillettes at room temperature with toasted croûtes.

INGREDIENTS:
½ pound skinned fresh salmon fillet, cut into large pieces
¼ teaspoon salt
9 tablespoons unsalted butter
1 shallot, minced
¼ cup dry white wine
¼ pound smoked salmon, diced fine
2 tablespoons olive oil
1 egg yolk
1 tablespoon lemon juice
⅛ teaspoon cayenne pepper
¼ teaspoon nutmeg
¼ cup clarified butter

TO MAKE THE CROÛTES:

INGREDIENTS:
*2 thin baguettes of sour-
    dough bread*
½ cup olive oil
*Optional: garlic powder,
    dried herbs such as
    thyme, oregano, basil,
    marjoram, rosemary*

INSTRUCTIONS:
Slice the baguettes, and spread the slices on baking sheets.
Place them in a 350°F. oven, and let them dry up without
turning brown.

Brush the warm slices with the olive oil, and return them
to the oven to brown. You may sprinkle garlic powder and
herbs to taste on the hot croûtes. Let them cool and store
them in a plastic bag. Keep the croûtes refrigerated for up to
1 week, or freeze them.

HARIRA

Makes 8 servings.

INGREDIENTS:
1 pound lamb bones
*½ pound lean lamb meat,
    cubed*
*1 large pinch of saffron,
    soaked in ¼ cup boiling
    water for 30 minutes*
*2 medium-sized onions,
    quartered*
2 cups red or brown lentils
*6 to 8 small tomatoes,
    peeled, seeded, and
    cubed, or 1 large can (1
    lb., 12 oz.) tomatoes,
    drained; reserve the
    tomato juice to add to
    the soup*
*2 large cloves of garlic,
    coarsely chopped*
¼ cup chopped parsley

INSTRUCTIONS:
TO MAKE LAMB STOCK:
Roast the lamb bones in a very hot oven until slightly charred.
Put them into a stockpot with the meat, saffron, 1 quart of
water, and salt and cayenne pepper to taste. Bring to a boil
and simmer 1 hour. Add 1 onion and simmer 30 more minutes.

Add water to the tomato juice to make 1 quart if using
the canned tomatoes, and pour it into a saucepan with the
tomatoes. Or place fresh tomatoes in a saucepan with 1 quart
of water. Season with salt and cayenne pepper and simmer
for 15 minutes.

Discard the bones from the lamb stock, add the lentils,
the second onion, the tomato mixture with the liquid, the
garlic, parsley, thyme, and bay. Simmer, covered, for 45 minutes.

Brown the chopped onion in 2 tablespoons of the butter
and reserve.

Purée the soup through a food mill or in a food processor.
Reheat it, stir in the lemon juice, cumin, and remaining butter.
Adjust the seasoning.

Serve the soup topped with the browned onion and lemon wedges and cilantro as garnish.

See Chapter 1 for the recipe for toasted pita bread.

2 each, thyme sprigs and
 bay leaves
¼ cup unsalted butter, 2
 ounces
¼ cup finely chopped
 onion
Juice of 1 lemon
2 teaspoons ground cumin
salt and cayenne pepper to
 taste
Lemon wedges and cilantro
 sprigs for garnish

SPINACH, LEEK, TOFU, AND CHEESE PIE

Makes 8 servings.

PREPARATION:

The pie should be made at home. As soon as it comes out of the oven, wrap it first in foil, then in several layers of newspaper and then in several dishcloths to keep it hot until served at the picnic site.

INSTRUCTIONS:

Pat the spinach dry and chop coarsely.

Heat the 2 tablespoons of butter in a large noncorrosive skillet, add the leeks and shallots; stir them briefly to coat with the butter.

Butter a large piece of foil and press it down on the vegetables to cover. Top the skillet with a lid and let the vegetables "sweat" for 5 minutes over low heat.

Remove the lid and the foil and add the spinach, garlic, mace, and cayenne pepper. Cook the vegetables, stirring until the spinach is tender and the liquid almost evaporated, 5 to 6 minutes. Remove the mixture from the heat, press out the remaining liquid, stir in the bread crumbs, and let cool.

INGREDIENTS:

2 pounds spinach, washed
 and with stems removed
4 leeks, white only,
 chopped
2 shallots, minced
2 tablespoons unsalted
 butter, and a little more
 to butter a large piece of
 foil
2 cloves of garlic, minced
1 teaspoon ground mace
⅛ teaspoon cayenne pepper
2 tablespoons dry bread
 crumbs
1 cup unsalted butter, 2
 sticks
4 large eggs, beaten to
 blend
10 ounces tofu

Preheat the oven to 375°F.

Melt the 1 cup of butter in a small saucepan. Mix together the beaten eggs, the tofu, Gruyère, blue cheese, and Parmesan. Stir into the vegetable mixture and blend.

Layer a 12-by-12-inch cake pan, or two 9-by-9-inch pans, with half the shredded dough, separating the shreds with the fingers to make an even layer. Brush with half the melted butter. Spread the spinach filling evenly and top with a second layer of shredded dough brushed with butter. Place the pie in the preheated oven and bake 30 to 40 minutes, until the dough is crisp and golden brown.

4 ounces Gruyère, grated
2 ounces crumbled blue cheese
1 ounce grated Parmesan cheese
1 pound (1 box) shredded phyllo dough

MARINATED OLIVES

Makes 1 quart.

PREPARATION:

Prepare the olives several days before using them. They keep up to 2 weeks very well in the refrigerator and improve in flavor with time.

INSTRUCTIONS:

Drain and rinse the olives under cold running water. Drain again. Place them in a quart-size jar.

Cut 8 thin slices of lemon from the center of 1 lemon and add them to the olives. Squeeze the juice from the remaining cut ends and the other lemon; pour the juice into the jar. Add all the remaining ingredients.

Seal the jar and shake it to mix well. Marinate for at least two days. Drain the olives to serve or use them in other recipes.

Use the marinade to make salad dressings.

INGREDIENTS:
2 cans pitted ripe olives
2 lemons
4 cloves of garlic, crushed but left in one piece
3 bay leaves
3 to 4 sprigs of thyme
1 sprig of rosemary
1 teaspoon whole fennel seeds
1 teaspoon whole coriander seeds
1½ teaspoons sea salt
20 black peppercorns
1½ cups olive oil

SUN-DRIED TOMATO SALAD WITH FRESH BASIL

Makes 8 servings.

PREPARATION:

Prepare the salad the day before serving it to let the dried tomatoes plump up and absorb the flavors of the marinade overnight. They will not reconstitute very much in salad dressing as they would in water; they will remain deliciously chewy with a concentrated tomato flavor.

INSTRUCTIONS:

In a wide shallow plastic box equipped with a tight-fitting lid, make layers of dehydrated tomato slices, basil leaves coarsely chopped (save a few whole leaves for garnish), and sliced marinated olives. Mix the vinegar into the olive marinade, and pour it over the vegetable layers. Place the whole marinated olives and basil leaves on top. Seal the box with the lid and some duct tape. Refrigerate it overnight.

INGREDIENTS:

6 ounces home-dehydrated tomates (equivalent to about 4 pounds of fresh tomatoes)

1 bunch fresh basil leaves, 1½ ounces

½ cup marinated olive marinade, with some of the herbs

24 marinated olives, sliced

A few marinated olives left whole

2 tablespoons red wine vinegar

FRENCH LEMON PIE

Makes 8 servings.

PREPARATION:

This pie can be made one day, kept refrigerated, and served the next day. It also can be kept frozen for longer storage. This recipe calls for a 10-inch pie plate.

INSTRUCTIONS:

SHELL:

Grind the almonds to a powder in a food processor. Add the flour, sugar, and butter; process until the mixture resembles coarse sand. With the motor running, pour in the lemon juice

INGREDIENTS:

SHELL:

1 cup blanched almonds

1½ cups unbleached organic white flour

½ cup raw sugar (turbinado)

6 tablespoons cold unsalted butter, cut into bits

2 tablespoons cold lemon juice

in a fine stream, and let the machine run just a few more seconds until the mixture begins to form a ball.

Preheat the oven to 375°F.

Transfer the dough to a marble or wooden pastry board. Press it together with the hand into a thick disk; wrap it in clear plastic film and refrigerate it for at least 30 minutes. Remove it from the plastic and roll it out to make a 14-to-15-inch circle. Drape it over a 10-inch pie plate. Trim some of the excess dough hanging over and fold the remaining edge back to form a roll around the shell. With the blade of a knife, carve slanted indents equally spaced on the rolled edge to form a rope pattern. Prick the bottom of the shell with a fork in many places. Bake it in the preheated oven for 10 minutes.

FILLING:

Whip together the eggs, sugar, ground almonds, grated lemon peel, and the juice of 1 lemon. Add the melted but cool butter. Taste, and add more lemon juice to taste. Pour the mixture into the partly baked shell.

Lower the oven temperature to 350°F. and bake the pie 30 minutes, or a little longer, until the filling is cooked through and the top begins to brown.

Let the pie cool on a wire rack. When completely cooled, wrap it with plastic and refrigerate it if it is to be served the next day.

FILLING:
3 large eggs
¾ cup raw sugar
¾ cup ground blanched almonds
2 lemons, peels finely grated and juice reserved
½ cup melted butter

ROCHERS CONGOLAIS

Makes 24 cookies.

PREPARATION:

Rocher Congolais means, in French, Congolese rock. Congolese, because traditionally, France used to get her coconut from Congo. But why "rock," when these little cookies just melt in your mouth? They are even better the next day! So make them 1 or 2 days before you want to serve them and keep them in an airtight box.

INGREDIENTS:
2 large eggs, separated
6 tablespoons raw honey
2 cups unsweetened finely shredded coconut

INSTRUCTIONS:
Preheat the oven to 350°F.

Whip the egg whites until very stiff peaks form. Whip together the yolks, honey, and coconut. Fold the whites gently into the yolk mixture; do not overmix.

Drop 1½-tablespoonful quantities of batter onto a greased baking sheet. You should get about 24 little mounds. Bake them in the prepared oven for 15 minutes, until well browned. Cool them on a wire rack.

3
Snow Camping

I may be "The Trekking Chef," but a sixty-day trek in the icy mountains of Wrangell-St. Elias, from the Yukon Territory into southwest Alaska? And in April to May with subzero temperatures? Thank you, Bob! I will pack your food, but I'll be damned if I spend sixty days of my life on that ice cap, even if it is the largest outside the poles, and this trek has never been accomplished before!

And yet the stories, the pictures, that Bob, Jim, John, and Jeff brought back depict a most unique, unforgettable experience: a succession of breathtaking glacier and mountain vistas, colored by the sun at all times of the day; the testimonies of an experience well enjoyed by four companions sharing every moment, living, laughing, marveling together.

However, I did get great satisfaction from this trip in the knowledge of the pleasure created by every single meal; the fun they had cooking together, following the instructions, the enjoyment of savoring great-tasting food, something new for those men who had known nothing on previous expeditions but salami, cheese, and freeze-dried food.

It was the first time that my "trek food" was to be used on a long, tough journey. I remember my numerous concerns while preparing it: They must retain a maximum energy, mentally and physically, from beginning to end; the weight must be reasonable, but they need to burn a lot of calories every day; variety and flavor are important, but not so much as is a balanced diet; this food has to be as fresh and well-preserved on the last as on the first day; the packaging is crucial. They are talking of caching some of the food as they venture on side trips with only a limited supply. They say that the pilot will "drop" the second half of their food supply when they reach the midpoint of the expedition. I am relieved to hear that the pilot does not actually drop boxes from the air, but lands on a glacier at a designated spot.

Once more, the climate is my ally: the cold will preserve everything. I can turn every lunch into a special treat with a variety of spreads, scrumptious blends of nut-butters, cheeses, meats, and vegetables with spices and herbs. I can freeze them as I make them, each day-spread individually sealed in a plastic pouch. It will remain frozen on the trip until the day it is on the menu, when they will expose it to the sun or carry it inside their parkas to warm it up with body heat.

Once more the sleds, too—one for each man—will permit a certain volume and weight. No matter what, with only one food drop and that one on Day 24, they are going to start at the trail head with a supply of food and beverage for thirty days—a considerable amount, even though the "Trekking Chef's" food is very comparable in weight and volume to freeze-dried food.

They want bread every day—the sleds can allow that: one pound of bread daily. I am packing the neat one-pound cubical loaves of compact, sliced pumpernickel, Jewish rye, German country breads, a total of sixty pounds. (We have found on many occasions that this bread remains intact for many days; it does not crumble or get squashed easily.)

What about the snack bars? At least two per person per day: a total of 480 bars! And the beverages? They want some "sweet powders" for their melted snow, enough for four quarts daily. (They found later that half this amount was enough.) I gave them three kinds: a good instant vitamin C drink, sweetened with fructose, and two less healthful drinks, sugar-loaded fruit punch and lemon-lime beverages. They want sugar. They think they cannot survive out there without sugar! They also have bags of turbinado sugar for their tea: three servings of herbal teas per person per day. The other hot beverage is our favorite at home and away: a delicious carob-flavored soy-milk powder, sweetened with pure cane sugar, proving that healthful food can also taste good, far better than a refined sugar-chocolate-dairy product. Three servings per person per day, too, add up to thirty-four pounds of the carob soy-milk powder alone. (It was not too much, they used it up.)

The main food was packed into sixty daily bags containing, from top to bottom, lunch, dinner, breakfast. Their first meal on the trail would be lunch, out of Bag 1, followed by dinner and breakfast at the first campsite, and this would be repeated fifty-nine times.

Each man carries his own snacks: fifteen pounds of dried fruit and nuts with 120 bars divided into two loads, before and after the food drop.

Indeed, weight is the primary concern. Even though I have dehydrated all the main food ingredients for dinners and breakfasts, I cannot cut down the huge amounts of bread, snacks, and beverages that they justly require. The best way to eliminate weight on such a trip is to cut down the amount of fuel used for cooking. No cooking time for any preparation should exceed ten or twelve minutes. Most of the fuel has to be used to melt snow to make water rather than just to cook. But how do you serve a healthful diet based on grains and legumes, when you cannot allow more cooking time?

I started to experiment, cooking rice, barley, lentils, kasha, then dehydrating them, and this is what I found: The cooked grain or legume dehydrates back to a volume only slightly larger than the volume of the raw food. The good news was that the resulting weight was actually lighter than the original one. Of course, the rehydrating time would be five minutes compared to thirty or forty-five minutes' cooking time, and, moreover, only half the amount of water needed to cook the food is necessary to rehydrate it, and this saves a lot of fuel, too!

The menu was designed to repeat itself every two weeks, so that each dish was not presented more than three times. On a forty-plus-day expedition, a seven-day menu cycle becomes tedious. In this chapter I am offering a seven-day menu. (Most of us do not wish to spend more than a week snow camping!) If you want to plan for a longer trip you can combine the seven-day menu of the backpacking trip—Chapter 5—with this one. Some adjustments will be necessary: Some recipes in Chapter 5 require a longer cooking time with the idea that many times a campfire will be used with no worry about the fuel. Other recipes are created with the knowledge that some wild foods will be available on the trail: mountain sorrel, blueberries. Nothing of the kind can be found on top of an ice cap, but the absence of life in an immaculate world of ice and snow enhances its beauty!

SNACKING

In this type of camping, I believe that the one-pot-meal prepared in less than twenty minutes is the best option for breakfast and dinner. Sometimes dinner is a two-course meal with a soup and vegetable patties to break the monotony. Lunch is a sandwich spread and bread, still very simple!

This rule is imposed by the necessity to strip down the kitchen equipment to a minimum, and the fact that the only fuel available is the white gas carried by the travelers.

To compensate for the starkness of this fare, I provide each person with a "snack bag." The snack bag is already a legend among us. Those who are aware of my food-planning habits look forward to it; those who aren't are happily surprised. It contains enough nuts, dried fruits, homemade and commercial sweet bars—even chocolate ones in moderation!—to give a quick pick-me-up on the trail when needed, to be enjoyed when the backpack is down for a break, and to add dessert to each meal.

The most popular item, next to the "decadently delicious" Cadbury fruit and nut bars, is my supposedly more healthful "Trek Bar," created one day when I felt like being extravagant and used almonds, carob, coconut, apricot, apple, dates—all at once! The recipe follows in this chapter. Many more recipes for delicious snack bars—using natural, non-refined ingredients—are found in every chapter of this book.

Here is a description of a typical daily snack allowance for one person:

- 2 ounces nuts and seeds: whole almonds, filberts, Brazil nuts, cashews, walnut halves, sunflower seeds, shredded unsweetened coconut...
- 2 ounces mixed dried unsulfured fruits: apricots, apples, pears, peaches, papaya, pineapple, banana chips, raisins...
- 2 homemade sweet bars: trek bar, apricot bar, protein bar, nutty-rye bar, buzz bar, orange-carob bar...
- 2 commercial candy bars: chocolate bar, granola bar, fruit leather, Guru-Shew...

Two ounces each of fruit and nuts a day doesn't seem like much, but think of the quantity you will have to carry if you are on the trail for sixty days, as my four heroes were. And this quantity did satisfy them!

I buy all the commercial candy bars, except the Cadburys, in a health food store, but don't let this encourage you. A candy bar is a candy bar no matter where it comes from; it still contains too much sugar to be considered healthful, whether the sugar is called saccharose, fructose, honey, or fruit juice! But don't the rigorous conditions of a hardy trail deserve a sweet touch?

MENUS

DAY 1
◆
LUNCH

Apricot-almond spread with bread
Turkey chips, cheese slices

DINNER

Turkey-barley casserole

BREAKFAST

Almond-pistachio couscous

DAY 2
◆
LUNCH

Ham-onion-mustard spread with bread
Turkey jerky and cheese slices

DINNER

Cherba
Felafel with nut and garlic sauce

BREAKFAST

Sesame coconut bulgur

DAY 3
◆
LUNCH

Berry-cheese spread with bread
Smoked trout

DINNER

Tomato-oats soup
Zucchini patties with vegetable sauce

BREAKFAST

Barley pudding

DAY 4
◆
LUNCH

Tahini-garbanzo spread with bread
Turkey chips, cheese slices

DINNER

Zarda: sweet spicy rice with chicken

BREAKFAST

Oats pudding

DAY 5

◆

LUNCH

Korean soup with bread
Smoked trout, cheese slices

DINNER

Bulgur wheat with lamb sauce

BREAKFAST

Kasha pudding

DAY 6

◆

LUNCH

Potato-horseradish spread with bread
Turkey jerky, cheese slices

DINNER

Sopa da panela
Spinach patties with tomato sauce

BREAKFAST

Cream of wheat pudding

DAY 7

◆

LUNCH

Tofu-chutney spread with bread
Turkey chips, cheese slices

DINNER

Potato and smoked fish casserole

BREAKFAST

Buckwheat pancakes, rice bran syrup

Notes on store-bought items:

Smoked trout: We are lucky here in Sun Valley, Idaho, to live close to the world's largest trout farm. Someone nearby smokes the fish as a business. I was able to get our smoked fish at a wholesale price, and to add some special requirements to my order such as less salt and NO nitrate. In Alaska, it is easy to find those local smoking enterprises; they also smoke salmon, halibut, and good sausages.

Korean soup: Soup is a good idea for lunch once a week. The group does not travel every day; there are some layover days or days when the weather is stormy and the visibility nil. On those days it is possible to fire up the stoves and enjoy a hot lunch. I wanted to serve for these occasions a quick-cooking ramen type of soup, but they all contain some MSG except for more expensive ones in the health food stores. Near a military air base I found a quaint Korean shop that had several varieties of these soups. Only two kinds did not have any MSG, and they sold me a case of each.

SPREADS

All the spreads are made at home, then sealed airtight in plastic pouches. Keep them in a freezer until the food is packed for the trip.

APRICOT-ALMOND SPREAD

Makes one cup spread.

WEIGHT: one pound

INSTRUCTIONS:
Grind the almonds in a food processor. Add the apricots and

INGREDIENTS:
2 tablespoons blanched almonds, toasted lightly and cooled

process to a paste. Add the cream cheese, almond butter, and honey with the lemon peel and cardamom. Blend the mixture, scraping the bowl occasionally with a spatula until homogeneous and smooth.

Keep the spread in the cooler during the trip. Let it come up to the ambient temperature before serving it.

¼ cup chopped dried apricots
½ cup cream cheese
¼ cup almond butter
1 tablespoon raw honey
½ teaspoon lemon peel
¼ teaspoon cardamom

HAM, ONION, MUSTARD SPREAD

Makes 2 cups, enough for 8 sandwiches.

WEIGHT: 1 pound, 2 ounces
Equipment: A food processor.

INSTRUCTIONS:
Purée the ham in the food processor. Add the remaining ingredients and run the food processor 1 more minute to blend them well together.

INGREDIENTS:
12 ounces ham, fat trimmed away
4 ounces butter, ½ cup
1 yellow onion chopped, about 1 cup
6 tablespoons Dijon mustard
2 teaspoons sweet paprika
⅛ teaspoon cayenne pepper, or more to taste

BERRY-CHEESE SPREAD

Makes 2 cups, enough for 8 sandwiches.

WEIGHT: 1 pound, 2 ounces
Equipment: A food processor.

INSTRUCTIONS:
Purée the berries in the food processor. Add the remaining ingredients and run the food processor until they are well blended.

INGREDIENTS:
12 ounces cream cheese, or 8 ounces cream cheese and 4 ounces tofu
12 ounces fresh or frozen berries: blueberries, blackberries, raspberries
2 tablespoons raw honey
2 teaspoons vanilla extract
1 teaspoon freshly grated lemon peel, or ½ teaspoon dry

TAHINI-GARBANZO SPREAD

Makes 2 cups, enough for 8 sandwiches.

WEIGHT: 1 pound, 2 ounces
Equipment: A food processor.

INSTRUCTIONS:
Process all the ingredients in the food processor. If the spread seems too thick, you may add some water up to ¼ cup to thin it.

INGREDIENTS:
1 cup tahini (sesame nut butter)
¾ cup mashed cooked garbanzo beans
¼ cup fresh lemon juice
2 tablespoons toasted sesame seeds
2 teaspoons sweet paprika
½ teaspoon garlic granules or dried minced garlic
½ teaspoon instant vegetable-stock powder
⅛ teaspoon cayenne pepper, or more to taste

TOFU-CHUTNEY SPREAD

Makes 2 cups, enough for 8 sandwiches.

WEIGHT: 1 pound
Equipment: a food processor.

INSTRUCTIONS:
Process the tofu in the food processor to make a smooth paste. Add the chutney and the apricots and process until blended. A few small chunks of mango or apricot may remain. Blend in the slivered almonds by hand.

INGREDIENTS:
10 ounces firm tofu
4 ounces mango chutney
⅔ cup dried apricots, chopped
⅓ cup slivered almonds, toasted

SNACKS

HERBAL TURKEY CHIPS

This recipe makes five 4-ounce bags; each bag serves four as a lunch snack.

PREPARATION:

Turkey chips are best made at home using a food dehydrator. You also need a food processor. For the cooked turkey called for in the recipe, I use whole turkey keels. I cook them in water with some vegetables, herbs, and spices and reserve the stock for other uses. A whole turkey breast yields 4 to 6 pounds of cooked meat. I use ½ breast in each batch of either herb chips or cranberry chips.

INSTRUCTIONS:

Peel the onions. Chop the turkey meat and the onions into large pieces, ½- to 1-inch size. Quarter the eggs. Process all the ingredients together in the food processor in batches and transfer each batch to a large mixing bowl. You should have about 5 pounds of mixture.

Line 5 12-by-12-inch dehydrator trays with waxed paper; to hold the paper in place, fasten it to the frames of the trays with an adhesive tape. Spread 1 pound of mixture on each lined tray, ¼ inch thick. Dry 10 to 12 hours at 120° F.

Each square weighs 4 ounces when dried. Break each one into pieces, chip size, and store in a sealed plastic pouch.

INGREDIENTS:

3 pounds cooked turkey breast
2 large yellow onions
6 cloves of garlic, peeled
6 hard-boiled eggs, peeled
1 cup packed fresh parsley leaves
1 cup mixed fresh herbs or ¼ cup dried: tarragon, chervil, basil, mint, thyme, rosemary...
¾ cup Dijon mustard (6 ounces)
¾ apple-cider vinegar
1 tablespoon Tabasco sauce, or more: the mixture should be very spicy, or the chips will be quite bland.

CRANBERRY TURKEY CHIPS

The preparation and the instructions are the same as for the herb turkey chips. Only the ingredients differ:

INGREDIENTS:

3 pounds cooked turkey

3 16-ounce cans of
  cranberry sauce
1½ whole oranges
¾ cup apple-cider vinegar
2 teaspoons nutmeg
1 teaspoon ginger
1 teaspoon dry mustard
1 teaspoon allspice

TURKEY JERKY

Makes 8 ounces of jerky, or 8 servings.

PREPARATION:

Turkey jerky is best made at home, using a food dehydrator.

INSTRUCTIONS:

Slice the turkey ¼ inch thick. Cut each slice into strips 2 to 5 inches long. Mix all the other ingredients together and pour the mixture over the turkey strips. Gently stir until all the strips are coated with the liquid. Let them marinate covered and refrigerated from 2 hours to overnight.

Drain the strips out of the marinade and place them on the dehydrator trays in a single layer. Make sure they do not touch each other. Dry 5 hours, or overnight, at 120° F.

Transfer the turkey jerky to plastic pouches in batches of 2 or 4 ounces (2 to 4 servings) and seal.

INGREDIENTS:

1½ pounds raw turkey
  breast (fat, skin, bones
  removed)
¼ cup tamari sauce
1 tablespoon fresh lemon
  juice
¼ teaspoon garlic powder
¼ teaspoon cayenne pepper
⅛ teaspoon ginger
⅛ teaspoon Chinese five
  spices

SOUPS

The soups, casseroles, vegetable patties, and breakfasts are prepared entirely in the field, using home- and commercially dehydrated ingredients. The ingredients are measured ahead of time and sealed into several plastic pouches, according to the instructions.

CHERBA: ARABIC TOMATO-MINT SOUP

Makes 4 servings.

WEIGHT: 8 ounces, without the oil or butter

PREPARATION TIME: 12 to 14 minutes

INSTRUCTIONS:
Have five cups hot water ready.

Use ½ cup of the water to reconstitute the onion. Let it stand 2 minutes.

In a soup pot, heat the olive oil and sauté the onion for 1 minute. Add the tomato slices, mint, cayenne pepper, and vegetable-stock powder with 4 cups of the hot water. Bring the soup to a boil and let it simmer, uncovered, for 5 minutes.

In the meantime, reconstitute the eggs with ½ cup of the warm water. Mix the cheese into the eggs and add the mixture to the soup, stirring. Let it simmer 3 more minutes and serve.

INGREDIENTS:
¼ cup dehydrated chopped onion
2 tablespoons olive oil, or 1 pouch clarified butter
1 cup dehydrated tomato slices, crushed lightly
1 tablespoon dried mint
1 pinch of cayenne pepper, or more to taste
4 teaspoons instant vegetable-stock powder
2 ounces freeze-dried eggs, ½ cup
½ cup dried grated Parmesan cheese

TOMATO-OATS SOUP

Makes 4 servings.

TOTAL WEIGHT: approximately 10 ounces

TOMATO-OATS SOUP

Makes 4 servings.

TOTAL WEIGHT: approximately 10 ounces

TOTAL COOKING TIME: 12 minutes

INSTRUCTIONS:
Have 4¾ cups of cold water ready. Pour 1 cup of the water into the oats, right in the bag, and stir to moisten them.

Pour the contents of Bag 2 (the tomato mixture) into a soup pot, add 1 cup of the water, and heat it gently until the liquid is absorbed. Add the clarified butter and cook the mixture for 5 minutes. Pour 2 more cups of water into the soup pot, stir in the oats mixture. Bring the soup to a boil, lower the heat, and cook for 5 minutes.

Rehydrate the eggs right in their bag with the remaining ¾ cup of water. Pour the eggs into the soup, stir 1 minute, and serve.

INGREDIENTS:
BAG 1: *1 cup quick-cooking oats*
4 teaspoons vegetable-stock powder
BAG 2: *4 ounces dehydrated tomatoes, powdered with some pieces left in them*
¾ cup dried onion, or ¼ cup if powdered
1 teaspoon dried thyme
1 dry bay leaf
⅛ teaspoon ground clove
⅛ teaspoon cayenne pepper
1 pinch of salt, optional, depending on how salty the stock is
BAG 3: *2 ounces freeze-dried scrambled-eggs mix*
1¾-ounce pouch clarified butter

SOPA DA PANELA

Makes 4 servings.

TOTAL WEIGHT: approximately 8 ounces

TOTAL COOKING TIME: 8 minutes

INSTRUCTIONS:
Mix the contents of Bag 1 (the garbanzo mixture) with 4 cups of water in a saucepan. Bring it to a boil, lower the heat, and cook gently until the garbanzo beans are soft, about 5 minutes. Add the croutons and serve.

INGREDIENTS:
BAG 1: *1 cup cooked and dehydrated garbanzo beans*
4 teaspoons vegetable-stock powder
½ teaspoon garlic granules
2 tablespoons dried mint
2 tablespoons dried parsley
⅛ teaspoon cayenne pepper

CROUTONS

INSTRUCTIONS:

Dry the bread slices in a 350° F. oven, until they feel dry to the touch but are not browned. Transfer them to a bread board and, with a serrated-edged knife, cut them into small cubes, about ⅜ inch across. Heat the olive oil in a large frying pan and sauté the bread cubes, shaking the pan constantly. When they are well browned, drain them on paper towels. Sprinkle the garlic powder on the croutons and let them cool completely.

Pack them in a plastic pouch and seal it. It is better to store the croutons in the refrigerator or the freezer, as the olive oil in them may turn rancid.

BAG 2: *1 cup croutons (Instructions to make the croutons follow this recipe.)*

INGREDIENTS:
2 slices of bread, whole wheat or sourdough
2 tablespoons of olive oil
¼ teaspoon garlic powder

DINNER CASSEROLES

TURKEY AND BARLEY CASSEROLE

Makes 4 servings.

TOTAL WEIGHT: approximately 20 ounces

TOTAL COOKING TIME: 15 minutes

INSTRUCTIONS:

Rehydrate the onion-turkey mixture in its bag with 1 cup very hot water. Rehydrate the barley mixture with 2 cups hot water. Heat the butter in a nonstick skillet; add the turkey mixture and cook until the onion begins to brown. Add ½ cup of water and let it simmer until all the liquid is absorbed and the turkey is soft.

Add the barley mixture, stir to mix well. Sprinkle the grated cheese on top; cover the skillet with a piece of foil. Keep the skillet over low heat until the cheese is melted, and serve.

INGREDIENTS:
1¾-ounce pouch clarified butter
BAG 1: *6 ounces cooked and dehydrated turkey meat*
¼ cup dehydrated onion
1 tablespoon vegetable-stock powder
½ teaspoon nutmeg
⅛ teaspoon cayenne pepper
BAG 2: *2 cups cooked and dehydrated barley*
¼ cup buttermilk powder
¼ teaspoon dry mustard

BAG 3: *½ cup grated and dehydrated mozzarella cheese*

ZARDA: SWEET SPICY RICE PILAF WITH CHICKEN

Makes 4 servings.

TOTAL WEIGHT: approximately 18 ounces

TOTAL COOKING TIME: 12 to 15 minutes

INSTRUCTIONS:

Heat the butter in a nonstick skillet or a wok. Add the spices (Bag 1) and sauté them until they are browned and puffy. Add the rice, stir, and cook 2 minutes. Add 3 cups of hot water to the contents of Bag 3 (chicken mixture). Lower the heat, cover the skillet or wok with a lid or a piece of foil. Let the food simmer until all the liquid is absorbed and the rice and chicken are tender: 8 to 10 minutes.

Note: I find it great fun to cook with whole spices, as they do in India: It fills up the tent with enchanting exotic aromas. I also love to chew on whole cloves, cardamom seeds, and cinnamon. Not only do they act as a breath freshener, but, like many other spices, they are natural antiseptics and preservatives; cardamom is a powerful cough remedy. In fact, in the old traditional Ayurvedic diet, so little distinction is made between medicine and foodstuffs that they are designated with the same word: *dravya.*

INGREDIENTS:

1¾-ounce pouch clarified butter

BAG 1: *8 whole cloves*
6 whole cardamom pods
3-inch cinnamon stick, broken up

BAG 2: *2 cups cooked and dehydrated brown rice*

BAG 3: *6 ounces cooked and dehydrated chicken*
6 tablespoons raisins
¼ cup honey flakes
¼ teaspoon saffron powder or turmeric
1 pinch of salt

BULGUR WHEAT WITH LAMB SAUCE

Makes 4 servings.

PREPARATION:

Bulgur is a fine cracked wheat that has been steamed and dried. Therefore, it takes very little time to cook, just like my precooked grains and legumes. The lamb sauce needs to be cooked ahead of time and dehydrated in a food dehydrator. If you prefer beef, it can be used instead of lamb. Since a certain amount of fat remains in the meat —and fat does not dehydrate—I recommend that the lamb sauce, after it has been dehydrated and sealed in a plastic bag, be refrigerated or frozen.

TOTAL WEIGHT: approximately 18 ounces

TOTAL COOKING TIME IN THE FIELD: 12 to 15 minutes

INSTRUCTIONS:

Empty Bag 1 (bulgur) into a saucepan; add 1½ cups boiling water, cover the pan, and let stand 10 minutes.

In the meantime, mix the lamb sauce with water to cover in a skillet and bring to a boil. Lower the heat and let simmer until the liquid is absorbed and the meat is tender, about 10 minutes.

Uncover the bulgur wheat, stir it with a fork to fluff it up. Stir in the butter and serve topped with the lamb sauce.

INGREDIENTS:

1¾-ounce pouch of clarified butter

BAG 1: *1½ cups bulgur wheat*
2 teaspoons vegetable-stock powder

BAG 2: *8 ounces dehydrated lamb sauce, made with 1 pound ground lamb; recipe follows*

LAMB SAUCE:

INSTRUCTIONS:

Heat the olive oil in a large frying pan. Add the ground meat and cook over medium-high heat, stirring, until it is all brown with no pink left. Transfer with a slotted spoon to a bowl and discard the fat out of the frying pan.

Wipe the pan with a paper towel, add a little more olive oil, and sauté the onion until limp but not brown. Add the green pepper and cook until soft.

Transfer the onion-pepper mixture to the bowl with the

meat. Add the tomato paste, the raisins, green olives, the egg, salt, cayenne pepper, thyme, and sugar. Blend all the ingredients together very thoroughly. It should be quite spicy and you may want to add more cayenne pepper.

Spread the mixture on dehydrator trays that have been lined with waxed paper held to the frames with adhesive tape. Since it is already cooked, the sauce can be dehydrated at 145° F, for about 6 hours or overnight.

INGREDIENTS:
2 tablespoons olive oil
1 pound ground lamb or beef, as lean as possible
1 medium onion, chopped
1 green pepper, chopped
1 tablespoon tomato paste
1/4 cup raisins
2 tablespoons minced green olives
1 large egg, beaten to blend
1/2 teaspoon salt
1/8 teaspoon cayenne pepper
2 teaspoons fresh thyme, or 1/2 teaspoon dried
Pinch of sugar

POTATO-SMOKED FISH CASSEROLE

Makes 4 servings.

WEIGHT: 24 ounces

PREPARATION TIME: 10 minutes

INSTRUCTIONS:
Pour 4 cups boiling water directly into the potato bag and 1/2 cup boiling water into the onion bag to rehydrate the vegetables. Let them stand a few minutes.

Heat the butter in a skillet and sauté the onion mixture for 2 minutes. Add the potato mixture and cook over low heat until the potatoes are soft and the liquid is absorbed. You may have to add a little more water if the liquid is absorbed before the potatoes are tender. Add the smoked fish in chunks, stir, cook 2 more minutes, and serve.

INGREDIENTS:
1 pouch clarified butter
BAG 1: *4 cups dehydrated cubed potatoes, about 10 ounces*
2 tablespoons dried parsley
1 tablespoon instant vegetable-stock powder
1/8 teaspoon cayenne pepper
BAG 2: *1/2 cup dehydrated onion*
1 teaspoon garlic granules
BAG 3: *12 ounces smoked fish (trout or salmon)*

VEGETABLE PATTIES

FELAFEL WITH NUT AND GARLIC SAUCE

Makes 4 servings.

TOTAL WEIGHT: 24 ounces

TOTAL COOKING TIME: 20 minutes

INSTRUCTIONS:

Mix 3 cups water with the contents of Bag 1 and stir to blend well. You should have a stiff batter; add a little more water if it is too stiff. Heat some of the butter in the skillet and fry small amounts of batter until browned on both sides. Transfer them to a plate and repeat until all the batter is used.

IN THE MEANTIME, MAKE THE SAUCE:

In a small saucepan gently warm up the butter from 2 of the pouches. Add the nut mixture (Bag 2), stir, and keep warm until ready to serve on top of the felafel patties.

WATCH POINT: do not let the nuts blacken in the butter as you keep it warm. If they do, remove the sauce from the heat.

INGREDIENTS:

3 pouches clarified butter

BAG 1: *1 cup bulgur wheat*

½ cup dry bread crumbs

1¾ cups ground dehydrated cooked garbanzos

2 teaspoons instant vegetable-stock powder

1 teaspoon dry lemon peel

1 teaspoon garlic granules

1 teaspoon ground cumin

1 pinch cayenne pepper, or more (felafel should be spicy)

BAG 2: NUT AND GARLIC SAUCE

¼ cup ground pine nuts

¼ cup ground pistachio nuts

½ teaspoon garlic granules

½ teaspoon ground dried mint leaves

1 pinch sea salt

1 pinch cayenne pepper

ZUCCHINI PATTIES WITH VEGETABLE SAUCE

Makes 4 servings.

WEIGHT: patties and sauce, 18 ounces

PREPARATION TIME: 20 minutes

INSTRUCTIONS:
Pour the contents of Bag 1 into a bowl and stir with 2 cups warm water. Let stand 5 to 10 minutes and stir again. The batter should be thick.

Heat some of the butter in the skillet and fry small amounts of batter for 3 to 4 minutes; turn them over and cook the other sides 2 to 3 minutes. Transfer the patties to a warm plate and repeat until all the batter is used. While the patties are cooking, make the sauce.

Just before serving, sprinkle the patties with the Parmesan cheese in Bag 2.

VEGETABLE SAUCE

INSTRUCTIONS:
In a small saucepan, bring 2 cups of water to a boil. Add the vegetable sauce bag contents, stir, and simmer the sauce over low heat for at least 10 minutes until the patties are ready.

INGREDIENTS:
2 pouches clarified butter
BAG 1: *2 ounces ground dehydrated zucchini*
¼ cup dehydrated onion
4 ounces freeze-dried eggs
½ cup wheat germ
½ cup whole-wheat flour
1 teaspoon garlic granules
1 teaspoon ground cumin
1 teaspoon vegetable-stock powder
⅛ teaspoon cayenne pepper
BAG 2: *½ cup dry grated Parmesan cheese*

INGREDIENTS:
2 teaspoons instant vegetable-stock powder
½ teaspoon ground cumin
2 tablespoons mixed dried herbs: parsley, oregano, thyme, mint, marjoram, cilantro . . .
2 ounces crushed or ground dehydrated tomatoes
¼ cup dehydrated onion, ½ ounce
½ cup dehydrated bell pepper, green and red, 1 ounce
¼ cup dehydrated celery leaves, ½ ounce

SPINACH PATTIES WITH TOMATO SAUCE

Makes 4 servings.

WEIGHT: patties and sauce, 14 ounces

PREPARATION TIME: 20 minutes

INSTRUCTIONS:

Stir the contents of Bag 1 into 2 cups of warm water until well blended, like a pancake batter. Heat some of the butter in the skillet; fry small amounts of batter 3 to 4 minutes until browned. Turn them over and brown the other side, 2 to 3 minutes. Transfer the patties onto a warm plate and repeat until all the batter is used. While the patties are cooking, make the sauce.

TOMATO SAUCE:

Mix the contents of Bag 2 with 2 cups of cold water in a small saucepan. Bring the mixture to a boil, lower the heat, and let it simmer for at least 10 minutes. When the patties are ready, serve them topped with the sauce.

INGREDIENTS:

2 pouches clarified butter

BAG 1: *2 ounces dehydrated spinach, ground, 1 cup*
¼ cup soy-milk powder
4 ounces freeze-dried eggs
6 tablespoons rye flour
¼ teaspoon ground mace
1 teaspoon vegetable-stock powder
⅛ teaspoon cayenne pepper

BAG 2: *2 ounces dehydrated tomatoes, ground*
1 ounce dehydrated bell peppers, green and red
½ teaspoon garlic granules
2 tablespoons dried parsley
1 bay leaf
1 teaspoon dried oregano
1 teaspoon dried thyme
1 teaspoon vegetable-stock powder
⅛ teaspoon each cayenne pepper, cloves, sugar

BREAKFASTS

ALMOND-PISTACHIO COUSCOUS

Makes 4 servings.

WEIGHT: 16 ounces

PREPARATION TIME: 10 minutes

INSTRUCTIONS:

Bring 3 cups water to a boil in a deep skillet. Add the couscous mixture—Bag 1—stir gently, cover the pot with a lid or a piece of foil. Turn the heat off, and let the couscous stand for 5 minutes. Uncover the pot and fluff up the couscous with a fork (do not use a spoon or you will crush the grains together). Stir the contents of Bag 2 into the couscous and serve topped with butter.

INGREDIENTS:
1 pouch clarified butter
BAG 1: *1½ cups couscous*
   ⅜ cup soy-milk powder
BAG 2: *¼ cup ground almonds*
   ¼ cup ground pistachios
   ¼ cup dehydrated honey
   ½ tablespoon cinnamon

SESAME-COCONUT BULGUR

Makes 4 servings.

WEIGHT: 18 ounces

PREPARATION TIME: 20 minutes

INSTRUCTIONS:

Heat the butter in a skillet. Sauté the contents of Bag 1 in the hot butter 2 to 3 minutes. Add 3 cups boiling water, stir; lower the heat, cover the skillet with a piece of foil or a lid, and let the mixture simmer until the liquid is absorbed, about 15 minutes.

   In the meantime, stir the contents of Bag 2 with 1 cup hot water until the soy-milk powder is totally dissolved. When the bulgur is ready, pour the soy-milk mixture on it, stir a little, and serve.

INGREDIENTS:
1 pouch clarified butter
BAG 1: *1 cup fine bulgur*
       wheat
   ½ cup sesame seeds
   ½ cup wheat germ
   ½ cup shredded
       unsweetened coconut
   Pinch of sea salt
BAG 2: *¾ cup raisins*
   ¼ cup soy-milk powder
   ¼ cup dehydrated honey

BARLEY PUDDING

Makes 4 servings.

For the situations in the backcountry where the cooking time has to be limited to conserve fuel, I use pressed barley, which is ready in 5 minutes, whereas pearl barley takes 30 minutes to prepare. Pressed barley can be found in specialty stores. If you cannot find it and want to use pearl barley, I recommend that you precook the barley and dehydrate it just as I do with rice or buckwheat.

WEIGHT: 20 ounces

PREPARATION TIME: 12 minutes

INSTRUCTIONS:
Combine the barley with 2 cups water. Bring to a boil, lower the heat and let it simmer, uncovered, 5 minutes. Add the contents of Bag 2, the dried fruit mixture; stir gently and continue cooking until the mixture becomes very thick, about 5 more minutes. Continue to stir occasionally to prevent sticking at the bottom. If the cereal gets too thick you may add a little water.

In the meantime, add 1 cup hot water to the contents of Bag 3 and stir until the soy-milk powder is totally dissolved. When the cereal pudding is ready, serve it topped with the almond-milk mixture.

INGREDIENTS:
BAG 1: *1½ cups pressed barley or cooked and dehydrated pearl barley*
BAG 2: *1 cup unsulfured dried apricots*
¾ cup raisins
½ cup dehydrated honey flakes
1 teaspoon cinnamon
Pinch of sea salt
BAG 3: *¾ cup toasted slivered almonds*
3 tablespoons soy-milk powder

OATS PUDDING

Makes 4 servings.

WEIGHT: 14 ounces

PREPARATION TIME: 10 minutes

INGREDIENTS:
BAG 1: *1½ cups quick-cooking oats*

INSTRUCTIONS:

Combine the oats mixture with 3 cups cold water and bring to a boil. Lower the heat and cook just 1 minute. Remove from the heat and cover the pot.

In the meantime, add ½ cup cold water to the egg mixture (Bag 2). Stir until well blended. Pour the egg mixture into the oats and cook the pudding 3 more minutes over low heat, stirring constantly. Use a fork to stir, rather than a spoon, to prevent the pudding from getting lumpy.

FRUIT SAUCE:

If you are using the instant baby food, add just enough water to it to make a sauce of the desired consistency. If you are using dehydrated berries, mix them in a small saucepan with 1 cup water. Bring to a boil and simmer over low heat until the texture is smooth, about 5 minutes. When the pudding is ready, serve it topped with the fruit sauce.

6 tablespoons soy-milk powder
Pinch of sea salt
BAG 2: *2 ounces freeze-dried eggs*
½ teaspoon dried grated lemon peel
¼ cup dehydrated honey flakes
½ teaspoon nutmeg
BAG 3: FRUIT SAUCE (OPTIONAL)
2 cans Heinz instant baby food: the mixed berries, or peach, banana, applesauce, as you wish, or
½ cup ground dehydrated berries: 2 ounces raspberries, strawberries, blackberries, blueberries, mixed with ¼ cup dehydrated honey flakes

KASHA PUDDING

Makes 4 servings.

WEIGHT: 20 ounces

PREPARATION TIME: 10 minutes if you precook the kasha and dehydrate it

INGREDIENTS:

1 pouch clarified butter
BAG 1: *2 cups dehydrated cooked toasted buckwheat groats*
6 tablespoons soy-milk powder
¼ cup dehydrated honey flakes
1 teaspoon cinnamon
¼ teaspoon nutmeg

INSTRUCTIONS:
Mix the contents of Bag 1 with 3 cups water in the skillet. Bring to a boil and simmer the mixture over low heat, 5 minutes, until the buckwheat groats, the kasha, is tender.

Reconstitute the eggs directly in their bag with ½ cup cold water. Add the eggs to the kasha with the dried fruit (Bag 2). Stir the pudding and cook it 2 more minutes. While the kasha is cooking, sauté the walnut pieces in the clarified butter. When the kasha is ready, serve it topped with the toasted walnuts.

¼ teaspoon ginger
Pinch of sea salt
BAG 2: *½ cup chopped dried*
apples
½ cup raisins
BAG 3: *2 ounces freeze-dried*
eggs
BAG 4: *½ cup coarsely*
chopped walnuts

CREAM OF WHEAT PUDDING

Makes 4 servings.

WEIGHT: 20 ounces

PREPARATION TIME: 6 minutes

INSTRUCTIONS:
Mix the cream of wheat mixture (Bag 1) with 5 cups water in the skillet. Bring to a boil, stirring; lower the heat and let it simmer 1 minute.

Reconstitute the eggs with ½ cup water right in their bag. Whip the eggs into the cream of wheat, add the dried fruit (Bag 2), and stir. Pour the clarified butter over the mixture, stir, and serve.

INGREDIENTS:
1 pouch clarified butter
BAG 1: *1 cup cream of wheat*
½ cup soy-milk powder
¼ cup dehydrated honey
flakes
1 teaspoon cinnamon
½ teaspoon cardamom
Pinch of sea salt
BAG 2: *½ cup golden raisins*
½ cup date bits
BAG 3: *2 ounces freeze-dried*
eggs

BUCKWHEAT PANCAKES

Makes 4 servings.

WEIGHT: 1 pound, 12 ounces

PREPARATION TIME: 20 minutes

INGREDIENTS:
2 pouches clarified butter
BAG 1: *1½ cups buckwheat*
flour

INSTRUCTIONS:

Mix the contents of Bag 1 with 3 cups cold water. Stir to have a smooth batter. If the batter is too thick, add up to ½ cup water.

Heat some of the butter in the skillet. Fry small amounts of batter 3 to 4 minutes on one side. Turn them over and cook the other side about 2 minutes, until browned. Transfer the hotcakes to a warm plate, and repeat until all the batter is used.

In a cold environment such as the snow-camping situation, you may want to let each person eat the hotcakes in turn as they come off the skillet rather than wait until they are all ready. Our rule in cold weather is, "Eat while the food is hot. Don't wait until everyone is served!"

While the hotcakes are cooking, prepare the maple syrup or fruit sauce according to the package instructions.

1 cup whole-wheat flour
½ cup wheat germ
2 ounces freeze-dried eggs
½ cup buttermilk powder
2 teaspoons baking powder
Pinch of sea salt

BAG 2: *your choice of topping: freeze-dried maple syrup or instant baby food: any fruit mixture with berries, bananas, apples, peaches. Personally, I don't like to use freeze-dried maple syrup—it is nothing but colored sugar.*

FOOD BARS

TREK BARS

Makes 24 to 32 bars, depending on how big you want them.

PREPARATION:

Individually wrapped in a plastic film, these bars keep

INGREDIENTS:
8 ounces unsalted butter
¾ cup raw honey
2 cups whole-wheat flour
1 cup quick-cooking oats

well three to four weeks, refrigerated. You can freeze them for longer storage.

INSTRUCTIONS:

Preheat the oven to 350°F.

Cream the butter with the honey until blended. Stir the flour, oats, wheat germ, and orange peel into the butter mixture. Spread the batter evenly in the bottom of a 13-by-9-inch baking pan. Reserve.

Stir the ¼ cup honey into the beaten eggs. Add the almonds, carob chips, date bits, chopped fruit, and coconut to the egg mixture. Stir until well coated.

Spread the nut mixture on top of the batter in the pan. Bake until browned, about 30 to 35 minutes. Let cool in the pan. Cut into bars.

½ cup raw wheat germ
2 tablespoons freshly grated orange peel, or 1 tablespoon dry peel
2 eggs beaten to blend
¼ cup raw honey
1 cup whole almonds
1 cup unsweetened carob chips
½ cup date bits
½ cup chopped dried apricots or apples
½ cup shredded, unsweetened coconut

RICE-BRAN SYRUP BARS

Makes 24 bars.

PREPARATION:

They keep for several weeks, wrapped individually in a plastic film. You can freeze them for longer storage.

INSTRUCTIONS:

Preheat the oven to 350°F.

Make sure you have all the ingredients ready to be mixed before you start warming up the syrup, because the mixture will stiffen as it cools.

Heat the rice-bran syrup over medium heat until liquid. Add the butter. Sift the flour with the baking powder into the syrup mixture away from the heat. Add the flavorings and nuts with the extra flour to form a sticky dough. Pat the dough into a greased 13-by-9-inch baking pan. Bake 20 to 25 minutes. Slice into bars while still hot and lift the bars out of the pan. Cool them on a wire rack.

INGREDIENTS:

1½ cups rice-bran syrup (you can use molasses)
3 tablespoons unsalted butter
2 cups whole-wheat flour
1 tablespoon baking powder
2 tablespoons freshly grated orange or lemon peel
1 tablespoon ground cinnamon
½ teaspoon ground cardamom
¼ teaspoon ground coriander
½ cup chopped filberts, lightly roasted
1½ to 2 cups more whole-wheat flour

4
Sea Kayaking

The very first "expedition food" I ever packed was for a sea kayak trip in Alaska. At the time I did not think I could be a member of such an adventure. I did not even know how much food, or should I say how little food, could be loaded into kayaks, and how it was to be cooked. I was doing this food preparation as a favor for my friend Bob Miller, an emergency room physician at the main hospital in Boise, Idaho. He had to work until the last minute before departure.

When I picked him up to drive him to the airport, he looked at the enormous duffle bag packed with the food I had assembled for him and his three companions.

"What did you put in there?" he asked kindly, with the amused smile he always kept for me.

"Well, a lot of 'compact foods,' as it says in a Sierra Club book: salami, cheeses, canned soup. But I felt sorry for you men, so I added a bag of potatoes, a bag of carrots, and some onions. I also took the time to bake some bread; I call it 'brown bread'; there's everything in it. You won't starve!"

Bob Miller had the same smile when he came back:

"The food was great! We loved the bread; we called it the 'Ten Pounder,' it was so heavy and indestructible!"

I did not know whether to take his observation about the bread as a compliment. Now I know it was really a compliment. A friend of Bob Miller's by the name of Bob Jonas was on that same trip; he never forgot me because of the bread; he remembers how they could stuff it inside the kayak with many other items. The bread did not crumble, it sliced well to the last piece, and tasted very good. One loaf doesn't weigh exactly ten pounds, but . . .

Right now, I am preparing the food for another sea kayak expedition: Bob Jonas will be paddling again with friends, on an Alaskan shore, next July. I wish I were going too. I feel chagrined that other obligations keep me at home. I know what an exciting adventure it can be! I was there three years ago, with Bob Jonas and his brother John, kayaking the magnificent fjords of the Kenai Peninsula. There, ice, water, and rock meet in fierce confrontation. Glaciers carve deep narrow gorges between the mountain spines, the ocean beats their flanks, reshaping the coast endlessly and carrying away huge blocks of glacier ice.

We used foldboats, finely crafted kayaks made of wood and canvas. They are easy to handle, stable, and offer more storage space than a regular hard-shell kayak. They can actually be "folded" and contained in a large duffle bag.

But I felt cheated because the two brothers decided to use a Zodiac as the main mode of transportation and the foldboats only for side trips. You probably remember the Zodiac from Jean-Jacques Cousteau's films—it is the big inflatable motor boat he has used in most of his expeditions. The Zodiac would allow us to travel in luxury with table and chairs, a cooler, a case of wine, and what not, with the foldboats neatly folded in their bags. It was most uncomfortable bouncing on top of those bags, as the Zodiac hit the waves that were made as hard as concrete by the speed. I felt certain that it was not the proper way to use foldboats on the ocean.

Overwhelming bouts of shame would assault me every time I looked at those aluminum-tube armchairs, disgracing the natural beauty of a glacier beach. A rock or a log, gently smoothed by the surf, is a gift offered by Nature to rest one's body. But I got my share of laughter and delight when I saw the metal chairs, one by one, unfasten their ties and gradually slide off the Zodiac as we were tossed around on a rough sea. Unfortunately, the crab pot went too!

A black bear probably thought that some of the Zodiac cargo was incongruous too. While we ventured on a side trip, he broke into our base camp cache. He tossed some bottles of wine around, but could not get to their contents, so he destroyed the case. He planted his teeth in the plastic of a gallon of fuel. The awful beverage must have surprised him, and surely kept him from visiting our camp again.

The only way I would do a sea kayak trip now is the way that Bob chose for his next one: to be flown with the foldboats into an area of special interest and then to gently, quietly, unobtrusively explore the coastline. Now, as I pack his food, I know what the advantages and disadvantages are: A kayak offers less storage capacity than any other means of adventure boating. The food has to be very compact, light in weight, and indestructible as it is stuffed into the narrow boat. However, fishing and foraging can supplement a restricted diet.

I am packing a great many dried vegetables, herbs, spices, and condiments with the recipes, to use with the fish in soups, sandwiches, and main entrées. But if for any reason the seafood is missing on the menu, I provide them with plenty of grains, legumes, flours, dried fruits, nuts, and powdered eggs. They could still put together complete and nutritionally balanced vegetarian meals. I will not forget to add the carrot cake, brownies, and food bars for their sweet tooth, and most of all the "Ten Pounder," now renamed "Miller's Bread."

MENUS

DAY 1

LUNCH

Potato hash cake
Antipasto salad
Mandel bread with dried fruit

DINNER

Stracciatella: egg and cheese soup
Poached fish Navarre
Potatoes in parsley sauce

DAY 2
♦

BREAKFAST

Granola with soy milk
Brown bread with creamed honey

LUNCH

Fish cakes on English muffins
Orange-carob brownies

DINNER

Cherba (recipe in Chapter 3)
Fish baked in foil, couscous stuffing
Apple-pear leather

DAY 3
♦

BREAKFAST

Potato cakes with applesauce
Brown bread with creamed honey

LUNCH

Salmon sandwiches
Orange-carob brownies

DINNER

Carrot-buttermilk soup
Broiled marinated fish with kasha
Banana-granola bars

DAY 4
◆
BREAKFAST

Guryevskaya
Miller's bread with creamed honey

LUNCH

Salmon chowder, rye bread
Fig bars, dried fruit

DINNER

Mushroom soup
Poached crab, horseradish herb sauce
Saffron rice
Campfire pie

DAY 5
◆
BREAKFAST

Tofu-lemon pancakes, maple syrup
Miller's bread with creamed honey

LUNCH

Crab cakes, horseradish sauce on English muffins
Pumpkin leather

DINNER

Lentil-herb soup
Poached fish à la Sétoise
Cracked wheat pilaf
Seashore salad

DAY 6
◆
BREAKFAST

Oatmeal panbread

LUNCH

Fish steak, tahini sauce on rye bread
Apricot-apple bar

DINNER

Onion soup with croûtes
Baked fish with lemon sauce
Linguini with vegetables
Fried tortillas with honey and cinnamon

DAY 7
◆
BREAKFAST

Porridge with fruit and nuts
Brown bread with creamed honey

The packaging is the most critical aspect of this trip, because the volume must be reduced as much as possible. For this reason, rather than packing each meal separately, I prefer to carry each ingredient in bulk, calculating how much is needed for the entire trip.

Plastic boxes must definitely be eliminated because they require extra space; all the dried ingredients are carried in plastic bags with hermetic closures; the liquid ingredients, such as lemon juice, olive oil, or soy sauce, are in bottles; some ingredients, like mayonnaise and honey, are in food tubes. In the hope that I will cook a lot of fresh-caught fish, I allow the luxury of several fresh ingredients: gingerroot, garlic, lemons, and my precious kitchen kit with its great variety of herbs and spices. The breads, cakes, sweet bars, and dried fruit make up the main bulk of the provisions. If some space is still available at the end, I may add some wasa bread as an accompaniment to the soups.

The cooking utensils needed for this trip are two large pots, one to heat water for drinks and cleaning, the other as a fish-and-crab-poaching pot; two smaller pots, one for soup, the other for the occasional sauces. Most of the cooking is done on a campfire, so it is imperative to have a grill. Also, one must not forget a large skillet for frying, and the measuring cup and spoons.

SANDWICHES

FISH CAKES ON ENGLISH MUFFINS

Makes 4 servings.

PREPARATION:

   This lunch preparation requires some cooking, so it should be served on a layover day, using a campfire. It is a way to use up leftover cooked fish. The fish cakes can also be made ahead of time and eaten cold on a picnic lunch.

INSTRUCTIONS:

Heat 1 tablespoon clarified butter (⅔ of one pouch) in a small saucepan. Add the flour, stir to blend the flour and butter together. Cook the mixture over medium heat for one minute, until brown.

   In the meantime, add ½ cup of hot water to the soy-milk powder and stir to dissolve. Pour the soy milk on the butter-flour mixture away from the heat. Stir vigorously with a whisk to obtain a smooth liquid. Season with a little salt and cayenne pepper.

   Return the saucepan to the heat; cook the mixture 1 minute until bubbly and thick.

   To reconstitute the eggs, put ¼ cup water into a mixing bowl; add the egg powder and blend; then add another ¼ cup of water and blend again. Slowly pour the flour mixture on the eggs, beating constantly. Add the flaked fish, the bread crumbs, lemon juice, spinach, basil, mace. Adjust the seasoning with salt and cayenne pepper to taste.

   Heat half the remaining butter in a skillet. Form 4 patties with the fish mixture. Fry them in the hot butter, turning them once to brown both sides, about 3 minutes on each side. Transfer them to a hot plate. Rapidly toast the muffin halves in the skillet, using all the remaining butter. Place one fish patty on each muffin half and serve.

INGREDIENTS:

2 pouches clarified butter, ¾ ounce each

1 tablespoon whole-wheat flour

1 tablespoon soy-milk powder

2 ounces freeze-dried eggs

2 cups cooked fish, flaked with a fork

2 tablespoons dry bread crumbs

2 tablespoons lemon juice

2 tablespoons powdered dried spinach

1 teaspoon dried basil

⅛ teaspoon mace

1 pinch each salt and cayenne pepper

2 English muffins

SALMON SANDWICHES

Makes 4 sandwiches.

PREPARATION:

The salmon mixture can be prepared in the morning before taking off for the day. If you want to assemble the sandwiches ahead of time, spread the bread slices with a thin layer of butter to prevent them from becoming soggy. In this recipe, you can use some leftover cooked salmon or other fish. You can also mix the fresh-cooked fish with some smoked fish. Smoked fish is so easy to find and affordable in Alaska, I take some on every trip to use as a snack or to supplement some dishes.

INSTRUCTIONS:

Mix the fresh and smoked fish together. Blend the mayonnaise, lemon juice, dill, scallion, garlic, and cayenne pepper.

Stir the fish blend into the mayonnaise mixture. Make four sandwiches, adding, if available, the beach greens or sorrel.

INGREDIENTS:

1 cup cooked fresh salmon, or other fish
½ cup smoked salmon, fluked
¼ cup mayonnaise
2 tablespoons lemon juice
1 tablespoon each, dried dill weed and dried scallion
1 teaspoon garlic granules
Cayenne pepper to taste
8 compact square slices of rye bread
If possible, some wild beach greens or sorrel

CRAB CAKES, WITH HORSERADISH HERB SAUCE

Makes 4 servings.

PREPARATION:

Like the fish cakes, the crab cakes can be cooked for lunch on a campfire, on a layover day, or made ahead of time and eaten cold on a picnic. Use some crab meat left over from the previous dinner.

INSTRUCTIONS:

Combine the mayonnaise, lemon juice, bread crumbs, celery seeds, dry mustard, and cayenne pepper. Stir in the crab meat.

INGREDIENTS:

¾ cup mayonnaise
¼ cup lemon juice
2 tablespoons dry bread crumbs
¼ teaspoon celery seeds
⅛ teaspoon dry mustard
⅛ teaspoon cayenne pepper
2 cups cooked crab meat, flaked

Form four patties. Sauté the crab cakes in some of the clarified butter for 4 to 6 minutes until browned, turning them once. Remove them to a warm plate and fry the muffin halves in the remaining butter. Top each muffin half with a crab cake and serve garnished with beach greens and lemon wedges if available.

1 pouch clarified butter
2 English muffins,
*   separated in halves*
Horseradish herb sauce:
*   instructions with the*
*   poached crab recipe.*

FISH STEAKS, TAHINI SAUCE ON RYE

Makes 4 servings.

PREPARATION:

If you are enjoying a layover day and have four fillets of fresh halibut (best) or any other firm white fish, this is a different way to serve them. The tahini sauce is also excellent on cold cooked fish.

INSTRUCTIONS:

Cook the fish fillets, lightly sprinkle them with salt and cayenne pepper. Brown them lightly in two tablespoons of the olive oil. Place each fillet on a square of heavy-duty foil. Sprinkle equal amounts of lemon juice, ground nuts, parsley, and garlic, with the remaining two tablespoons of olive oil, on top of the fillets. Enclose the fillets inside the foil pieces, sealing them well. Place them on a grill over the campfire and let them bake 20 minutes, until the fish flakes easily.

In the meantime, make the sauce. Combine the tahini with a little water to give it a sauce consistency. Add the remaining ingredients and stir to blend well.

When the fish is ready, spread some of the sauce on the slices of rye bread. Top each one with a fish fillet. Serve extra sauce on the side.

INGREDIENTS:

4 uncooked halibut fillets
Salt and cayenne pepper
4 tablespoons olive oil
¼ cup lemon juice
¼ cup ground almonds or
*   pistachios*
1 tablespoon dried parsley
1 tablespoon garlic
*   granules*

TAHINI SAUCE:

½ cup raw tahini (sesame
*   seed butter)*
2 tablespoons lemon juice
2 teaspoons paprika
½ teaspoon garlic powder
Salt and cayenne pepper to
*   taste*
8 slices of firm, square rye
*   bread*

RELISHES, SALADS, SAVORY CAKES

POTATO HASH CAKE

Makes 4 servings.

PREPARATION:

Make the potato hash cake at home any time before a trip as it freezes very well for long storage. Each serving should be wrapped individually in a plastic film. Keep it in the cooler during the trip until ready to serve.

INSTRUCTIONS:

Peel the potatoes and cut them into ¼ inch cubes. Keep the cubes in cold water as you cut them, to prevent browning. Drain them and drop them into boiling salty water to simmer 5 minutes; they should be just tender. Drain them and rinse them under cold water. Transfer them to a large bowl.

Heat the 1½ tablespoons olive oil in a skillet; sauté the ½ cup bread crumbs until golden and add them to the potatoes. Add the Parmesan, the egg, ham, mozzarella, parsley, garlic, thyme, salt, and cayenne. Stir to blend well.

Preheat the oven to 375°F. Coat a nonstick 8-inch-square baking pan with olive oil. Press the potato mixture in one even, firm layer into the pan. Bake it in the oven 12 to 15 minutes.

Mix the topping ingredients together and spread the mixture on top of the potato cake. Place it under the broiler, 4" from the heat, for 2 to 3 minutes until it begins to brown.

Let the cake cool completely in the pan. Run a thin knife blade around the cake to loosen the edges. Cut it into 4 equal squares. Wrap each square in a plastic film. They will keep up to a week refrigerated and inside a cooler.

INGREDIENTS

10 to 12 ounces potatoes
1½ tablespoons olive oil
½ cup fresh bread crumbs
¼ cup grated Parmesan cheese
1 egg, beaten
3 ounces prosciutto ham, diced
3 ounces mozzarella cheese, grated
2 tablespoons parsley, minced
1 clove of garlic, minced
½ teaspoon dried thyme leaves
¼ teaspoon sea salt
1 pinch Cayenne pepper, or more to taste
Topping: 1 tablespoon olive oil
  1 tablespoon grated Parmesan
  1 tablespoon fresh bread crumbs

ANTIPASTO SALAD

Makes 4 servings.

PREPARATION:

This is a salad-relish you can prepare at home and keep chilled for several days as the flavor improves.

INSTRUCTIONS:

Combine in a large skillet the tomato purée, lemon juice, olive oil, horseradish, oregano, chili powder, garlic, fennel seeds, thyme, and red pepper sauce or cayenne. Bring the mixture to a boil and simmer over low heat 5 minutes. Add the vegetables: celery, pepper, zucchini, cauliflower and pepperoncini. Simmer uncovered 10 to 12 minutes, stirring often until the vegetables are tender-crisp. Let cool. Transfer to a plastic bag with hermetic closure. Chill overnight. Double-bag for transportation.

INGREDIENTS:

1 cup tomato purée
¼ cup fresh lemon juice
¼ cup olive oil
1 teaspoon prepared horseradish
1 teaspoon dried oregano leaves
1 teaspoon chili powder
1 clove of garlic, minced
1 teaspoon crushed fennel seeds
½ teaspoon dried thyme leaves
Optional: a few drops of hot red pepper sauce or cayenne pepper to taste
2 stalks of celery, peeled and cut into ½" pieces
1 large red or green pepper cut into strips
2 medium zucchini, sliced
1 small head of cauliflower separated into flowerets
1 cup pepperoncini

SEASHORE SALAD

Make as much as you want.

INGREDIENTS:

Here is a selection of wild edible plants we were able to find on the coast of the Kenai Peninsula:

- Beach Greens, also called Seapurslane and sea-chickweed. This plant forms large sprawling mats; the leaves are fleshy, succulent, juicy, and a good source of vitamins A and C.
- Sourgrass, or Mountain Sorrel. It can be found at sea level in sheltered gulches. The wide, kidney-shaped leaves rise straight from the root. They are acid-tasting and a good source of vitamin C.
- Wintercress. The first growth of dark-green shiny leaves have a bitter radish flavor.
- Scurvygrass. It was the plant sought by early explorers to cure scurvy. The leaves are simple, spoon-shaped, with a broad base. Upper leaves have no stem. It is a very rich source of vitamin C.
- Seashore Plantain. It has many long narrow leaves arising from the root crown. The young tender leaves are available in May and June.
- Salad Greens or Wild Cucumber. The leaves grow at the base, broad, kidney-shaped, or circular. Young tender leaves can be found late in the season in shoreline gulches where the snow has persisted until midsummer.

Salt and cayenne pepper to taste
Garlic granules
Mixed dried herbs to taste: parsley, tarragon, basil . . .
Optional: ½ teaspoon dry mustard, a pinch of cumin
1 tablespoon vinegar
3 tablespoons olive oil

FOR THE SALAD DRESSING

INSTRUCTIONS:

Pick some wild edible greens, the ones you recognize for sure or those that are familiar to you. (It is good to carry a booklet on wild and poisonous plants of Alaska, because there *are* poisonous ones.) Combine the dressing ingredients together in a bowl. Add the greens, picked and washed. Toss and serve. What a treat!

SOUPS

The four following soup recipes, stracciatella, carrot-buttermilk, mushroom, and lentil with herbs, are ideal for extreme backpacking, kayaking conditions, or any adventure trip when the space and weight allowed for food are very restricted. Most of the ingredients are dehydrated, with the exception of olive oil. If you want to eliminate even the bottle of olive oil, use pouches of clarified butter instead.

STRACCIATELLA: EGG AND CHEESE SOUP

Makes 4 servings.

WEIGHT: 6 ounces

PREPARATION TIME: about 10 minutes

INGREDIENTS:
4 teaspoons instant vegetable-stock powder
2 ounces freeze-dried eggs, ½ cup
½ cup dried grated Parmesan cheese
¼ cup dried parsley
½ teaspoon nutmeg
1 pinch cayenne pepper or more to taste

INSTRUCTIONS:
Bring four cups of water with the stock powder to a boil. In the meantime, reconstitute the eggs with ½ cup water. Mix the egg with the Parmesan, parsley, nutmeg, and cayenne pepper. As the stock simmers over medium-low heat, gradually pour in the egg mixture, stirring constantly. The egg should form filaments in the broth. Serve immediately, piping hot.

CARROT-BUTTERMILK SOUP

Makes 4 servings.

WEIGHT: 8 ounces without the butter

PREPARATION TIME: 12 to 15 minutes

INGREDIENTS:
1 pouch clarified butter
2 tablespoons whole-wheat flour

INSTRUCTIONS:

Mix the carrot powder and the onion in a plastic bag or a bowl. Add 1 cup hot water and let the mixture rehydrate for 5 minutes.

In the meantime, heat the clarified butter in a soup pot. Add the flour and cook it 1 minute until brown and bubbly.

Add the carrot-onion mixture with the water and stir to blend. Add 2 more cups of water, bring the soup to a boil. Lower the heat and let it simmer 2 minutes.

Add 1 cup cold water to the buttermilk powder, stir to blend. Add the buttermilk to the soup, reheat, and serve.

¼ to ½ cup dehydrated carrot powder, made with 1 pound fresh carrots, grated, dehydrated, and powdered in a food processor (some larger bits of carrot can be left in the powder)
¼ cup dehydrated onion
3 teaspoons instant vegetable-stock powder
½ teaspoon garlic granules
½ teaspoon ginger
½ teaspoon orange peel
½ teaspoon marjoram
1 pinch of cayenne pepper, or more to taste
¼ cup buttermilk powder
Optional: ¼ cup toasted sesame seeds

MUSHROOM SOUP

Makes 4 servings.

WEIGHT: 5 ounces without the butter

PREPARATION TIME: 12 to 15 minutes

INSTRUCTIONS:

Mix the onion, mushrooms, parsley, tarragon, stock powder, mace, and cayenne pepper in a bowl or plastic bag. Add 2 cups hot water to rehydrate the vegetables, let stand 5 minutes.

Heat the butter in a soup pot; add the flour and cook for 1 minute.

INGREDIENTS:
¼ cup dehydrated onion
About 1 cup dehydrated mushrooms, 2 ounces
2 tablespoons dried parsley
2 tablespoons dried tarragon
3 teaspoons instant vegetable-stock powder
¼ teaspoon mace
1 pinch cayenne pepper, or more to taste

Add the vegetable mixture with the water to the flour-butter mixture. Stir to blend, add 2 more cups of water and stir. Bring the soup to a boil, lower the heat, and let it simmer 2 to 3 minutes. Stir the soy-milk powder into 1 cup hot water, and pour into the soup. Stir and serve.

1 pouch clarified butter
2 tablespoons whole-wheat flour
2 tablespoons soy-milk powder

LENTIL-HERB SOUP

Makes 4 servings.

WEIGHT: 12 ounces without the butter

PREPARATION TIME: 12 minutes

INSTRUCTIONS:
Rehydrate the onion in a small bowl or a plastic bag with ¼ cup hot water. Let stand while you prepare and measure the other ingredients.

Heat the butter in the soup pot. Sauté the onion for one minute; add 4 cups of water (hot or cold), with the vegetable-stock powder, the lentils, spinach, herbs, and garlic. If you are using lemon peel, add it too. Bring the soup to a boil, and simmer it 5 minutes. Stir the buttermilk powder in ¾ cup cold water until dissolved. Pour the buttermilk into the soup with the lemon juice, if using the latter. Reheat and serve.

Optional: you may add 1 teaspoon ground cumin with the vegetable and herb mixture.

INGREDIENTS:
¼ cup dehydrated onion
1 pouch clarified butter
4 teaspoons instant vegetable-stock powder
1 cup dehydrated cooked lentils
1 ounce dehydrated spinach, ¾ cup crushed and packed
2 tablespoons mixed dried herbs: parsley, oregano, basil, marjoram, chervil, thyme, tarragon, mint...
1 tablespoon lemon juice or 1 teaspoon lemon peel
½ teaspoon garlic granules
3 tablespoons buttermilk powder

FRENCH ONION SOUP WITH CROÛTES

Makes 4 servings.

PREPARATION:
This soup differs a little from the first four in this chapter because it requires fresh "croûtes" made with slices of

INGREDIENTS:
½ cup dehydrated chopped onion
2 pouches clarified butter

sourdough bread. Often it is not practical to have sourdough bread in the backcountry. However, you can substitute herb croutons for the croûtes.

INSTRUCTIONS:

Rehydrate the onion with ½ cup hot water, letting it stand for 10 minutes. Heat the butter over medium-low heat, and sauté the onion until soft, about 2 minutes. Add the flour, stir and cook 2 to 3 minutes. Add 2 cups cold water and stir to blend. Bring to a boil and cook 1 minute. Add 2 more cups of cold water, the stock powder, bay leaves, marjoram, cardamom, and cayenne to taste, and bring it again to a boil. Lower the heat and simmer the soup 10 to 15 minutes.

To make the croûtes, heat 1 tablespoon of the olive oil in a skillet. Fry the bread slices until lightly browned on one side. Turn them over, add the remaining olive oil, and brown the other side. Transfer the croûtes to paper towels to absorb the oil. Sprinkle the croûtes to taste with mixed dried herbs and garlic.

To serve the soup, place 1 croûte at the bottom of each individual soup bowl. Top each one with 2 tablespoons of grated Parmesan and pour 1 cup of soup on top.

2 tablespoons whole-wheat flour
4 teaspoons instant vegetable-stock powder
2 bay leaves
1 teaspoon dried marjoram
½ teaspoon cardamom
1 pinch cayenne pepper, or more to taste
4 slices of sourdough bread
2 tablespoons olive oil
Mixed dried herbs and garlic granules to taste
½ cup dried grated Parmesan cheese

SALMON CHOWDER

Makes 4 servings.

PREPARATION:

This recipe differs from the five preceding ones, in that it requires fresh salmon and, optionally, smoked salmon. But most of the other ingredients can be dehydrated food. If you want to use this recipe where no fresh fish is available, you can substitute dehydrated shrimp for the salmon. In this case, rehydrate the onion and shrimp with hot water and sauté them in hot clarified butter, add the flour and the milk mixture, as in the following instructions.

INGREDIENTS:

1 cup dehydrated cubed potatoes, about 1 pound fresh
2 tablespoons soy-milk powder
½ teaspoon salt
¼ cup dehydrated chopped onion
2 pouches clarified butter

INSTRUCTIONS:

Combine the dehydrated potatoes and the soy-milk powder with 4 cups cold water and the salt. Bring to a boil, stirring to dissolve the milk powder. Lower the heat and simmer 10 minutes.

In the meantime, rehydrate the onion with ¼ cup hot water. Heat the butter in a skillet, add the onion, and cook until soft, 2 minutes. Add the fresh salmon, some salt and cayenne pepper to taste, and the lemon juice. Cover the fish with a piece of foil and let it cook over medium heat 8 to 10 minutes, turning it over once. Transfer the fish to a warm plate.

Sprinkle the flour over the onion mixture and cook it 3 minutes. Add about 1 cup of the hot milk, and blend to make a smooth sauce. Pour the whole skillet contents into the potato-milk mixture and simmer 5 minutes. Break the cooked salmon into flakes, chop the smoked salmon if using it, and add each to the chowder. Stir in the dill and adjust the seasonings. Heat the chowder until the fish is thoroughly hot, and serve.

1 pound fresh salmon fillet cut into 4 pieces
1 pinch cayenne pepper, or more to taste
2 tablespoons lemon juice
2 tablespoons whole-wheat flour
4 ounces smoked salmon, ½ cup (optional)
4 teaspoons dried dill weed

FISH AND SEAFOOD DISHES

POACHED FISH NAVARRE

Makes 4 servings.

INSTRUCTIONS:

Lay the fish in one layer in the skillet. Combine all the remaining ingredients and pour the mixture on top of the fish. Let the fish marinate for at least 30 minutes, turning it over once.

Place the skillet on a grill or rack that sits over the camp-

INGREDIENTS:

2 pounds fresh whole fish cleaned, heads and tails removed. It can be 4 small fish or 1 whole fish.
½ cup dry red wine; it

fire, which should have some good red coals. Bring the liquid to a simmer, then cover the skillet with a piece of foil. Let it simmer for 20 minutes or more, depending on the size of the fish. The fish should be cooked through and flake easily, but be careful not to overcook.

Transfer the fish to a platter, cover it with the foil, and keep it warm near the fire.

Strain the cooking liquid into a saucepan, pressing the solids to extract the juices. Stir ½ cup cooking liquid with the freeze-dried eggs to reconstitute them; pour the eggs into the cooking liquid and heat slowly over the fire, whisking constantly. Do not let it boil or the sauce will curdle. Taste and adjust the seasoning. Pour the sauce over the fish and serve.

would not be realistic to try to take wine on a trip where the storage capacity is so limited, but, just as I have a small bottle of olive oil or lemon juice, I allow a small plastic bottle of wine for cooking. If wine is not available, substitute vinegar.

¼ cup olive oil
1 tablespoon apple-cider vinegar
¼ cup dehydrated chopped onion
1 teaspoon dried mint leaves
½ teaspoon dried rosemary
½ teaspoon dried thyme
1 bay leaf
¼ teaspoon ground coriander
⅛ teaspoon cayenne pepper
1 teaspoon sea salt
4 slices fresh lemon, if available
¼ cup freeze-dried eggs, 1 ounce

FISH BAKED IN FOIL, COUSCOUS STUFFING

Makes 4 servings.

INSTRUCTIONS:
Season the fish inside and outside with salt, cayenne pepper, and paprika. Lay it on a piece of foil large enough to wrap the fish in it.

Pour ¼ cup hot water over the onion and celery to re-hydrate. Let them stand 5 to 10 minutes. Heat the butter in a skillet. Drain the onion and celery; add them to the hot butter and sauté 2 to 3 minutes. Add 1½ cups cold or hot water with the herbs and the vegetable-stock powder. Bring to a boil. Season with salt and cayenne pepper and, away from the heat, stir in the couscous. Cover the skillet with foil and let it stand in a warm place, but not over direct heat, for 10 minutes.

Uncover the skillet and fluff up the couscous with a fork. Use a fork to avoid crushing the soft grains together. Stuff the fish with as much couscous as can fit inside the cavity. Wrap the fish inside the foil to make it airtight and place it on a grill or rack over the glowing coals of the campfire. Reserve the remaining couscous, keeping it covered and warm. Cook the fish until it is firm and flakes easily. The time will depend on the size and thickness of the fish—20 to 30 minutes. Serve the fish with the extra couscous stuffing as a side dish.

INGREDIENTS:
*1 whole fish, about 2
    pounds, cleaned, head
    and tail removed
sea salt, cayenne pepper,
    and paprika*
STUFFING:
*1 pouch clarified butter
2 tablespoons each
    dehydrated onion and
    celery
2 tablespoons mixed dried
    herbs
2 teaspoons instant
    vegetable-stock powder
1¼ cups couscous*

BROILED MARINATED FISH

Makes 4 servings.

INSTRUCTIONS:
Combine the lemon juice, honey, soy sauce, gingerroot, garlic, and olive oil in a plate or bowl. Add the fish morsels. Turn them over in the mixture to coat them well. Let the fish

INGREDIENTS:
*1½ pounds of fish morsels,
    1- to 2-inch size; a firm
    fish is best, such as rock
    fish or halibut*

marinate at least 2 hours and up to 6 hours, covered.

In the meantime, soak several bamboo skewers in water. Bamboo skewers are handy to have in the kitchen kit. If you do not have any, use some thin twigs to broil fish pieces. You can also broil the fish directly on the grill over the fire if the morsels are big enough and will not fall through; you can even fry them in the skillet.

Just before cooking the fish, dry toast the sesame seeds in the skillet. Reserve.

Impale the fish morsels on the skewers and broil over glowing coals, basting with the marinade, about 5 minutes. Coat the fish with sesame seeds and serve.

¼ cup lemon juice
1 tablespoon honey
1 tablespoon soy sauce
1 tablespoon minced fresh
  gingerroot
garlic granules to taste
2 tablespoons olive oil
¼ cup sesame seeds

POACHED FISH À LA SÉTOISE

Makes 4 servings.

INSTRUCTIONS:
Combine all the poaching liquid ingredients with 1½ quarts cold water. Bring to a boil, let it simmer 10 minutes.

Place the fish in the poaching liquid and cook it for 10 to 20 minutes, depending on the size of the fish. The liquid should be just barely simmering: boiling makes the flesh of the fish fall apart. Keep the fish warm in the liquid but away from the heat while you prepare the sauce.

To make the sauce, pour the vinegar into a small saucepan, and boil it until reduced to a half. Let it cool and add the garlic (cloves mashed to a paste if using the whole cloves), the cayenne pepper, olive oil, ¼ cup hot poaching liquid, and the parsley.

Remove the fish from the liquid and serve it with the sauce and lemon wedges, if available.

INGREDIENTS:
1 to 4 whole fish, cleaned
POACHING LIQUID:
  ½ cup dehydrated onion
  2 tablespoons dried parsley
  2 bay leaves
  1 teaspoon dried thyme
  1 teaspoon orange or
    lemon peel
  1 teaspoon fennel seeds
  1 teaspoon celery seeds
  4 whole cloves
  ¼ teaspoon cayenne pepper
  1 tablespoon instant
    vegetable-stock powder
SAUCE:
  1 cup vinegar
  6 whole cloves of garlic,
    peeled, or 1 tablespoon
    garlic granules
  1 tablespoon dried parsley
  ¼ cup olive oil
  Pinch of cayenne pepper

BAKED FISH WITH LEMON SAUCE

Makes 4 servings.

INSTRUCTIONS:

Wash and pat the fish dry. Rehydrate the onion in ¾ cup hot water. Sprinkle the fish cavity with salt and cayenne pepper. Stuff it with ⅔ of the onion and the slices of 1 lemon. Spread the remaining onion and the slices from the second lemon on a large piece of foil. Place the fish on the onion bed, sprinkle it with salt and cayenne pepper. Mix the olive oil and the garlic together and brush the fish with the mixture. Wrap the fish in the foil, seal it well. Place it on a grill over red-hot coals and cook it from 45 minutes to 1 hour or more, depending on the size of the fish and how hot the fire is. Turn the fish over occasionally. The fish is done when it flakes easily and no more pink can be seen near the bone.

To make the lemon sauce, warm up the butter in a small saucepan. Add the other ingredients. Keep warm until ready to use.

When the fish is cooked, lift off parts of the fillets and place them on individual plates. Spoon some of the stuffing on each serving, and pour a little sauce over the fish.

INGREDIENTS:

- 1 4- or 5-pound salmon or other fish
- ¾ cup dehydrated chopped onion
- 2 lemons, thinly sliced
- ½ cup olive oil
- 2 teaspoons garlic granules

FOR THE LEMON SAUCE:

- 3 pouches clarified butter
- 2 tablespoons lemon juice
- 1 teaspoon garlic granules, or more to taste
- 2 tablespoons dehydrated parsley
- 1 pinch cayenne pepper

POACHED CRAB, WITH HORSERADISH HERB SAUCE

Makes 8 servings.

PREPARATION:

There is enough crab and sauce in this recipe to serve eight. But the menu shows that half the crab and sauce should be left over for the next day's lunch—the crab cakes. This explains why the quantities are doubled for this dinner.

INGREDIENTS:

- ½ cup dehydrated chopped onion
- 1 pouch clarified butter
- 1 tablespoon garlic granules
- ¼ teaspoon cayenne pepper

INSTRUCTIONS:
Rehydrate the onion in a little hot water for about 10 minutes. Heat the clarified butter in the skillet, and sauté the onion until soft. Transfer the onion to a large pot. Add two quarts cold water with the garlic, cayenne pepper, parsley, bay leaves, thyme, vegetable-stock powder, and any other spices of your choice. Bring the broth to a boil, let it simmer 10 minutes. Add the crab, in their shells, cover the pot, and simmer 10 minutes. Ladle the crab into individual plates. Pass the sauce around with lemon wedges to squeeze over the crab meat.

HORSERADISH SAUCE

INSTRUCTIONS:
Combine all the ingredients together and blend thoroughly.

If you have more sourdough bread slices, toast them in the skillet over the fire. Spread a little clarified butter on each slice, sprinkle garlic granules and dry grated Parmesan cheese on top, and serve.

or more; the broth should be very spicy
2 tablespoons dried parsley
2 bay leaves
1 teaspoon dried thyme
1½ tablespoons instant vegetable-stock powder
Optional: celery seeds, fennel seeds, whole clove, whole coriander, mixed herbs...
8 pounds fresh crab in the shell

INGREDIENTS:
1½ cups mayonnaise
2 tablespoons lemon juice, or 1 tablespoon each lemon juice and vinegar
1 tablespoon dried chopped scallions
1 teaspoon each dried tarragon and prepared horseradish
½ teaspoon dry mustard, salt, and cayenne pepper to taste

DINNER SIDE DISHES

POTATOES IN PARSLEY SAUCE

Makes 4 servings.

INSTRUCTIONS:

Rehydrate the potato and onion mixed together in 2½ cups of hot water. Drain them. Heat the oil in a skillet, add the potato and onion mixture, and sauté until it begins to brown. Add the garlic, parsley, salt, cayenne pepper, and nutmeg, if using it. Pour in the boiling water. Do not stir. Shake the pan back and forth 1 to 2 minutes to distribute the water evenly. Cover the skillet tightly with a piece of foil and simmer the vegetable mixture 20 minutes, until the potatoes are tender but do not fall apart. If the liquid is gone before the potatoes are cooked, add a little more boiling water and continue the cooking.

INGREDIENTS:
2 cups dehydrated cubed potatoes
¼ cup dehydrated chopped onion
¼ cup olive oil
1 teaspoon garlic granules
2 tablespoons dehydrated parsley
Salt and cayenne pepper to taste
Optional: nutmeg to taste
2½ cups hot water
1½ cups boiling water

KASHA

Makes 4 servings.

INSTRUCTIONS:

Rehydrate the onion with a little hot water and drain. Heat the butter in a skillet and sauté the onion with the walnuts. When the onion is soft and the walnuts begin to brown, transfer the mixture to a bowl and reserve. In the same skillet, put the buckwheat, tamari or soy sauce, thyme, and vegetable-stock powder with 1 cup hot water. Let the mixture simmer over medium heat until all the liquid is absorbed and the kasha is tender, just a few minutes. Add the walnut mixture

INGREDIENTS:
¼ cup dehydrated chopped onion
¾ cup chopped walnuts
1 pouch clarified butter
1½ cups dehydrated cooked roasted buckwheat groats
1 tablespoon tamari or soy sauce

to the kasha and cook a little longer, until the walnuts are hot throughout.

1 teaspoon dried thyme leaves
2 teaspoons instant vegetable-stock powder
Pinch of cayenne pepper

SAFFRON RICE

Makes 4 servings.

PREPARATION:

You can choose to cook saffron rice at home and dehydrate it. You can then use portions of it on any adventure trip you embark on. But when it is possible to cook on a campfire, as in this case, and therefore the quantity of fuel and the cooking time are of no concern, I prefer to cook the rice at the location.

INSTRUCTIONS:

Rehydrate the onion in a little hot water and drain. Heat the olive oil in a saucepan or skillet. Sauté the onion, 2 to 3 minutes. Add the rice, stir it to coat all the grains with oil, and cook it 2 more minutes. Do not let it brown. Add the water, stock powder, cardamom, saffron, and cayenne pepper. Bring the liquid to a boil. Move the pan to a place over the fire where the heat is reduced; it may be on one of the stones that surround the campfire. Cover the pan tightly and let the rice simmer, undisturbed, for 35 to 45 minutes, until all the liquid is absorbed and the grains are soft and still firm, not mushy. Fluff up the rice with a fork, gently. Do not use a spoon from fear of crushing the grains and making them stick together.

The rice can wait in a warm place near the fire for up to 20 minutes.

INGREDIENTS:

2 tablespoons dehydrated chopped onion
2 tablespoons olive oil
1½ cups raw brown rice
3 cups boiling water
1 tablespoon instant vegetable-stock powder
1 teaspoon cardamom
⅛ teaspoon ground saffron
Pinch of cayenne pepper

CRACKED WHEAT PILAF

Makes 4 servings.

INSTRUCTIONS:

Rehydrate the onion in a little hot water and drain. Heat the butter or olive oil in a deep skillet or a saucepan. Sauté the onion with the cracked wheat, 2 to 3 minutes. Add 3 cups hot water, the stock powder, garlic, cardamom, and cayenne pepper. Bring the liquid to a boil. Move the pan to a place over the fire where the heat is reduced; it may be on one of the stones surrounding the campfire. Cover the pan tightly with foil and let the wheat pilaf simmer about 20 minutes. The liquid should be absorbed and the wheat tender but still firm. If some liquid is left, boil it away with the pan uncovered over high heat. Use a fork to fluff up the grain without crushing it.

INGREDIENTS:

- ¼ cup dehydrated chopped onion
- 2 pouches of clarified butter or ¼ cup olive oil
- 1½ cups cracked wheat
- 1 tablespoon instant vegetable-stock powder
- ½ teaspoon garlic granules
- ½ teaspoon ground cardamom
- 1 pinch cayenne pepper or more, to taste

LINGUINI WITH VEGETABLES

Makes 4 servings.

INSTRUCTIONS:

Heat the butter from one of the pouches in a skillet. Add the flour and stir to mix it with the butter and cook until browned, 1 minute. Add 2 cups hot water and stir to blend with the flour and make a smooth sauce. Add the stock powder, lemon juice, cilantro, basil or tarragon, garlic, and seasonings. Bring the sauce to a boil and let it simmer 1 minute. Reserve the sauce in a warm place near the fire.

Heat 2½ quarts of salty water in a large pot. Use 2 cups hot water to pour on the vegetables. Let them dehydrate while cooking the linguini. Add 1 tablespoon olive oil to the water in the large pot. When it boils, add the linguini and cook it as long as indicated on the package directions. When the

INGREDIENTS:

- 2 pouches of clarified butter
- 1½ tablespoons whole-wheat flour
- 2 teaspoons instant vegetable-stock powder
- 1 tablespoon lemon juice
- 1 tablespoon dried cilantro
- 1 tablespoon dried basil or tarragon
- 1 teaspoon garlic granules
- salt and cayenne pepper to taste

linguini is almost ready, drain the vegetables out of their water and add them to the herb-lemon sauce. Reheat the vegetable and sauce mixture, stirring to prevent sticking. Drain the linguini and mix it with the butter from the second pouch. Serve the linguini, topped with the vegetable sauce and with some grated Parmesan cheese.

2 cups dehydrated vegetables of your choice: red or green bell pepper, zucchini, green peas, broccoli flowerets, celery root, mushrooms, artichoke heart...
1 pound thin dry linguini
1 tablespoon olive oil
½ cup dry grated Parmesan cheese

BREAKFAST DISHES

GRANOLA

Makes about 8 cups.

PREPARATION:

I always make granola in large quantities at any time, when I feel like it. But it is important to store it either in the refrigerator or even in the freezer if it is to be kept for more than a month. Granola turns rancid easily; nuts do it naturally (mine are always refrigerated), but the roasting process seems to make it worse.

INGREDIENTS:
3 cups old-fashioned oats
1 cup coarsely shredded coconut
½ cup chopped almonds or pistachios
½ cup sesame seeds
½ cup sunflower or pumpkin seeds
½ cup raw wheat germ
Optional: ¼ cup bee pollen, great source of energy!
⅓ cup soy-milk powder
½ cup honey or fruit juice concentrate: apple, grape, pineapple...

INSTRUCTIONS:
Combine in a bowl the oats, coconut, almonds or pistachios, sesame seeds, sunflower or pumpkin seeds, wheat germ, bee pollen, and soy-milk powder. In another bowl, combine the honey or fruit concentrate and the oil. Stir into the oat mixture. Spread the mixture out in two rimmed baking pans. Bake in a preheated 300°F. oven for a total of 45 to 50 minutes, stirring every 15 minutes. Remove the granola from the oven and let it cool in the pans on a wire rack, stirring it frequently to prevent lumping. Stir in the apricots and raisins. Store in airtight plastic bags.

¼ cup pure light sesame or
safflower oil
1 cup chopped dried
apricots
1 cup raisins

POTATO CAKES WITH APPLESAUCE

Makes 4 servings.

INSTRUCTIONS:
Combine the potato flakes, raisins, freeze-dried eggs, soy-milk powder, dehydrated honey, cinnamon, and nutmeg. Add 3 cups cold water and stir to make a well-blended batter. Heat some of the butter in a skillet; add small amounts of batter and fry 2 to 3 minutes on each side, turning the cakes over once, just as in making pancakes. Transfer the cakes to a plate. Cover with foil and keep in a warm place near the fire. Repeat until all the batter is used.

Mix the instant applesauce with water according to directions. Serve the potato cakes topped with clarified butter and applesauce.

INGREDIENTS:
2 cups potato flakes as for
instant mashed potatoes
¼ cup raisins
½ cup freeze-dried eggs, 2
ounces
2 tablespoons soy-milk
powder
1 tablespoon dehydrated
honey
1 teaspoon cinnamon
¼ teaspoon nutmeg
2 pouches clarified butter
2 cans instant applesauce
(Heinz baby food)

GURYEVSKAYA

Guryevskaya is a Russian baked pudding made with "manna-croup" or semolina. I have adapted the recipe to use couscous, and to cook it in a pot instead of the oven.

Makes 4 servings.

COOKING TIME: 10 minutes

TOTAL INGREDIENT WEIGHT: 20 ounces

INSTRUCTIONS:
Bring 3 cups water to a boil. Add the couscous, soy-milk powder, sugar, vanilla powder, and 1 pinch of sea salt if desired. Remove the pot from the heat and cover it tightly with a lid or a piece of foil. Let it stand 5 minutes. Remove the foil or lid and fluff up the couscous with a fork, not a spoon, to prevent crushing the grain into lumps. Reconstitute the eggs with ½ cup water and stir into the couscous mixture. Return the mixture to the heat and cook 2 or 3 minutes until thickened to a pudding consistency. Top each serving with some butter and toasted almonds.

INGREDIENTS:
1½ cups couscous
⅜ cup soy-milk powder
½ cup raw sugar
½ teaspoon vanilla powder
½ cup freeze-dried eggs, 2 ounces
¼ cup toasted, slivered almonds
1 pouch clarified butter
Optional: pinch sea salt

TOFU-LEMON PANCAKES

Makes 4 servings.

INSTRUCTIONS:
Pour ½ cup hot water on the blueberries and let them stand 5 to 10 minutes to rehydrate.

Combine the soy-milk powder, freeze-dried eggs, sugar, lemon peel, and sea salt with 2½ cups water. Stir thoroughly until well blended. Combine the flour, baking powder, and baking soda. Add the wet ingredients to the dry ingredients, stirring just to moisten; be careful not to overmix. If the batter

INGREDIENTS:
½ cup dehydrated blueberries, or 1 cup fresh
½ cup soy-milk powder
1 cup freeze-dried eggs, 4 ounces
¼ cup raw sugar
1 teaspoon dry lemon peel
¼ teaspoon sea salt

is too thick you may add up to ½ cup more water. Drain the blueberries and stir them into the batter. Heat some of the butter in a skillet and make pancakes. Serve them with re-constituted freeze-dried maple syrup.

1½ cups whole-wheat flour
2 teaspoons baking powder
1 teaspoon baking soda
2 pouches clarified butter

OATMEAL PANBREAD

Makes 4 servings.

INSTRUCTIONS:
Pour ¼ cup hot water over the onion to rehydrate. When it is soft enough, combine with the oats, soy-milk powder, parsley, baking powder, thyme, sage, salt, cayenne pepper, and nutmeg. Add 1 cup cold water and let it stand 1 minute.

Reconstitute the eggs by adding, first, ½ cup cold water, blending it in, then another ½ cup water, blending thoroughly. Add the eggs to the oats mixture, stir to blend. Heat half the content of 1 butter pouch in a skillet. Spread half the amount of oat batter in the skillet and cook it 6 to 8 minutes. Turn it over and cook the other side 5 minutes or so. Remove it from the pan, and cook the other half. Top the pan bread with extra clarified butter.

INGREDIENTS:
¼ cup dehydrated chopped onion
2 cups quick-cooking oats (baby oats)
2 tablespoons soy-milk powder
2 tablespoons dried parsley
2 teaspoons baking powder
1 teaspoon dried thyme
½ teaspoon dried sage
½ teaspoon salt
½ teaspoon nutmeg
1 pinch of cayenne pepper
1 cup freeze-dried eggs, 4 ounces
2 pouches clarified butter

PORRIDGE WITH FRUIT AND NUTS

Makes 4 servings.

INSTRUCTIONS:
Combine the oats, wheat germ, prunes, raisins, pine nuts, cinnamon, and salt with 3 cups boiling water. Simmer the mixture

INGREDIENTS:
1½ cups old-fashioned oats
¾ cup raw wheat germ

over low heat until the liquid is absorbed. Serve the porridge topped with sugar. Add 1 cup hot water to the soy-milk powder and pour ¼ cup over each serving.

¾ *cup chopped dried prunes*
½ *cup raisins*
½ *cup pine nuts*
1 *teaspoon cinnamon*
Optional: salt to taste
¼ *cup raw sugar*
2 *tablespoons soy-milk powder*

BREADS, DESSERTS, SWEET SNACKS

MILLER'S BREAD

Makes one 9-by-5-inch loaf.

PREPARATION:
As mentioned before, this bread is perfect for trips where the storage capacity is limited and the food has to be stuffed into a small compartment. Moreover, this bread keeps very well for several days.

INSTRUCTIONS:
Preheat the oven to 350°F.

In the large bowl of the electric mixer, cream the butter; add the sugar and beat until creamy. Add the molasses and the buttermilk and beat until blended.

Stir together the flours, wheat germ, baking soda, and salt. Add to the buttermilk mixture and beat until combined. Stir in the raisins and walnuts.

Pour the batter into a well-greased 9-by-5-inch loaf pan. Bake 1 hour and 20 minutes, until a wooden pick inserted in the center comes out clean. Cool the bread in the pan for 10 minutes. Turn it out on a wire rack to let it cool completely. Wrapped airtight in a plastic film or a foil, this bread will keep for several days. Freeze it for longer storage.

INGREDIENTS:
3 *tablespoons unsalted butter*
½ *cup raw sugar*
6 *tablespoons molasses*
2 *cups buttermilk*
1 *cup whole-wheat flour*
1 *cup whole-rye flour*
1 *cup unbleached flour*
½ *cup wheat germ*
2 *teaspoons baking soda*
1 *teaspoon salt*
1 *cup raisins*
1 *cup chopped walnuts*

CAROB-ORANGE BROWNIES

Makes 8 4-by-2-inch bars.

PREPARATION:

I love this brownie recipe so much that I have adapted it to make snack bars for the backcountry. The trick is to let it cook a little longer. The result won't be the rich and chewy dessert, but a crisper, drier bar that can be packed with other foods and will not lose its flavor.

INSTRUCTIONS:

Preheat the oven to 350°F.

Line an 8-inch-square pan with foil, and grease the foil with a little unsalted butter.

Melt the carob chips with the butter in a small saucepan. Stir to blend, then remove it from the heat.

Let the carob mixture cool two minutes. Stir in the sugar, blend well; add the egg, orange peel, and extract.

Sift together the flour, baking powder, and salt. Blend thoroughly into the carob mixture.

Spread the batter in the prepared pan. Bake on the center rack 18 minutes for chewy brownies; they are done when the edges pull away from the sides of the pan. Cook 4 to 5 minutes longer for a drier bar.

Let the whole cake cool in the pan on a rack for 5 minutes. Invert the pan to unmold cake onto the rack. Let it cool completely. Cut into four pieces to serve the chewy brownies as dessert. You can top them with whipped cream.

If you use the drier version as trail bars, cut the cake into eight or sixteen bars, wrap each one individually in a plastic film, and refrigerate or freeze until the time to pack them.

INGREDIENTS:

4 ounces unsweetened carob chips

2 ounces unsalted butter, plus a little more for greasing the pan

6 tablespoons raw sugar

1 large egg, beaten to blend

1 teaspoon dried orange peel

1/2 teaspoon pure orange extract

1/2 cup whole-wheat flour

1/4 teaspoon baking powder

1 pinch of salt (optional)

FIG BARS

Makes 32 to 36 bars.

PREPARATION:

These bars require baking, so they should be made at home and cut and wrapped individually in a plastic film. They keep well for several days. They also freeze well for longer storage.

INSTRUCTIONS:

Preheat the oven to 325°F.

Combine the eggs, rice-bran syrup, and vanilla. Combine the flour, bran, baking powder, salt, cinnamon, and nutmeg in another bowl. Stir the dry and liquid ingredients together.

Grease and flour a 9-by-13-inch baking pan. Spread the batter in the pan; form 4 rows, lengthwise, of evenly spaced figs, 8 or 9 figs to each row, to cover the batter. Bake in the preheated oven 25 minutes. Let the pan cool on a rack. Cut 32 to 36 bars with a fig in the center of each.

INGREDIENTS:

2 large eggs, beaten
½ cup rice-bran syrup
1 teaspoon vanilla extract
¾ cup whole-wheat flour
¼ cup wheat bran
1 teaspoon baking powder
1 pinch of salt
1 teaspoon cinnamon
¼ teaspoon nutmeg
32 or 36 dried figs,
    preferably calimyrna figs

CAMPFIRE PIE

Makes 4 servings.

PREPARATION:

This dessert was created on July 14 of the year I was kayaking the fjords of the Kenai Peninsula in Alaska. July 14 is the French National Day, and I decided to do something special to celebrate. I wanted a special dessert. The ingredients on hand were ground nuts, sugar, and spices, and some instant chocolate pudding. I took my own eating plate, which is a metal pie plate. I like to use it because it is deep enough and the food won't spill out on a sometimes uneven terrain. In addition, because it is metallic,

I can set it by the fire to keep the food warm. The special dessert was a success, so the campfire pie has been made again many times with many variations. Any desired nuts and toppings can be used, as well as different pudding flavors, fruit preserves, etc.

INGREDIENTS:

½ cup ground walnuts
½ cup ground pistachios
2 tablespoons raw sugar
1 teaspoon cinnamon
1 pouch clarified butter
1 box instant pudding, 4-serving size, in chocolate or other flavor

INSTRUCTIONS:

Mix the ground nuts, sugar, and clarified butter in a metal pie plate, and press them at the bottom to form a crust. Press a piece of foil on top of the crust. Place the plate on a grill over red-hot coals in a campfire and let the crust cook for 10 to 15 minutes, depending on how hot the fire is. In the meantime, prepare the pudding following the package instructions. When the crust is baked, remove the foil and pour onto it the pudding preparation. Let it set.

FRIED TORTILLAS WITH HONEY AND CINNAMON

Makes 4 servings, 2 small tortillas each.

PREPARATION:

I recommend your making your own tortillas in the field. It is more fun, and commercial tortillas are going to break to pieces during the transportation. However, if you use ready-made tortillas, proceed with the second part of the recipe: Fry the tortillas and coat them with honey and cinnamon.

INGREDIENTS:

TO MAKE 8 SMALL TORTILLAS:
1 cup whole-wheat flour
¼ teaspoon salt
½ teaspoon baking powder
½ pouch clarified butter, 2 teaspoons
⅓ cup water

TOPPING:
3 to 4 tablespoons honey
cinnamon to taste

INSTRUCTIONS:

Combine the flour, baking powder, and salt. With the fingers, work the clarified butter into the flour mixture until it resembles coarse sand. Add the water and work the mixture lightly with the hands. You should obtain a soft, pliable dough. Place it in a plastic bag and let it rest at least 15 minutes.

Divide the dough into eight equal balls. Work with one

at a time, keeping the others in the bag to prevent their drying out. Using the fingers and pressing the dough down with the palm of the hand, form a flat circle about 3½ inches in diameter. When all 8 rounds of dough are ready, heat some clarified butter in the skillet and fry the tortillas, 3 or 4 at a time, as many as the skillet will hold in 1 layer. Fry them 1 minute on each side and transfer them to a plate. Repeat until all the tortillas are cooked. Top them with a little honey, sprinkle cinnamon to taste on top, and serve.

MANDEL BREAD

Mandel bread is a not-too-sweet cookie, baked twice like the Italian biscottis.

In order to transport the Mandel bread on our trips, I reshape parts of the loaves, in groups of 6 or 8 cookies, and wrap them very tightly in several layers of foil. This gives strength to the little bundles, which are then transported together in a bag.

This recipe makes about 4 dozen cookies.

INSTRUCTIONS:

Preheat the oven to 350°F. Brown the ground almonds in the hot oven, 10 minutes.

Melt the butter. Mix it with the sugar and almond extract until well blended. Beat in the eggs with a wooden spoon. Combine the flour, baking powder, and salt; sift into the butter mixture. Stir until well blended. Stir in the ground almonds. Shape the dough into a ball and refrigerate for 2 hours.

Flour a marble or wooden pastry board. Divide the dough into 2 equal amounts. Working on the floured surface, shape each piece of dough into a roll 12 inches long, 2 inches wide, and 1 inch thick. Place the 2 rolls on a buttered baking sheet. Bake in a 350°F. oven, 30 minutes, until firm and brown. Cool the loaves on the baking sheet until you can touch them.

Using a serrated edged bread knife, cut each loaf into

INGREDIENTS:
*1 cup ground, blanched
    almonds
1 cup raw sugar
    (turbinado)
½ cup butter, 4 ounces
2 teaspoons almond extract
4 eggs
3 cups unsifted whole-
    wheat flour
1½ teaspoons baking
    powder
¼ teaspoon sea salt*

½-inch-thick slices. Lay them flat on 2 baking sheets and return them to the hot oven 15 more minutes, turning them over once, until lightly browned. Cool on wire racks. Store them airtight up to 2 weeks.

FRUIT LEATHERS

Making fruit leathers is a wonderful way to use a food dehydrator. It allows you to use a lot of any kind of fruit when it is plentiful in season, in large quantities, and low in price. On the trail, the fruit leathers bring the pleasure of a snack bar quite different from that of the baked ones, with the flavor and the beneficial nutrients of fresh fruits; and fresh fruits are what we miss most often on a long trek. There are some exceptions, as in the Wrangell National Park of Alaska, where we walked across carpets of blueberries.

Every kind of fruit and even some vegetables can be turned into leather with an unlimited number of recipes. I have included here only two of my favorites—the apple-pear leather and the pumpkin leather, for those who enjoy .the flavor of pumpkin pies at times other than Thanksgiving.

APPLE-PEAR LEATHER

Makes 4 snacks.

INSTRUCTIONS:

Purée the fruit in a food processor. You should obtain about 5 cups of purée. Line 4 dehydrator trays with plastic wrap and fasten the pieces to the frames with adhesive tape. Spread one fourth of the fruit purée on each tray, making a rectangle ⅛ to ¼ inch thick, 9 by 12 inches. A plastic bowl scraper with a straight edge is the best tool for spreading. Sprinkle about ⅛ teaspoon spice of your choice on each prepared tray, with 2 tablespoons coconut or ground almonds as desired. Dehydrate 8 to 10 hours at 115°F to 120°F, until the leather pulls away from the lining.

INGREDIENTS:

3 cups diced apple, with or without the peel
3 cups diced pear, with or without the peel
¼ cup fresh lemon juice
Optional: you may choose to flavor the leather with various spices: cinnamon, nutmeg, clove, ginger, etc., or to add unsweetened, finely shredded coconut or ground almonds.

PUMPKIN LEATHER

Makes 4 snacks.

INSTRUCTIONS:

Process all the ingredients together in the food processor. Line 4 dehydrator trays with plastic film held to the frame with adhesive tape.

Spread one fourth of the pumpkin mixture on each prepared tray into a rectangle ⅛ to ¼ inch thick and 10 by 14 inches. Dehydrate 8 to 10 hours at 120°F, until the leather pulls away from the lining.

INGREDIENTS:

1 pound cooked pumpkin

2 eggs, well beaten

⅓ cup rice-bran syrup or molasses or honey

1 teaspoon ground cinnamon

½ teaspoon ground nutmeg

½ teaspoon ground clove

¼ cup soy-milk powder dissolved in ½ cup warm water

BANANA-GRANOLA BARS

Makes 64 bars.

INSTRUCTIONS:

Run the granola in the food processor very briefly 4 or 5 times with the on-off switch just to reduce the size of the pieces of granola, but don't grind it. Transfer to a large mixing bowl. Stir in the banana purée and the lemon juice until blended.

Line 4 dehydrator trays with plastic film held in place with adhesive tape. Spread one fourth banana mixture on each tray into a rectangle about 9 by 12 inches. Dehydrate 8 to 10 hours at 120°F, until the mixture pulls away from the lining. Using kitchen shears, cut each rectangle into 16 bars.

INGREDIENTS:

2 cups granola (recipe in breakfast section of this chapter)

5 cups puréed bananas (10 or 12)

¼ cup lemon juice

APRICOT-APPLE BARS

Makes 64 bars.

INSTRUCTIONS:

Line 4 dehydrator trays with plastic film held to the frames with adhesive tape.

Mix the apricot purée, honey, and lemon juice evenly; you may want to warm up the honey to liquefy. Spread one fourth apricot mixture on each tray into a rectangle about 10 by 12 inches. Sprinkle ½ cup chopped apples, ¼ cup chopped almonds, and ¼ cup shredded coconut on each tray. Dehydrate 8 to 10 hours at 120°F until the mixture pulls away from the lining.

Using kitchen shears, cut each rectangle into 16 bars.

INGREDIENTS:

5 cups apricot purée

¼ to ½ cup honey, taste to adjust the amount; it depends on how sweet the apricots are

¼ cup lemon juice

2 cups chopped apples, with or without the peel and dipped into pineapple juice to prevent discoloration

1 cup finely chopped almonds

1 cup shredded, unsweetened coconut

5
Backpacking

It's raining!

It's south central Alaska!

I am lying on the top bunk of a small cabin, reading, writing.

Three men go on with their favorite activities: Bob is stretching on the floor, following his daily yoga routine; Jake is making himself a belt; Cliff is busier than a honeybee, now stoking the wood stove, now doing some last-minute mending, now showing his pictures around, now emptying and restuffing his backpack, now looking all over the place for a can of beans, and simultaneously, incessantly, talking, talking, talking. . . . I think to myself: "Are we really going to spend three weeks backpacking with this man?"

Cliff has lived alone in this cabin for many years. Bob helped him homestead here twenty years ago, and we are now ready to celebrate this anniversary with a one-hundred-mile hike: up the Chitistone Canyon to the Skolaï Pass, up and down several glaciers to the Nizina River. We plan to do it in three weeks, with one food drop on the Skolaï Pass. Bob, Jake and I arrived by bush plane the day before, a beautiful, clear, late summer sunny day, August 21, and autumn had already succeeded summer. The cottonwood gold was shimmering in the sun, the Alaskan cotton grass spread a vaporous blanket over the ground. A multitude of succulent ripe berries were hanging from the bushes or carpeting the ground. Could anyone choose a better time to wander in wild Alaska?

We took off from McCarthy, a small mining community at the end of a sixty-three-mile dirt road that started in Chitina. There is a saying: "If you can find a cranny to put more stuff into a loaded Cessna 180, it will still fly." We proved it with all our equipment and the three of us, plus the pilot, jammed in the cockpit from McCarthy to May Creek.

May Creek, at the edge of the Wrangell Wilderness area. May Creek, two miles from the hill chosen by Cliff to homestead. A wonderful hill, with fabulous views all around, and covered with a dozen varieties of berry-bearing bushes: cranberries, raspberries, bearberries, lingonberries . . .

Cliff was the first human to discover this Garden of Eden, but not the first creature: Those berry-bearing bushes were already a favorite feeding spot for bears, grizzlies. Ever since Cliff settled on this hill, they have regularly attempted to regain their territory. Cliff found what could keep them at a distance—not the metal sheets on the windows, not the spikes planted, point side out, through the door, not the saw blades, but moth balls! Bears are repelled by moth balls. I feel repelled too. I wish I were a mile away, rather than breathe the moth-ball fumes, but I am a human being, and I can force my will to overcome my natural instincts.

I also used my strong will the day before to walk the two miles from May Creek to Cliff's cabin, bearing a pack much too heavy for me. The tops of my thigh bones were rubbing against my ribs. So today I have taken advantage of this rainy, inside-the-cabin morning to redo my pack.

I took out the six-hundred-page hardcover book. "Maybe, if it rains long enough, I'll be able to read it before we leave!"

I took out half a dozen cassettes and kept only three to play in my Walkman.

One hairbrush is enough, no more than one outfit for each weather condition. But I am the "Chef." I will not give up my kitchen kit that contains twenty different herbs and spices and miniature tools—spatula, whisk, chopping block —and all the nonfood paraphernalia: foil, plastic bags, cheese-cloth, menu cards, a seven-day plan with recipes, to be re-peated three times.

In earlier expeditions the Trekking Chef was in her in-fancy. I already had fun mixing dried foods to create various dishes; I was aware of nutritional needs—the necessity to provide a complete diet on such a strenuous trek, the neces-sity to provide energy through the food.

However, this trip was a learning experience in many respects: I got to know myself much better, to recognize my strengths and weaknesses. I learned about human relation-ships, that three men and one woman do not automatically create a harmonious, balanced situation. But these are topics for other books. As far as the food was concerned, I observed:

1. Freeze-dried food is not my choice. I already knew enough
   to avoid the prepared, flavorless meals pompously named

Stroganoff, Cordon Bleu, à la King. I thought I could use some plain, freeze-dried vegetables—carrots, corn, tomatoes, beans, peas. I was disappointed—they all had the same dustlike taste! They also appeared to travel through my digestive system like pieces of plastic, and I worried about not getting any vitamins or minerals from those pellets.

2. Serving pancakes for breakfast every other day was too often: it required too much fuel, which, with two quarts of maple syrup, ended being too much extra weight. Now I serve them once or twice a week. I create my own "complete" mixes, playing with a variety of ingredients; I do use freeze-dried eggs in the mixes. Even if those eggs have lost their nutritional value, they are needed as a binder, and the missing nutrients, essentially the amino acids, are provided by the combinations of nuts and grains. Baby foods, such as Heinz's natural dehydrated applesauce, fruit purées, banana cream, are pleasant toppings for the hotcakes.

3. In many places, at the right time, wild edible foods add an element of fun and excitement to the adventure of finding and gathering them; they also enrich the diet with fresh, unadulterated vitamins and minerals. We used mushrooms, mountain sorrel, and a wealth of berries—Juneberries, blueberries, nagoonberries, red raspberries, cranberries.

4. I have learned, since, to precook grains and legumes: rice, buckwheat, and lentils are ready in minutes; all the dried beans, such an excellent source of protein, were eliminated from the diet until I decided to precook and dehydrate them. Now garbanzos, white, black, and red beans can be enjoyed in the backcountry.

The following menus, which are different from what we had on that trip, are a result of these observations. They work!— and provide without effort the pleasures of creating together a "gourmet" fare that satisfies the body's requirements.

Now the rain has stopped. Hurriedly we fasten our boots, buckle our packs, lock the cabin. One group picture in front of the porch—a smiling, clean-looking team, and off we go. Our silhouettes fade away in the mist and the golden foliage of a wet Alaskan autumn evening.

MENUS

The menus here are presented in groups of meals that are packed together in one bag. Each bag contains one lunch, one dinner, one breakfast, for the whole group; lunch is on top, dinner in the middle, and breakfast at the bottom. The reason is, that the first meal on the trail is likely to be lunch. Then, at the first campsite, the bag that was opened for lunch will offer dinner and breakfast for this site. The next bag is opened for the next lunch and so on.

Each lunch includes a sandwich-spread with the bread, some side items such as chips, nuts, cheese, smoked fish, jerky, and a food bar for each person. Extra snacks such as dried fruit and nuts, candy bars, and more food bars, are carried by each individual for his/her own munching on the trail.

BAG 1

LUNCH

Roasted garlic-almond-cheese spread
Black pumpernickel bread
Smoked fish, shrimp chips
Almond butter bars

DINNER

Red pepper and tomato soup
Potato galettes, herb butter

BREAKFAST

Apple-date granola

BAG 2

LUNCH

Protein spread with pumpernickel bread
Sliced cheese, spiced walnuts
Buzz bars

DINNER

Curry-coriander soup
Shrimp curry with couscous

BREAKFAST

Millet porridge with raisins

BAG 3

LUNCH

Lentil-apricot spread, country bread
Turkey jerky, bean chips
Molasses pecan bars

DINNER

Sour dahl with tadka
Cornmeal patties with red pepper sauce

BREAKFAST

Zapekanka with strawberry soup

BAG 4

LUNCH

Tofu-feta spread with capers and rye bread
Smoked fish, shrimp chips
Apricot-nut bars

DINNER

Buttermilk dill soup
Linguini primavera

BREAKFAST

Russian blinchiki, blueberry filling

BAG 5

LUNCH

Tahini with apple chutney spread, black bread
Sliced cheese, spiced walnuts
Buzz bars

DINNER

Broccoli soup
Lentil-rice casserole

BREAKFAST

Couscous in fruit sauce

BAG 6

LUNCH

Smoked salmon spread, pumpernickel bread
Turkey jerkey, bean chips
Almond butter bars

DINNER

Green's beans and tomato soup
Buckwheat kasha with wild mushrooms

BREAKFAST

Barley-lemon pudding

BAG 7

LUNCH

Energy spread with rye bread
Smoked fish, shrimp chips
Molasses pecan bars

DINNER

Cinnamon milk soup with rice
Winter squash with coconut

BREAKFAST

Quick pancakes with honey butter

SPREADS

ROASTED GARLIC-ALMOND-CHEESE SPREAD

Makes 2 cups, enough for 8 sandwiches.

INSTRUCTIONS:
Heat the oven to 300°F.

Roast the whole garlic cloves in the oven for 20 to 30 minutes until the cloves are lightly browned and very soft.

Purée the garlic with the oil in a food processor. Add all the remaining ingredients except the almonds, and blend thoroughly. Stir in the almonds.

Seal the mixture inside a plastic bag, leaving as little air in it as possible. The spread can be refrigerated for several days or frozen for longer storage.

INGREDIENTS:
12 whole cloves of garlic, peeled
3 tablespoons olive oil
1 cup cream cheese (8 ounces)
½ cup soft tofu
½ teaspoon Dijon mustard
2 tablespoons chopped fresh mint leaves or 2 teaspoons dried mint leaves
1 teaspoon chopped fresh rosemary leaves or ¼ teaspoon dried rosemary leaves
¼ cup coarsely chopped almonds
¼ cup finely chopped shallots or green onions
1 teaspoon vegetable-stock powder
⅛ teaspoon cayenne pepper, or more to taste

PROTEIN SPREAD

Makes 2 cups, enough for 8 sandwiches.

INSTRUCTIONS:
Process the banana chips in the food processor until they are finely crushed. Transfer them to a bowl and reserve.

Process the almond butter or tahini in the food processor with the honey until well blended. Add all the other ingredients and the crushed banana chips, and process the mixture until well mixed.

Seal the mixture in a plastic bag, pressing out as much air as possible.

The spread can be refrigerated for a few days or frozen for longer storage.

INGREDIENTS:
- 1½ cups almond butter or tahini, about 15 ounces
- ½ cup raw honey
- ⅓ cup roasted wheat germ
- 3 tablespoons soy-milk powder
- ¼ cup apple juice concentrate mixed with ¼ cup water
- ¼ cup protein powder
- ½ cup dried banana chips

LENTIL-APRICOT SPREAD

Makes 2 cups, enough for 8 sandwiches.

INSTRUCTIONS:
Mix the lentils, onion slices, bouquet garni, cloves, salt, and cayenne pepper in a saucepan with a quart of cold water. Bring to a boil and simmer the mixture, covered, over low heat for 30 minutes, until the lentils are tender.

In the meantime, pour 1 cup boiling water on the apricots and let them soak for 20 minutes.

Drain the lentils and remove the bouquet garni. Transfer the lentils to the food processor and purée.

Drain the apricots and chop them coarsely.

Chop the small onion. Heat the oil in a frying pan and sauté the onion until soft. Add the apricot and cook it with the onion for 5 minutes. Transfer the apricot mixture to the food processor. Add the walnut pieces, lemon or lime juice, and paprika. Process the mixture until well blended. Season

INGREDIENTS:
- ½ cup dry lentils
- 2 slices raw onion
- 1 bouquet garni: 1 bay leaf, 1 sprig each parsley, thyme
- 2 whole cloves
- salt and cayenne pepper to taste
- 2 ounces dried unsulfured apricots
- 1 small onion
- 1 ounce chopped walnut pieces
- 2 tablespoons pure vegetable oil

to taste with salt and cayenne pepper.

Seal the spread in a plastic bag. Refrigerate it for a few days' storage, or freeze it for longer storage.

*2 tablespoons lemon or
lime juice
1 teaspoon paprika*

TOFU-FETA SPREAD WITH CAPERS

Makes about 2 cups, enough for 8 sandwiches.

INSTRUCTIONS:
Process all the ingredients except the capers in the food processor until well blended. Stir in the capers, adjust the seasoning with salt and more tabasco sauce to taste.

Seal the mixture in a plastic bag and refrigerate it for a few days, or freeze it for longer storage.

INGREDIENTS:
*1 cup soft tofu, 8 ounces
½ cup feta cheese, 4 ounces
2 cloves of garlic, minced
2 scallions, chopped
2 tablespoons chopped
fresh herbs: cilantro,
tarragon, chervil, basil,
oregano . . .
1 tablespoon apple-cider
vinegar
½ teaspoon ground
coriander
¼ teaspoon tabasco sauce
2 tablespoons drained and
rinsed capers*

TAHINI WITH APPLE CHUTNEY SPREAD

Makes 2 cups, enough for 8 sandwiches.

INSTRUCTIONS:
Blend the tahini and the apple chutney together in the food processor.

Seal the mixture in a plastic bag, pressing out all the air.

Refrigerate the spread for a few days' storage, or freeze it for longer storage.

INGREDIENTS:
*1 cup tahini, about 12
ounces
1 cup apple chutney (see
Chapter 7 for the recipe)*

SMOKED SALMON SPREAD

Makes one cup spread.

PREPARATION:

Make the spread at home and refrigerate it up to three days before the trip. Just before the trip, transfer to a plastic pouch and seal. On the trip, keep it in a plastic box or bag inside the cooler. Assemble the sandwiches just before eating.

INSTRUCTIONS:

In a food processor blend all the ingredients until smooth, add salt to taste. You may not need any if the salmon is salty. Store the spread in a box, refrigerated, until ready to pack for the trip.

INGREDIENTS:

4 ounces smoked salmon, skin removed and chopped fine
4 ounces cream cheese, soft
1 tablespoon chopped herbs: chives, cilantro, tarragon or basil
1 tablespoon fresh lemon juice
1 teaspoon paprika
⅛ teaspoon cayenne pepper or more to taste

ENERGY SPREAD

Makes 2 cups, enough for 8 sandwiches.

INSTRUCTIONS:

Blend all the ingredients together in a food processor.

Seal the mixture in a plastic bag, pressing out as much air as possible. Refrigerate the spread for a few days' storage, or freeze it for longer storage.

*Licorice extract can be found in a good health-food store.

INGREDIENTS:

1 cup tahini, about 12 ounces
½ cup raw honey
¼ cup lemon juice
½ cup sesame seeds, toasted on a dry pan
¼ cup bee pollen
1 teaspoon licorice extract*

SNACKS

SPICED WALNUTS

Makes 3 cups.

INSTRUCTIONS:
Combine all the ingredients in a skillet. Bring the mixture to a boil, stirring. Cook and keep on stirring until the liquid is evaporated and the nuts are coated and sugary—5 to 10 minutes.

Spread the nuts on baking sheets. Break them apart as they cool to keep them separate. When they are completely cooled, store them in plastic bags. They can be refrigerated for a brief storage or frozen for longer storage.

INGREDIENTS:
3 cups walnut halves or pieces
¾ cup raw honey
¼ cup water
1 tablespoon grated fresh orange peel or 1 teaspoon dried orange peel
½ teaspoon cinnamon
¼ teaspoon ginger
¼ teaspoon cardamom or coriander or ground cloves
¼ teaspoon nutmeg

SHRIMP CHIPS

Makes 5 ounces of chips, enough snacks for 4, for 2 lunches.

INSTRUCTIONS:
Purée the shrimp in the food processor with the lime and lemon juices, the tomato purée, the ketchup, the red pepper sauce, and the salt. Add the herbs, garlic, and eggs and process again until well blended. The mixture should have the consistency of a soft paste.

Line two 10-by-15-inch dehydrator trays with waxed paper, held in place with adhesive tape. Divide the shrimp paste equally between the 2 trays. Spread it thinly on each tray.

INGREDIENTS:
¾ pound cooked small shrimp (cleaned and shelled)
Juice of 1 lime
Juice of 1 lemon
¼ cup tomato purée
2 tablespoons ketchup
¼ teaspoon hot red pepper sauce
½ teaspoon salt

Dehydrate at high temperature (145°F) for 5 to 6 hours, until very crisp. Break each rectangle into small pieces and place them into a plastic bag. It is not necessary to refrigerate them.

½ teaspoon paprika
2 tablespoons mixed
chopped fresh herbs:
chives, parsley, rosemary,
thyme, cilantro, mint...
2 cloves of garlic, minced
4 hard-boiled eggs, shelled
and chopped

BEAN CHIPS

Makes 12 ounces of chips.

INSTRUCTIONS:
Soak the dry beans overnight. Drain them, place them in a saucepan with water to cover about 2 inches above the beans. You may want to add a few seasonings such as thyme, bay leaves, marjoram, and several whole cloves, but do not add any salt or the beans will remain tough. Add salt in the last fifteen minutes of cooking. Bring the liquid to a boil, lower the heat and simmer the beans, covered, for from 1 to 1½ hours. Let the beans cool and drain them.

Place them in a food processor with all the remaining ingredients and purée. You should have about 3 cups of purée. Adjust the seasonings. The purée should be spicy because the flavors mellow a lot during the drying process. Spread the purée on 3 dehydrator trays, and dry at 145°F. for several hours until completely dehydrated. The chips are crumbly but delicious.

INGREDIENTS:
1 cup dry navy beans, or
2½ cups cooked
1 large onion, chopped
1 tablespoon minced garlic,
about 3 cloves
½ teaspoon ground cumin
¼ cup apple cider vinegar
¼ teaspoon cayenne
pepper, or more to taste
¼ cup minced fresh mint
leaves
½ teaspoon sea salt
2 hard-boiled eggs

SOUPS

For ease of preparation I recommend that the ingredients be carefully weighed or measured according to the recipe before the trip, and sealed in plastic bags in groups, as shown in the following instructions. More information on how to package the food in sealed plastic bags is in Chapter 1.

RED PEPPER AND TOMATO SOUP

Makes 4 servings.

WEIGHT: 8 ounces without croutons

PREPARATION TIME: 15 minutes

INSTRUCTIONS:
Rehydrate the onion with some hot water right in its bag.

    Heat the butter in a soup pot; add the onion and sauté 1 minute. Add the contents of Bag 2, and 4 cups hot water. Bring to a boil and simmer, uncovered, over low heat, for 10 minutes. Reconstitute the egg mixture with ¼ cup cold water. Stir 1 cup of soup into the egg mixture and pour back into the soup. Stir and serve with croutons, if desired.

INGREDIENTS:
1 pouch clarified butter
BAG 1: *¼ cup dehydrated onion*
BAG 2: *½ ounce dehydrated red pepper*
1 ounce dehydrated crushed tomato slices
4 teaspoons instant vegetable-stock powder
½ teaspoon dried thyme leaves
1 dried bay leaf
⅛ teaspoon ground clove
1 pinch cayenne pepper
BAG 3: *1 ounce freeze-dried eggs*
¼ cup dried grated Parmesan cheese
BAG 4 (optional):
1 cup garlic croutons

CURRY-CORIANDER SOUP

Makes 4 servings.

WEIGHT: 8 ounces

PREPARATION TIME: 12 minutes

INSTRUCTIONS:

Bring three cups of water to a boil and reserve.

Heat the butter in the soup pot. Stir the contents of Bag 1 (spice-flour mix) in the hot butter and cook it 1 minute, until bubbly. Add the hot water and stir vigorously to blend the flour mixture smoothly. Add the contents of Bag 2. Bring the soup to simmering. Mix the contents of Bag 3 with 1 cup cold water; stir to dissolve the buttermilk powder, pour it into the soup. Stir and cook the soup, without letting it boil, for 5 minutes, until the rice is tender.

INGREDIENTS:

1 pouch clarified butter

BAG 1: *1 teaspoon ground coriander*

½ teaspoon ground cumin

2 tablespoons whole-wheat flour

BAG 2: *1 tablespoon instant vegetable-stock powder*

2 tablespoons lemon juice or 1 teaspoon dried lemon peel

BAG 3: *½ cup dehydrated cooked rice*

½ cup buttermilk powder

¼ cup dried coriander leaves

SOUR DAHL WITH TADKA

Makes 4 servings.

WEIGHT: 12 ounces

PREPARATION TIME: 10 minutes

INSTRUCTIONS:

Mix the contents of Bag 1 (lentil mixture) in a soup pot with 4 cups cold water. Stirring occasionally, bring to a boil. Lower the heat and let it simmer until the lentils are tender, about 7 or 8 minutes.

Heat the butter from the 2 pouches in a small frying pan,

INGREDIENTS:

2 pouches clarified butter

BAG 1: *1½ cups dehydrated cooked lentils*

1 teaspoon dry lemon peel

1 teaspoon ground ginger

1 teaspoon garlic granules

½ to 1 teaspoon sea salt, to taste

½ teaspoon turmeric

add the cumin seeds, and cook until they darken, one minute or less. Don't let them burn. This is the tadka. Pour it into the soup and serve.

¼ teaspoon cayenne or more, this soup should be spicy hot
BAG 2: *1 teaspoon cumin seeds*

BUTTERMILK-DILL SOUP

Makes 4 servings.

WEIGHT: 6 ounces

PREPARATION TIME: 15 minutes

INSTRUCTIONS:
Heat 3 cups of water. Use 1 cup hot water to rehydrate the leeks in their bag, 5 minutes. Heat the butter in the soup pot, add the leeks and sauté for 1 minute.

Add the remaining 2 cups hot water with the contents of Bag 2. Stir over medium heat until well blended and hot; lower the heat and let the soup simmer 8 minutes.

In the meantime, add the buttermilk powder to 1 cup cold water; stir until well dissolved. When the soup is ready, pour the buttermilk into it, stir, and reheat, but do not let it boil.

INGREDIENTS:
1 pouch clarified butter
BAG 1: *1½ ounces dehydrated leeks, about 2 cups*
BAG 2: *1 ounce potato flakes*
1 tablespoon instant vegetable-stock powder
1 tablespoon dried dill weed
¼ teaspoon curry powder
1 pinch cayenne pepper
BAG 3: *½ cup buttermilk powder*

BROCCOLI SOUP

Makes 4 servings.

WEIGHT: 6 ounces

PREPARATION TIME: 10 minutes

INGREDIENTS:
BAG 1: *2 ounces (2 cups) dehydrated broccoli, crushed*

INSTRUCTIONS:
Place the contents of Bag 1 into a soup pot. Add 4 cups of cold water. Bring to a boil, stirring occasionally. Lower the heat and let it simmer 5 minutes.

In the meantime, mix the soy-milk powder with 1 cup hot water and stir to dissolve the powder. When the vegetables are soft, pour the soy milk into the soup, reheat, stirring, and serve.

¼ cup dehydrated onion
½ teaspoon garlic granules
2 tablespoons dehydrated leeks
2 tablespoons dehydrated celery
1 tablespoon crushed dried mixed herbs (thyme, bay, basil, oregano, mint...)
½ teaspoon ground cumin
⅛ teaspoon cayenne pepper
1 tablespoon instant vegetable-stock powder
BAG 2: *¼ cup soy-milk powder*

GREEN'S BEANS AND TOMATO SOUP

Makes 4 servings.

WEIGHT: 8 ounces

PREPARATION TIME: 12 minutes

INGREDIENTS:
¾ cup dry navy beans cooked ahead of time and dehydrated. To cook them, soak them in water overnight. Drain them and place in a large pot with 6 fresh sage leaves, 3 cloves of garlic (peeled), 2 bay leaves, 6 sprigs of fresh thyme, and 1 tablespoon olive oil. Add 10 cups cold water; bring to a boil, lower the heat, and cook the beans for 1 hour, until tender but not mushy. In the last half hour of cooking add 1 teaspoon salt. Drain the beans and dehydrate them. For instructions on dehydrating, look in the Introduction of this book. You should have 1 cup dehydrated cooked beans.

1 pouch clarified butter
BAG 1: *½ teaspoon dried sage leaves, crumbled*
1 teaspoon garlic granules
1 bay leaf
¼ cup dehydrated onion
BAG 2: *1 cup dehydrated beans, as prepared above*
1½ ounces dehydrated tomato slices, crumbled
4 teaspoons instant vegetable-stock powder
1 pinch cayenne pepper, or more to taste
BAG 3: *Parsley sauce, recipe follows*

INSTRUCTIONS:

Add ¼ cup hot water to the contents of Bag 1 to rehydrate. Heat the butter in the soup pot and sauté the onion mixture 1 minute.

Add 4 cups cold water with the contents of Bag 2. Bring to a boil, lower the heat, and let it simmer 10 minutes, until the beans are soft again.

Adjust the seasoning with salt and cayenne pepper. Stir the parsley sauce into the soup and serve.

PARSLEY SAUCE

This sauce can be made ahead of time, and can be sealed airtight in a plastic bag, but it will keep, refrigerated, for no more than 2 weeks. This is true for the first recipe that follows. If you want to use dried ingredients that will keep much longer and that you can use to make the sauce in the field, I give a second recipe as an alternative to the first one.

INSTRUCTIONS RECIPE #1:

Place all the ingredients in a food processor, and purée until smooth. Seal airtight in a plastic bag.

INSTRUCTIONS RECIPE #2:

In the field, heat the butter in a small saucepan or metal cup. Add all the other ingredients, stir, and pour on the soup before serving.

Note: I call this soup "Green's beans and tomato soup" because it comes from my favorite cookbook, *The Green's Cookbook*, by Deborah Madison and Edward Brown. I love this soup recipe so much that I have created this adaptation for the backcountry.

RECIPE #1:
INGREDIENTS:

> 1 cup fresh parsley leaves, packed
> 2 cloves of garlic, peeled and coarsely chopped
> ¼ teaspoon sea salt
> 3 tablespoons olive oil
> 3 tablespoons grated Parmesan cheese
> lemon juice to taste

RECIPE #2:
INGREDIENTS:

> ¼ cup dehydrated parsley leaves
> ½ teaspoon garlic granules
> ¼ teaspoon sea salt
> 2 pouches clarified butter
> 3 tablespoons dry grated Parmesan cheese
> Lemon peel to taste

CINNAMON MILK SOUP WITH RICE

Makes 4 servings.

WEIGHT: 7 ounces

PREPARATION TIME: 12 minutes

INSTRUCTIONS:

Heat to boiling 4 cups water in the soup pot. Lower the heat and add the contents of Bag 1. Stir to dissolve the soy-milk powder, and let it simmer until the rice is tender, about 5 minutes. Reconstitute the eggs right in their bag with ¼ cup cold water. Stir the eggs into the soup with the clarified butter. Cook 1 more minute and serve.

INGREDIENTS:
1 pouch clarified butter
BAG 1: *½ cup soy-milk powder*
½ cup dehydrated cooked rice
1½ teaspoons or more, ground cinnamon
¼ cup dehydrated honey
Pinch of salt
BAG 2: *¼ cup freeze-dried eggs*

DINNER CASSEROLES

SHRIMP CURRY WITH COUSCOUS

Makes 4 servings.

WEIGHT: 18 ounces

PREPARATION TIME: 15 minutes

INSTRUCTIONS:

Mix the shrimp and peas with 1 cup hot water in a small bowl and keep warm near the fire, on a hot stone, to rehydrate.

Pour ¼ cup hot water into Bag 2 (onion-spice mixture) and let the onion rehydrate too, for 5 minutes.

Heat the butter from one pouch in a saucepan. Add the onion-spice mixture and cook it 1 or 2 minutes. Add the

INGREDIENTS:
2 pouches clarified butter
BAG 1: *3 ounces dehydrated cooked small shrimp*
1 ounce dehydrated green peas
BAG 2: *¼ cup dehydrated onion*
1 teaspoon curry powder
¼ teaspoon kelp or sea salt
⅛ teaspoon cayenne pepper
¼ teaspoon ground mace

whole-wheat flour, stir it into the onion mixture, and cook 1 more minute.

Separately, stir the soy-milk powder with 1 cup hot water to dissolve the powder. Pour the hot soy milk on the onion mixture and stir vigorously, scraping the sides of the pan to obtain a smooth-textured sauce. Cook the sauce over a medium-low heat until it thickens. Add the rehydrated shrimp and peas, and let them cook in the sauce until heated through.

In the meantime, heat 2 cups of water in the skillet; add the couscous mixture, stir it, cover the skillet with a foil, and keep the couscous warm but away from direct heat for 5 minutes. Uncover the skillet, fluff up the couscous with a fork. Stir the butter from the second pouch into the contents of bag 6. Serve hot and topped with the shrimp curry.

BAG 3: *2 tablespoons whole-wheat flour*

BAG 4: *¼ cup soy-milk powder*

BAG 5: *2 cups couscous*
¼ cup dehydrated onion
2 teaspoons instant vegetable-stock powder
¼ teaspoon turmeric

BAG 6: *¼ cup raisins*
¼ cup sunflower seeds
2 tablespoons dried parsley
½ teaspoon celery salt
¼ teaspoon cinnamon

LINGUINI PRIMAVERA

Makes 4 servings.

WEIGHT: 1 pound 4 ounces

PREPARATION TIME: 12 minutes

INSTRUCTIONS:
Heat 3½ cups of water to boiling. Use 1½ cups hot water to rehydrate the tomato mixture (Bag 1) and 2 cups to rehydrate the vegetable mixture (Bag 2). Also, fill a large pot with salty water for the linguini. When the tomatoes are soft, after about 5 minutes, heat the butter from one pouch in the skillet and sauté the tomato mixture in it, for 2 to 3 minutes. Add the vegetable mixture and keep warm.

When the water in the large pot begins to boil, add the linguini and cook for 6 to 8 minutes, until tender but still firm.

In the meantime, pour ¾ cup water into a small saucepan and add the contents of Bag 4, the cheese mixture. Stir over medium heat until the soy-milk powder is dissolved, and keep

INGREDIENTS:
2 pouches clarified butter

BAG 1: *1½ ounces dehydrated tomatoes, crushed to 1 cup*
¼ cup dehydrated mushrooms
2 tablespoons dehydrated parsley
½ teaspoon crushed red-pepper flakes
½ teaspoon garlic granules

BAG 2: *1 ounce dehydrated broccoli, crushed to 1 cup*
¾ ounce dehydrated zucchini, ½ cup

warm.

When the linguini is ready, drain it, discard the cooking water, and place the linguini back in the large pot. Toss it with the cheese mixture, the butter from the second pouch, and half the vegetable mixture. Serve topped with the remaining vegetable mixture and the toasted pine nuts.

*½ ounce dehydrated green
    beans, ¼ cup*
*½ ounce dehydrated green
    peas, ¼ cup*
*1 tablespoon dried basil
    leaves*
BAG 3: *12 ounces linguini,
    broken up to pack easily*
BAG 4: *3 tablespoons soy-milk
    powder*
*½ cup dry grated Parmesan
    cheese*
*1 teaspoon vegetable-stock
    powder*
BAG 5: *⅓ cup toasted pine
    nuts*

LENTIL-RICE CASSEROLE

Makes 4 servings.

WEIGHT: 20 ounces

PREPARATION TIME: 10 minutes

INSTRUCTIONS:

Place all the ingredients except the butter in the skillet. Add 4 cups cold water and bring it to a boil. Lower the heat and let the casserole simmer until the rice is soft. Stir in the butter and serve.

INGREDIENTS:
1 pouch clarified butter
BAG 1: *2 cups dehydrated
    cooked rice*
*1 cup dehydrated cooked
    lentils*
*2 ounces dehydrated
    tomatoes, crushed to 1
    cup*
*1 ounce dehydrated onion,
    ¼ cup*
*4 teaspoons instant
    vegetable-stock powder*
1 teaspoon ground cumin
½ teaspoon garlic granules
*1 pinch cayenne pepper or
    more, to taste*

BUCKWHEAT KASHA WITH WILD MUSHROOMS

Makes 4 servings.

WEIGHT: 1 pound 5 ounces with dehydrated mushrooms

PREPARATION TIME: 15 minutes, does not include the soaking time

INSTRUCTIONS:

If using dried mushrooms, let them soak in 4 cups cold water for 1 hour, or 4 cups hot water for 10 minutes.

Lift the mushrooms out of the water, reserving the soaking liquid. Cut the mushrooms into fine strips and sauté them in half the butter.

If you are using fresh edible wild mushrooms, wash them thoroughly and cut them into fine strips. Sauté them in half the butter.

Adjust the soaking liquid, if using dried mushrooms, to 4 cups and add it to the mushrooms. If using wild fresh mushrooms, add 4 cups plain water.

Add the contents of Bag 1 to the mushrooms and water. Bring it to a boil, lower the heat, and let the mixture simmer uncovered until the kasha is tender, about 5 minutes.

In the meantime, rehydrate the onion with ½ cup hot water. Sauté the onion in the remaining butter and reserve, keeping it warm.

When the kasha is cooked, serve it topped with the sautéed onion.

INGREDIENTS:

1 pouch clarified butter
2 to 3 cups wild edible boletus mushrooms, or 2 ounces dehydrated mushrooms
BAG 1: *4 cups dehydrated cooked kasha*
1 tablespoon instant vegetable-stock powder
1 teaspoon dried parsley
1 teaspoon dried tarragon
½ teaspoon dried thyme
¼ teaspoon ground mace
¼ teaspoon ground clove
1 pinch cayenne pepper
BAG 2: *½ cup dehydrated onion*

WINTER SQUASH WITH COCONUT

Makes 4 servings.

WEIGHT: 8 ounces

PREPARATION TIME: 8 minutes

INSTRUCTIONS:
Add 2 cups water to the contents of the bag in a saucepan or skillet. Bring it to simmer and cook gently over low heat until all moisture is absorbed and the squash is rehydrated. Stir in the butter and serve.

INGREDIENTS:
1 pouch clarified butter
BAG 1: *4 ounces dehydrated*
cubed winter squash
4 ounces shredded coconut,
about 1 cup
1 teaspoon ground cumin
½ teaspoon sea salt
½ teaspoon ground mace
½ teaspoon ground clove
¼ teaspoon cayenne pepper

VEGETABLE PATTIES

POTATO GALETTES WITH HERB BUTTER

Makes 4 servings.

WEIGHT: 15 ounces

PREPARATION TIME: 20 minutes

INSTRUCTIONS:
Pour the contents of Bag 1 into a mixing bowl and add enough water to make a thick pancake batter, about 6 cups. Heat some of the clarified butter in a skillet. Fry small amounts of potato batter in the skillet, cooking them about 5 minutes, turning them over, and cooking 5 more minutes on the other side,

INGREDIENTS:
2 pouches clarified butter
BAG 1: *4 cups potato flakes*
(instant mashed
potatoes)
¼ cup soy-milk powder
¼ cup dehydrated scallions
4 ounces freeze-dried eggs
(1 cup)
1 teaspoon instant
vegetable-stock powder

until well browned. Transfer the potato galettes to a warm plate. If you are cooking on a campfire, a metal plate covered with a piece of foil and kept on a hot stone is a perfect food warmer.

Repeat until all the batter is used. Serve the potato galettes topped with herbed butter, the recipe for which follows:

For the herb butter, gently heat the clarified butter from one pouch in a metal cup. Stir in the contents of Bag 2 (the herb mixture). Add ¼ cup hot water and keep warm until the herbs are soft.

¼ teaspoon ground nutmeg
1 pinch cayenne pepper, or more to taste
BAG 2: *2 tablespoons dried parsley*
2 tablespoons mixed dried herbs of your choice (cilantro, basil, oregano, dill, mint...)
1 teaspoon garlic granules
¼ teaspoon sea salt

CORNMEAL PATTIES WITH RED PEPPER SAUCE

Makes 4 servings.

WEIGHT: 1 pound 12 ounces

PREPARATION TIME: 20 minutes

INSTRUCTIONS:
Place the contents of Bag 1 in a mixing bowl. Add 3 cups cold water and stir until well blended. The batter should have the consistency of pancake batter; if it is too thick, add up to ½ cup water.

Heat some of the clarified butter in the skillet. Fry small amounts of batter: about 5 minutes on 1 side, then turn it over and cook the other side 3 to 4 minutes until lightly browned.

Transfer the patties to a metal plate set on a hot stone near the fire. Cover it with a piece of foil to keep the food warm. Repeat until all the batter is used.

To make the red pepper sauce, combine the ingredients of Bag 2 with 1 cup water. Heat to simmer and keep it warm near the fire until ready to use.

INGREDIENTS:
1 pouch clarified butter
BAG 1: *1½ cups yellow cornmeal*
1½ cups whole-wheat flour
4 ounces freeze-dried eggs
½ cup soy-milk powder
¼ cup dehydrated scallions
¼ cup dehydrated red and green bell peppers
3 tablespoons dehydrated honey
1 tablespoon instant vegetable-stock powder
2 teaspoons baking powder
BAG 2: **Red Pepper Sauce**
1 ounce dehydrated red pepper processed to a powder in a food processor
2 tablespoons buttermilk powder

When the patties are ready, serve them topped with the red pepper sauce.

1 teaspoon crushed basil leaves
¼ teaspoon garlic granules
¼ teaspoon sweet paprika
¼ teaspoon sea salt
⅛ teaspoon cayenne pepper

BREAKFASTS

APPLE-DATE GRANOLA

Makes 4 servings.

WEIGHT: 1 pound

PREPARATION TIME: 45 minutes to make the granola at home; 6 to 8 minutes in the field

When the granola is ready, pack it into a sealed plastic bag as Bag 1.

INSTRUCTIONS:
To make the granola, mix together the oats, barley, cracked wheat, wheat germ, soy-milk powder, rice-bran syrup, and vegetable oil. Spread on a baking sheet and roast in a 300°F oven for 45 minutes. Stir the granola every 15 minutes. Take the granola out of the oven and transfer to another baking sheet to cool. Stir it occasionally while it is cooling, to keep the grains separate. When completely cooled, add the chopped dates and apples.

Store the granola in a sealed plastic bag. Keep it refrigerated for up to 2 weeks or freeze it for longer storage.

At the campsite, bring 6 cups water to a boil. Add the granola with the contents of Bag 2. Stir and cook 2 to 3 minutes.

INGREDIENTS:
To make the granola at home:
1 cup rolled oats
½ cup pearl barley
½ cup cracked wheat
¼ cup raw wheat germ
2 tablespoons soy-milk powder
2 tablespoons rice-bran syrup
1 tablespoon pure vegetable oil
½ cup chopped dates
½ cup chopped dried apples

BAG 2: *½ cup soy-milk powder*
1 teaspoon ground cinnamon

MILLET PORRIDGE WITH RAISINS

Makes 4 servings.

WEIGHT: 16 ounces

PREPARATION TIME: 8 minutes

INSTRUCTIONS:
Bring 4 cups water to a boil. Add the contents of Bag 1, stir, and cook over low heat 5 minutes, until the millet is tender.
Stir in the butter and the raisins and serve.

INGREDIENTS:
1 pouch clarified butter
BAG 1: *2 cups dehydrated cooked millet*
½ cup shredded coconut
1 tablespoon dehydrated honey
½ cup soy-milk powder
1 pinch sea salt
BAG 2: *1 cup raisins*

ZAPEKANKA WITH STRAWBERRY SOUP

Makes 4 servings.

The word zapekanka means "pudding" in Russian. The basic zapekanka is made with flour, milk, butter, eggs, and sugar, and baked in the oven. Sometimes potato flour is used, or a cereal like millet. I made up this version to use cream of rice, a pretty bland cereal normally. The eggs make it set like a pudding, but it can cook on top of the fire if you are careful to stir it constantly to prevent sticking at the bottom. Russians also make a lot of fruit soups or sauces. My recipe for back-country strawberry soup is a delicious complement to the zapekanka. It can also be eaten with dinner, hot or cold, as hors d'oeuvre or dessert.

INGREDIENTS:
1½ cups cream of rice
1 cup freeze-dried eggs, 4 ounces
6 tablespoons soy-milk powder
1 pouch clarified butter
¼ cup raw sugar
Strawberry soup, recipe follows

INSTRUCTIONS:
Combine the cream of rice, freeze-dried eggs, soy-milk powder, clarified butter, and sugar in a saucepan. Add 4 cups of water and cook over medium heat until the liquid begins to

boil. Stir constantly, and continue to cook the pudding 1 more minute, always stirring, until it thickens and sets. Serve, topped with strawberry soup.

STRAWBERRY SOUP

INGREDIENTS:

2 cups dehydrated strawberries, 2½ ounces
1 teaspoon dried orange peel
¼ cup raw sugar
½ teaspoon cinnamon
2 tablespoons cornstarch
¼ cup buttermilk powder

INSTRUCTIONS:

Mix the strawberries, orange peel, sugar, and cinnamon with 3 cups of water in a saucepan. Bring to a boil, stirring occasionally. Simmer over low heat until the strawberries are very soft, about 5 minutes.

In the meantime, combine the cornstarch with ¼ cup cold water and stir to blend. Pour the cornstarch into the strawberry mixture and cook it a little longer until it thickens, 1 to 2 minutes. Reconstitute the buttermilk with 1 cup cold water. Pour it into the soup, reheat, and serve.

BLINCHIKI WITH BLUEBERRY FILLING

Makes 4 servings (16 blinchiki)

WEIGHT: 22 ounces with the dried blueberries

PREPARATION TIME: 30 minutes

INGREDIENTS:

1 pouch clarified butter
2 cups fresh blueberries or 1 cup dried
BAG 1: *½ cup dehydrated honey*
1 teaspoon lemon peel
½ teaspoon nutmeg
BAG 2: *2 tablespoons cornstarch*
BAG 3: *4 ounces freeze-dried eggs*
1 pinch sea salt
1 tablespoon dehydrated honey

INSTRUCTIONS:

TO MAKE THE FILLING:

Place the fresh blueberries in a saucepan with ¼ cup water, or the dried ones with 1 cup water. Add the contents of Bag 1, stir over medium heat, and bring to a boil.

Stir the cornstarch with ¼ cup water; add a little hot blueberry mix to the cornstarch and pour it back into the sauce. Cook 2 to 3 minutes until thickened. Keep on a warm stone near the campfire.

TO MAKE THE BLINCHIKI:

To reconstitute the eggs, add first ½ cup water, stir to blend. Add another ½ cup water and stir again.

Add ½ cup water to the eggs, and the contents of Bag 4. Stir until smooth, and add 1 more cup water. The batter should be thin.

Heat some of the butter in the skillet; pour about ¼ cup batter and cook about 2 minutes until browned on one side. Do not brown the other side; remove the thin pancake to a warm plate, brown side up. Place about two tablespoons' filling on the pancake and fold it like an envelope. Repeat until all the batter has been used.

Add more butter to the skillet and fry the rolled pancakes until browned.

BAG 4: *1 cup buckwheat flour*
3 tablespoons soy-milk powder

COUSCOUS IN FRUIT SAUCE

Makes 4 servings.

WEIGHT: 16 ounces

PREPARATION TIME: 10 minutes

INSTRUCTIONS:

Bring 3 cups water to a boil in a skillet with the butter. Add the couscous mixture, stir, turn the heat off. Cover the skillet tightly with a piece of foil and let it stand 5 minutes. Uncover the pan, fluff up the couscous with a fork; do not use a spoon or the soft grain will form lumps. Stir in the contents of Bag 2 and serve.

INGREDIENTS:
1 pouch clarified butter
BAG 1: *1½ cups couscous*
½ cup ground dehydrated berries, choice of raspberries, blueberries, strawberries...
¼ cup ground dehydrated bananas
BAG 2: *½ cup pineapple bits*
¼ cup raw sugar (turbinado)
½ teaspoon ground cinnamon

BARLEY-LEMON PUDDING

Makes 4 servings.

WEIGHT: 16 ounces

PREPARATION TIME: 10 minutes

INSTRUCTIONS:
Mix the barley mixture with 4 cups cold water. Bring to a boil. Lower the heat and cook 5 minutes until the barley is tender.

Reconstitute the eggs with ½ cup cold water. Add the egg mixture to the barley, stir and cook 1 minute until you have a pudding consistency. Serve the pudding topped with the walnut pieces.

INGREDIENTS:
BAG 1: *1½ cups pressed barley or 2 cups dehydrated cooked pearl barley*
½ cup soy-milk powder
¼ cup dehydrated honey flakes
BAG 2: *½ cup freeze-dried eggs, 2 ounces*
1½ teaspoons dry lemon peel
½ teaspoon nutmeg
BAG 3: *½ cup walnut pieces*

QUICK PANCAKES WITH HONEY BUTTER

Makes four servings.

WEIGHT: 22 ounces

PREPARATION TIME: 20 minutes

INSTRUCTIONS:
Add ½ cup water to the egg mixture to rehydrate. Beat the mixture with 3 cups water. Add the flour and stir until the texture is very smooth. Dissolve the cream of tartar in 1 cup water and pour it into the batter. Use 1 pouch clarified butter to make the cakes.

Stir the other pouch clarified butter with the dehydrated honey and ¼ cup warm water until blended. Top the cakes with the honey butter.

INGREDIENTS:
2 pouches clarified butter
BAG 1: *2 ounces freeze-dried eggs*
1 tablespoon raw sugar
½ teaspoon baking soda
¼ teaspoon sea salt
BAG 2: *18 ounces whole-wheat flour*
BAG 3: *½ teaspoon cream of tartar*
BAG 4: *¼ cup dehydrated honey*

FOOD BARS

ALMOND BUTTER BARS

Makes 32 bars.

INSTRUCTIONS:
Mix all the ingredients thoroughly in a food processor. Pat the dough evenly into an 8-by-8-inch baking pan.

These bars require no cooking. Refrigerate several hours. Cut into 32 pieces. Wrap each one in a plastic film. The bars can be refrigerated for several days or frozen for longer storage.

INGREDIENTS:
½ cup almond butter
½ cup ground blanched almonds
½ cup raw honey
½ cup toasted wheat germ
½ cup soy-milk powder
Optional: ¼ teaspoon pure almond extract

BUZZ BARS

Makes 24 bars.

INSTRUCTIONS:
Preheat the oven to 350°F.

Mix all the ingredients thoroughly. You should have a stiff batter. Pat and press it in a greased baking pan, 9 inches square. Bake in the preheated oven for 15 minutes.

Cut while still warm into 24 bars. Wrap each bar individually in a small piece of plastic film. The buzz bars keep well for several days. You may freeze them for a long storage.

INGREDIENTS:
½ cup light pure vegetable oil, sesame or safflower
½ cup raw honey
½ cup whole-wheat flour
½ cup raw wheat germ
½ cup toasted sesame seeds
2 tablespoons bee pollen
½ teaspoon ground nutmeg
¼ teaspoon ground cardamom

MOLASSES PECAN BARS

Makes 12 bars.

INSTRUCTIONS:

Preheat the oven to 350°F.

Beat the molasses in the electric blender with the water. Sift together the flour, baking soda, and spices. Add the flour mixture to the molasses and beat until well combined. Stir in the pecans.

Pour the batter into a greased 8-by-8-inch pan. Bake in the preheated oven for 30 to 35 minutes, until a wooden pick inserted in the center of the cake comes out clean.

Cool on a rack, in the pan, for 10 minutes. Cut the cake into 12 bars. Transfer them to the rack to cool completely. Wrap each bar individually in a plastic film. The bars will keep well for several days, refrigerated. Freeze them for longer storage.

INGREDIENTS:

1 cup unsulfured dark molasses
½ cup hot water
1½ cups whole-wheat flour
½ teaspoon baking soda
¼ teaspoon each cinnamon, ginger, and nutmeg
1 cup pecans, toasted lightly and chopped

APRICOT-NUT BARS

Makes 32 bars.

INSTRUCTIONS:

Preheat the oven to 350°F.

Combine the chopped apricots and the currants with 1 cup boiling water. Let stand 20 minutes; drain.

Cream together the butter and honey until light.

Sift together the flour, baking powder, and salt. Beat the dry ingredients into the butter mixture. Stir in the apricots and currants with the water. Stir in the coconut.

Pour the batter into a greased 13-by-9-inch baking pan. Bake in the preheated oven 30 to 35 minutes. Cool the cake on a wire rack. Cut it into 32 bars. Wrap each bar individually

INGREDIENTS:

1½ cups chopped dried unsulfured apricots
½ cup currants
½ cup unsalted butter, soft
½ cup raw honey
1½ cups whole-wheat flour
½ teaspoon baking powder
¼ teaspoon salt
¾ cup shredded coconut

in a plastic film and refrigerate for a few days' storage. Freeze them for longer storage.

All the following recipes in this chapter—soups, dinner dishes, breakfasts, are made mostly from dehydrated ingredients. They can be totally prepared in the field.

Instructions on how to dehydrate vegetables, herbs, even cooked grains, and legumes are in the first section of this book. Some dehydrated foods, such as soy milk, buttermilk, eggs, honey, and spices, can be purchased at the grocery or specialty shops.

6
Llama Trekking

If you want to be made aware of every sign of wildlife on your backcountry trails, take an animal along.

A dog is so much fun! His joy is contagious. He spots every animal scent or track, and the game is to find out what creature made him stop, point, run, or dig. At night he can be a warm protecting companion. However, once I wondered who was protecting whom, as I camped one night alone with a female Akita, an impressive husky type of dog. All evening long she stayed very close to me, ears twitching at every creaking noise, refusing to venture outside the circle of light from the campfire.

Horses are all right; they carry a lot of weight, but they are generally too nervous out there, and their unpredictable reactions can cause some troubles. Moreover, you can always tell when and where horses have walked and camped, so noticeable is their impact on the environment.

What animal can be as affectionate as a dog, docile as a sheep, and freight a hundred pounds or more? What is this animal that moves with perfect ease in the forest, responds open-mindedly, without fear, to signs of wildlife, has very little impact upon the environment, and whose double cloven hooves provide a sure footing on rocky steep terrain? This animal is a llama!

Llamas are becoming popular in this country both as pack animals and pets. Indeed, they can be extremely loving and attached to their masters. Though their attitude is almost "snobbish" toward newcomers, once they adopt you as a friend, they express their esteem. Their sharp memory allows them to remember you months later and demonstrate their affection again—that is, they may allow you to touch their necks, caress their foreheads; typically, they blow gentle warm breath on your cheek, an affectionate "llama kiss." Yes, they can spit, but you have to push their buttons really hard to cause them to spit, and they are trained at an early age not to do so.

Bob and I have outfitted a number of "llama treks" in the Pioneer Mountains, south of Sun Valley. It has always been a joy to see the animals respond kindly to people's desire to become friends; they seem to be instinctively more caring for children, perhaps as a result of their loving concern for their own offspring. With the patience of a nice uncle, they let children take them by the lead, pat them playfully, and ride on their backs.

However, don't let all this make you think that llamas are as submissively devoted to man as are dogs. Whatever you do to them—pat them, lead them, load them, they have a way of letting you know they are doing you a big favor. And if, for any reason, they decide to stop the favor, they can be as stubborn as mules. This can happen with animals lacking sufficient training for the trail.

I remember a certain "Max," an unusual character. All day, Max had shown signs of independent thinking, walking his own trail, at his own pace, stopping to eat or urinate in the most awkward places; then he decided that the day had been long enough for him. Without fuss, without a warning sign, he simply sat down on the trail, half a mile from our destination camp, and refused to budge. Suddenly, we had lost all control. Max, without a wink in his eye, without a twitch of his tail, dictated that we were to divide his load among all of us and carry it for the rest of the day; that we were to come back for him only when the camp was set up. Three hours later, when one of us, the strongest male, came back and humbly begged Max to stand up and walk, he condescendingly followed him to camp.

Llamas blend wonderfully into the natural element, just as wild animals do. One day, I was running on a trail to catch up with five llamas. Jeff, who was leading them, had taken off ahead of our group, and I was aware that he did not know where we were going to leave the trail to move in another direction. I did not trust that he would stop and wait for us, but he did—off the trail! I ran right past him and the five llamas, totally unaware of their presence in the bushes. I ended up running up and down the wrong trail, over two mountain passes, to take a short cut to the picnic site, hoping to be there in time to serve lunch. To every person I met on my way, I would ask:

"Have you seen five llamas?"

This is not the usual phrase with which you greet strangers on the trail! They would look at me suspiciously because no one ever saw the llamas. That is how well they dissolve into the scenery!

Without mentioning the necessity of good communication between the guides, the success of a llama trek depends on the loading process. It is most important that the saddle-bags be equally weighted on each side of the llama's back and that no sharp edges or corners dig into its flanks. I can't blame them if any cause of discomfort prompts them to sit down and refuse to move, or buck and run a few feet away, dropping the whole harness on the ground when you thought you had it well secured!

In any case, with some precautions—I made special padded stuff sacks—and much consideration for the noble llamas, we were able to live royally in the wild environment. Thanks to our loving helpers, who carried the cast-iron gear, the campfire grills, the insulated containers, and the fishing equipment in addition to the tents, sleeping bags, etcetera, we enjoyed the types of foods that are in the following menus:

MENUS

DAY 1
♦
LUNCH

Broiled duck sandwiches with
fresh tomato relish and garlic jam
Fresh fruit salad, lime dressing

DINNER

Spinach-bulgur salad
Indian poached trout
Yogurt rice, peach chutney
Grilled pita bread
Baklava

DAY 2
♦
BREAKFAST

Grilled fruit and cheese sandwiches
with fruit sauce
and cut-up fresh fruit—
oranges, kiwi, strawberries

LUNCH

Roquefort-walnut loaf
Zucchini-tofu dip with crackers
Date bonbons

DINNER

Green bean soup with coriander
Angel Lake trout
Wilderness tempura
Steamed rice
Gingersnaps

DAY 3
◆
BREAKFAST

Trout Hemingway
Oatmeal biscuits with Moroccan
apple-date butter

LUNCH

Oriental cabbage slaw
Shrimp-paste ribbon sandwiches
Anise biscotti

DINNER

Vegetable soup with wild sorrel
Orange trout with wild rice
Zucchini-carob bars

DAY 4
◆
BREAKFAST

Thin cornmeal hotcakes with rice-bran syrup
Stewed dried-fruit salad

LUNCH

Coucous salad sandwiches
Green olive spread with crackers
Tahini-granola bars

SANDWICHES

BROILED DUCK SANDWICHES

Makes 8 servings.

INSTRUCTIONS:
TO COOK THE DUCK:

A few days before departure, slash the skin crosswise on the duck breasts. Mix together the sea salt, thyme, allspice, and cayenne pepper. Cover the breasts with the spice mixture and refrigerate, covered, for 12 to 24 hours.

Pat the duck pieces dry with a paper towel, and place them in a broiler pan. Broil them in the oven, 3 inches from the heat. Cook 12 minutes for medium rare, or longer to your liking. Let them cool completely. Store them in a plastic bag and refrigerate until departure time.

TO ASSEMBLE THE SANDWICHES:

Spread a thin film of soft butter on the bread slices. Spread the garlic jam and the fresh tomato relish on every other slice. Slice the duck breasts across the grain at a 45° angle. Fan the breast slices on the tomato relish. Add the garnishes of your choice. Top with the other slices of bread. Wrap each sandwich in a plastic film if it is to be served later.

INGREDIENTS:
TO COOK THE DUCK:

3 whole raw duck breasts

1½ teaspoons coarse sea salt

1 tablespoon fresh thyme leaves

½ teaspoon ground allspice cayenne pepper to taste

TO ASSEMBLE THE SANDWICHES:

16 slices of your choice of bread: whole wheat, sourdough, or rye

A little soft butter if the sandwiches are to be made ahead of time

Garlic jam and fresh tomato relish (recipes follow under "Relishes")

Your choice of the following: lettuce or spinach leaves, slices of tomato, cucumber, bell pepper, avocado, alfalfa sprouts, sunflower seeds . . .

ROQUEFORT-WALNUT LOAF

Makes 4 servings.

For this recipe you need a firm type of bread, shaped into round loaves. The recipes for the Italian or Finland country breads in Chapter 1 are very well suited. On this canoe trip I use small individual loaves—each recipe from Chapter 1 would make 8 or 10 individual loaves—and prepare them as directed. For a buffet display or a larger picnic, I would use a large loaf, about 10 inches in diameter, which could serve 6 or 8 persons. The loaves are stuffed at home, preferably on the day before the trip, and should be served the next day while still fresh. Wrap them tightly in a heavy-duty foil, place in a cooler, and let them warm up to the ambient temperature before lunch.

INGREDIENTS

4 ounces Roquefort cheese
4 ounces cream cheese
4 ounces finely chopped walnuts
1 teaspoon dried thyme leaves
1 teaspoon dried oregano leaves
½ teaspoon ground mace
½ teaspoon Worcestershire sauce
⅛ teaspoon cayenne pepper
4 small individual loaves of Italian or Finland country bread, or one 6-to-8-inch loaf.

INSTRUCTIONS:

Place the Roquefort cheese, cream cheese, walnuts, herbs, spices, and Worcestershire sauce in a food processor, and process until well blended.

Cut a lid off the top of one loaf. Take a good serrated bread knife, hold it blade down, vertically, and cut round the soft inside part of the loaf, leaving a ½ -inch-thick crust around and at the bottom. Don't cut all the way through! Now, using the knife horizontally, insert the blade at one point half an inch above the bottom of the loaf and move the blade over the surface of the bottom crust, without enlarging the insert point, to release the soft inside part of the bread. Remove the blade and lift the inside part of the bread in one piece. Slice this piece into an even number of ¼-inch-thick slices: you will get 4 or 6 slices, depending on the size of the loaf. Then, if you have 4 loaves, spread a quarter of the cheese mixture between all the slices of one loaf; if you have one large loaf, spread all the filling between the slices of bread. Restack them together evenly and cut four or six wedges through the whole stack. Place the whole stack back inside the crust as one piece, place the lid on top, and wrap tightly in foil. Repeat with the other loaves, if you have more than one.

SHRIMP-PASTE RIBBON SANDWICHES

Makes 8 servings.

PREPARATION:

These are sandwiches that are best prepared ahead of time, cut, and wrapped tightly in a plastic film. They can be kept refrigerated for 3 to 4 days.

INSTRUCTIONS:

Combine all the ingredients in a food processor and purée until the mixture is pastelike.

TO MAKE THE RIBBON SANDWICHES

You need 16 slices of very compact cocktail pumpernickel, country, or rye bread: the thin slices are 4½ inches square and come in a perfectly cubical stack of . . . unfortunately, 15 slices!

Spread on one slice a layer of shrimp paste ⅛ to ¼ inch thick, about two tablespoons. Top it with a second slice of bread. Spread another layer of shrimp paste on it, and repeat until you have a neat stack of 4 slices with 3 layers of paste in between.

Make 3 more stacks with the remaining 12 slices. Cutting through all the slices and layers together, separate each stack into 2 equal halves and cut each half again lengthwise to form 4 long "ribbon sandwiches" with each stack. Serve 2 ribbon sandwiches per person.

INGREDIENTS:

½ pound cooked medium-size shrimp, shelled, deveined

2 large egg whites

6 ounces clarified butter

2 tablespoons dry sherry

1 tablespoon minced fresh ginger

1 clove of garlic, minced

2 teaspoons cornstarch

½ teaspoon sea salt

¼ teaspoon stevia

¼ teaspoon Chinese five spices

⅛ teaspoon cayenne pepper

Optional: 1 tablespoon fresh lemon juice

1 tablespoon toasted sesame seeds

COUSCOUS SALAD SANDWICHES

Makes 8 servings of 2 pita bread halves each.

The couscous salad can be made at home, one day before the trip. It keeps very well in a sealed airtight plastic box.

INSTRUCTIONS:

Melt the butter with the turmeric. Add 2 cups of water and the instant vegetable-stock powder. Bring to a boil. Stir in the couscous, cover the pan, and turn the heat off. Let it stand 5 minutes. Uncover and fluff up the couscous with a fork. Do not use a spoon or the grain will get crushed and ball together. Add the currants, scallions, sunflower seeds, parsley, and celery salt. Whisk the lemon juice with the cinnamon. Add the olive oil in a stream, beating until emulsified. Pour the dressing on the couscous, stir, and transfer to a plastic box. Refrigerate until departure time.

To assemble the sandwiches, cut 8 rounds of pita bread in halves. Open each half to form a pocket and fill it with couscous salad. Wrap each pocket sandwich in a plastic film if you are going to serve them later. Serve 2 halves per person.

Note: I have used this recipe often as a lightweight, quick, and easy-to-prepare casserole for trips such as snow camping or kayak expeditions. I substitute the unsalted butter and olive oil with clarified butter and serve it hot with or without the bread. Dehydrated scallion and parsley replace the fresh ingredients.

INGREDIENTS:
COUSCOUS SALAD:

4 tablespoons unsalted butter
¼ teaspoon turmeric
2 teaspoons instant vegetable-stock powder
2 cups couscous
1 cup currants plumped in hot water 15 minutes
½ cup sliced scallions
½ cup sunflower seeds, toasted lightly
¼ cup fresh minced parsley
1 teaspoon celery salt
¼ cup lemon juice
¼ teaspoon cinnamon
½ cup olive oil

GRILLED FRUIT AND CHEESE SANDWICHES

Makes four sandwiches.

INSTRUCTIONS:

Spread four of the slices of bread with the cream cheese and the four others with the fruit spread. Assemble each cream cheese slice with a fruit spread slice to form four sandwiches.

Reconstitute the eggs with ½ cup water and the soy milk with one cup warm water. Mix the eggs and milk together, add the nutmeg. Dip each sandwich into the egg-milk mixture until the bread has absorbed most of the liquid.

Heat half the butter on the griddle and fry the sandwiches about 3 minutes on 1 side. Add more butter, turn the sandwiches over, and brown the other side, another 2 to 3 minutes. Serve 1 sandwich per person, topped with the fruit compote.

FRUIT SAUCE FOR THE GRILLED SANDWICHES

Makes two cups.

Note: Stevia is an herb found in South America. For more than 100 years the natives have used it as a sweetener for drinks and foods. Although it contains no sugar, its taste is very similar to that of sugar. Japanese researchers report that it is expected to be the main natural sweetener in the future. They also conclude that there are no harmful effects from ingesting Stevia.

INSTRUCTIONS:

Purée the fruit in a food processor with the lime juice, nutmeg, and Stevia.

Store the compote in a box, refrigerated, for a day or two. Keep it chilled in a cooler during the trip until ready to use.

INGREDIENTS:

8 slices firm whole-wheat bread
4 ounces cream cheese
4 ounces (½ cup) commercial fruit spread: unsweetened or sweetened with honey, or your own fruit spread recipe
2 ounces freeze-dried eggs
2 tablespoons soy-milk powder
½ teaspoon nutmeg
1 pouch clarified butter
1 cup fruit compote (recipe follows)

INGREDIENTS:

2 peaches, peeled, seed removed
2 bananas, peeled
1 cup pineapple chunks
¼ cup lime juice
½ teaspoon nutmeg
¼ teaspoon stevia or more to taste

RELISHES*

FRESH TOMATO RELISH

Makes about two cups.

INGREDIENTS:
2 ripe tomatoes
1 red or green pepper
½ cup chopped parsley
¼ cup chopped mint leaves
1 cucumber, peeled and
    seeded
¼ teaspoon ground cumin
Sea salt and cayenne
    pepper to taste

INSTRUCTIONS:
Dip the tomatoes in 1 quart boiling water for 1 minute. Lift the tomatoes out, cool them under cold running water, and peel. Cut them in half, crosswise, squeeze the seeds out and chop. Seed and chop the pepper and the cucumber. Place all the vegetables with the parsley, mint, cumin, in a food processor and purée. Season to taste with salt and cayenne pepper. Transfer to a plastic container and seal with duct tape. The tomato relish keeps well, refrigerated, for 3 to 4 days.

GARLIC JAM

Makes about 1½ cups.

INGREDIENTS:
1 pound fresh garlic cloves
¾ cups raw sugar
½ cup water

INSTRUCTIONS:
Dip the whole, unpeeled garlic cloves into boiling water for 1 minute. Let them cool in the water and drain. The cloves are then very easy to peel. Chop the garlic coarsely and place it in a heavy saucepan with the sugar and water. Bring it to a boil over high heat; reduce the heat to very low and simmer

---

Note: All relishes have to be prepared at home. They keep for several days, refrigerated. They should be transported in plastic containers, well sealed with duct tape. Carrying the food in the llama's saddlebags allows insulated containers to be used. This helps preserve the food on hot summer days.

the mixture, stirring it occasionally until the garlic is very soft. The mixture should be light golden and slightly syrupy after 20 to 25 minutes.

Let it cool to room temperature and transfer it to a plastic container. The garlic jam can be kept refrigerated up to 1 week.

PEACH CHUTNEY

Makes about 5 cups.

Chutney can be made anytime in anticipation of a trip and for home use too. I like to make a lot when the fruit are at their best and when the price is low. Chutney can be canned or frozen for a year's storage.

INGREDIENTS:
- *2 cups apple cider vinegar*
- *2 cups turbinado sugar (raw sugar)*
- *3" cinnamon stick*
- *Seeds from two cardamom pods*
- *½ teaspoon fennel seeds*
- *1 teaspoon coriander seeds*
- *½ teaspoon mustard seeds*
- *2 cloves of garlic, minced*
- *2 tablespoons sea salt*
- *¼ teaspoon ground mace*
- *⅛ teaspoon cayenne pepper*
- *1 large green pepper, diced*
- *1 cup raisins*
- *1 cup dried apricots, coarsely chopped*
- *½ cup sliced candied ginger*
- *1½ pounds ripe but firm peaches*

INSTRUCTIONS:
Mix the vinegar and sugar in a large noncorrosive pan. Tie the cinnamon, cardamon, fennel, coriander, mustard, and garlic in a piece of cheesecloth. Add the spice bag to the pan with the salt, mace, and cayenne pepper. Bring the liquid to a boil; lower the heat and let it simmer, uncovered, for 30 minutes. Add the green pepper, raisins, apricots, and candied ginger, and simmer another 30 minutes.

In the meantime, boil a large saucepan of water. Remove it from the heat and dip the peaches into it for just 1 minute. Rinse them under cold water and peel the skins off. Halve the peaches, remove the seeds. Cut the peaches into 4 or 5 wedges per half, and the wedges crosswise into 2 or 3 pieces.

Add the peach chunks to the simmering mixture in the pot and let them simmer for 45 minutes, stirring occasionally. Remove the pot from the heat and let the chutney cool completely. Remove the spice bag. You can pack the chutney into sterilized jars, seal them, and process them to can; or freeze it in 1-cup boxes or plastic bags.

ZUCCHINI-TOFU DIP

Makes about 2½ cups.

INSTRUCTIONS:

Coarsely shred the zucchini and place it in a colander, mixed with salt, to draw out the juice.

Squeeze the tofu between paper towels to expel as much water as possible.

Process the tofu, garlic, and oil in a food processor until well combined. Transfer the mixture to a bowl. Add the remaining ingredients and blend thoroughly.

Transfer the dip to a plastic container. It keeps well, refrigerated, for up to 4 days.

INGREDIENTS:

6 ounces small firm zucchinis, trimmed and rinsed
1 pound firm tofu
3 cloves garlic
2 tablespoons olive oil
¼ cup coriander leaves, chopped
1 tablespoon apple-cider vinegar
1 teaspoon ground coriander
Sea salt and cayenne pepper to taste

GREEN OLIVE SPREAD

Makes 1¼ cups.

INSTRUCTIONS:

Roast the pepper under the broiler in the oven, turning it around until charred on all sides, about 15 minutes. Wrap it in a piece of foil and let it cool for 20 minutes. Unwrap it and seed and peel it. Chop it coarsely.

Process the olives in a food processor with the roasted pepper and the garlic. Add the oil, parsley, and lemon juice and blend to a smooth paste.

Transfer to a plastic container. Refrigerated, it will keep well for up to 4 or 5 days.

INGREDIENTS:

1 small red pepper
7 ounces pitted green olives
1 large clove of garlic, peeled and minced
3 tablespoons dark-green unrefined olive oil
2 tablespoons minced parsley leaves
2 teaspoons fresh lemon juice

SALADS

FRESH FRUIT SALAD WITH LIME DRESSING

Makes 8 servings.

This salad is best served on the first day's lunch, when the fruit are still freshly cut from the morning and have not lost their juices, flavors, and colors. The dressing can also be mixed into the fruit before departure. Keep it cold in an insulated container or in a plastic box, placed inside a larger bag with other foods that need to stay cold, and blue-ice packs or some frozen foods.

INGREDIENTS:
6 tablespoons freshly squeezed lime juice
1 tablespoon grated lime rind
2 tablespoons raw honey
1 medium-size honeydew melon
1 pint raspberries
1½ tablespoons minced fresh mint leaves

INSTRUCTIONS:
Mix together the lime juice, rind, and honey. You may want to heat the honey to make it blend easily with the other ingredients.

Slice the melon in half, discard the seeds and scoop the flesh out into balls. Stir the melon and the raspberries together with the dressing and the mint leaves.

SPINACH-BULGUR SALAD

Makes 8 servings.

To carry fresh spinach leaves or lettuce into the backcountry, I clean them, remove the stems at home, then layer them flat in a wide plastic container lined with paper towels. This saves a lot of space compared to throwing them loosely into a large box, or, even worse, into a bag that will get

INGREDIENTS:
10 ounces fresh spinach leaves, washed, stems removed
2 to 3 scallions thinly sliced, green and white parts

crushed. For this salad, the scallions can be premixed in the spinach layers. The bulgur and dressing are combined together inside a small plastic container. Both components should remain cool during transportation inside an insulated container or next to blue-ice packs or frozen foods.

INSTRUCTIONS:

Layer the spinach leaves mixed with the scallions in a plastic box and refrigerate.

Cover the bulgur with boiling water to cover by 2 inches. Let it soak until cool and soft, about 1 hour. Drain.

Toast the cumin seeds on a dry frying pan over medium heat. Watch carefully, they burn easily. Crush them with a mortar and pestle.

Blend together the tofu, olive oil, and vinegar in an electric blender or food processor. Add the garlic, cumin seeds, salt, and cayenne pepper to taste. Process a few more turns just to mix well. Pour the dressing over the bulgur, stir to blend well. Transfer this mixture to a small plastic box and seal it well with duct tape. Refrigerate until ready to pack the food.

This salad can be prepared the day before departure.

½ cup bulgur wheat
8 ounces (1 cup) soft tofu
¼ cup olive oil
2 tablespoons apple-cider vinegar
2 cloves of garlic, minced
½ teaspoon whole cumin seeds
½ teaspoon sea salt
1 pinch cayenne pepper or more to taste

ORIENTAL CABBAGE SLAW

Makes 8 servings.

PREPARATION:

Prepare the vegetable mixture ahead of time and chill. Mix the dressing together and keep it separately in a plastic bottle. Toss the dressing into the vegetables just before serving.

INSTRUCTIONS:

Shred the cabbage and mix it with the snow peas, water chestnuts, bamboo shoots, and chopped scallions. Place in a plastic container and chill.

Dry toast the sesame seeds on a frying pan and reserve.

INGREDIENTS:

1 small head chinese cabbage, about 1¼ pounds
½ pound snow peas, trimmed and cut in 1" pieces
1 can (6½ ounces) sliced water chestnuts, drained
1 can (8½ ounces) sliced bamboo shoots, drained

When cool, store in a plastic bag.

Combine well the vinegar, honey, soy sauce, ginger, and cayenne pepper. Whisking constantly, add the oil in a fine stream until emulsified. Store the dressing in a plastic bottle and chill.

⅔ cup sesame seeds
½ cup chopped scallions, 3 or 4
⅓ cup apple-cider vinegar
2 tablespoons honey
2 tablespoons soy sauce
1 teaspoon ground ginger
1 pinch cayenne pepper, or more to taste
½ cup sesame oil

STEWED DRIED-FRUIT SALAD

Makes 8 servings.

INSTRUCTIONS:

Before departure, layer the dried fruit in a clear plastic bowl that has a well-fitting lid. Alternate the colors of each layer; the clear plastic bowl lets you see the colors. There should be 2 to 3 inches left between the top layer and the top of the box to allow the fruit to expand later.

Stuff some waxed paper in the empty space to keep the layers together during transportation.

At the campsite: The night before serving the fruit salad, make a strong licorice tea, add the spices and honey if they are to be used. Pour the hot tea over the dried fruit layers, top the container with the lid, and let the fruit soak overnight. Serve cold the next morning.

INGREDIENTS:
1 cup each dried apricots, prunes, peaches, raisins, pears, figs, golden raisins (make sure all the fruit is unsulfured)
Licorice tea for 6 cups (bags or bulk), plain or spiced
Cinnamon, 1 teaspoon if using plain licorice tea, ¼ teaspoon each nutmeg and clove, if using plain tea

Note: If you use spiced licorice tea, reduce the amount of spices to taste. You may also add a little honey to the tea.

SOUPS

GREEN BEAN SOUP WITH CORIANDER

Makes 8 servings.

This is one of the soups described earlier in this book. These soups are cooked at home with one-third or less of liquid. The result is a thick purée that can be transported in a small container and that weighs a lot less than the regular soup. The liquid is added at the campsite when the soup is reheated just before serving.

INSTRUCTIONS:

Heat the oil in a heavy-bottomed saucepan. Sautée the onion until soft but not brown.

In the meantime, drain the tomatoes out of their liquid, reserve the liquid. Chop the tomatoes, add them to the onion with their liquid and the vegetable-stock powder. Bring it to a boil. Add the beans, cauliflowerets, potatoes, sea salt, and cayenne pepper to taste. Lower the heat, cover the pan, and let the soup simmer 15 minutes until the vegetables are tender. Transfer 1½ cups of vegetables to a food processor or electric blender. Add the garlic, Parmesan, and coriander leaves, and purée. Stir the purée into the rest of the vegetables, adjust the seasoning.

Let the mixture cool completely and store in a plastic box. Seal it tightly with duct tape and refrigerate until departure time. If you have to keep it for more than 2 days, you can freeze it. Actually, if it is put frozen into the food bag with the other preparations it will help keep the other foods cool.

INGREDIENTS:
2 cups chopped onion (about 1 medium onion)
¼ cup olive oil
4 teaspoons instant vegetable-stock powder
14 ounces canned tomatoes
2 pounds green beans, trimmed and cut in ½" lengths
½ head cauliflower separated in flowerets
½ pound small red potatoes, scrubbed, cubed, and reserved in cold lemony water
3 cloves of garlic, chopped
½ cup dry grated Parmesan cheese
1 cup loosely packed coriander leaves
Sea salt and cayenne pepper to taste

VEGETABLE SOUP WITH WILD SORREL

Makes 8 servings.

Wild sorrel grows all over the Rockies and in Alaska. It has a delicious sour flavor and is very rich in vitamin C. Just in case wild sorrel is nowhere to be found, take some dehydrated domestic sorrel along.

Most of the soup is prepared ahead of time with very little liquid and puréed. At the campsite simply reheat the soup with extra liquid and add the sorrel.

INSTRUCTIONS:

Melt 4 tablespoons of the butter in a heavy-bottomed large pot and spread the other tablespoon of butter on a piece of foil. Into the pot put the leeks, sliced, the potatoes, and the celery, with 1 teaspoon sea salt and 2 cups water. Place the foil, buttered side down, over the vegetables, cover the pot, and cook over low heat 15 minutes. Uncover the pot, remove and discard the foil. Add the peas, herbs, and the spinach. Cover and continue to cook until the spinach has wilted, about 5 minutes. Add 4 cups water, bring to a boil, and simmer 10 minutes.

Transfer the vegetables to a food processor and purée. Season the purée with nutmeg, lemon juice, cayenne pepper, and more salt to taste.

Let the purée cool completely and pour it into a plastic container with a well-fitting lid. Seal the box with duct tape. The purée can be refrigerated or frozen until the food is packed for the trip.

At the campsite, reheat the soup with 6 cups water and the sorrel, and serve. Croutons can be served with this soup.

INGREDIENTS:
5 tablespoons unsalted butter
6 or 7 leeks, white part only (12 ounces)
2 medium potatoes, scrubbed, sliced, and reserved in water
4 or 6 celery stalks, peeled with a potato peeler and diced (1½ cups)
1 teaspoon sea salt, and more for later
1 cup fresh or frozen green peas
1 cup loosely packed parsley
2 or 3 sprigs fresh mint
2 sprigs fresh thyme
1 bay leaf
1 large bunch spinach, washed, stems removed (1 pound)
Nutmeg to taste
Lemon juice to taste
Cayenne pepper to taste
2 handfuls wild sorrel leaves

TROUT DISHES

INDIAN POACHED TROUT

To cook 8 trout, 1 per serving.

INSTRUCTIONS:

Melt the butter in a cast-iron skillet large enough to hold the 8 trout in 1 layer. You may have to use 2 skillets and divide all the ingredients equally between each. Sauté the onion in the butter until soft, add the garlic, and cook until the onion begins to brown. Add all the spices with 1 cup water. Bring to a boil and let the mixture simmer 10 minutes.

If you are using fresh tomatoes, peel them—plunge them into boiling water to peel the skin easily—cut them crosswise, press the seeds out, and chop the tomatoes.

If you are using dehydrated tomatoes, crush them to small pieces and add 1 cup of water to the sauce. Drop the tomatoes into the skillet(s) and let the sauce cook 10 more minutes.

Clean the fish and pat it dry with paper towels. You may choose to bone and skin the trout and cook the fillets or to cook them whole and remove bones and skins later.

Lay the fish on the sauce, covering it with some of the juices. Cook the fillets 6 to 7 minutes, or the whole trout 10 to 12 minutes, basting them frequently. The fish is done when it flakes easily with a fork.

Lift the fish out. Serve it with the sauce spooned over and lemon wedges as a garnish.

INGREDIENTS:

2 onions, finely chopped (3 cups) or ½ cup dehydrated onion, rehydrated in 1 cup hot water

6 to 8 cloves of garlic, finely minced

8 ounces unsalted butter (1 cup)

1 teaspoon each ground coriander, paprika, cumin, ginger, and sea salt

¼ teaspoon cayenne pepper

4 ripe fresh tomatoes or 2 ounces dehydrated tomatoes

2 fresh lemons cut in wedges

ANGEL LAKE TROUT

Makes 8 servings.

INSTRUCTIONS:
Combine the scallions, gingerroot, 2 tablespoons of sake and the sea salt. Rub the fish all over with the mixture and let it marinate half an hour.

Pour 4 quarts of water into a large pot with the ¼ cup sake and the sesame oil. Bring to a boil. Poach the fish in the boiling liquid for 5 minutes. Turn the heat off and let the fish cook in the hot liquid for 20 minutes.

In the meantime, lift out 2 cups poaching liquid. Pour it into a small saucepan. Add the sugar, soy sauce, and apple vinegar. Bring the mixture to a boil. Lower the heat and simmer. Mix the cornstarch with 2 tablespoons of cold water. Stir into the sauce and let it simmer 3 more minutes until thickened. Adjust the seasoning with salt and cayenne pepper. Transfer the fish to a platter, pour the sauce over it, and sprinkle the garnish on top.

INGREDIENTS:
*4 large or 8 small trout
4 scallions, chopped, green part included
1 inch piece gingerroot, minced
2 tablespoons sake (rice wine)
2 teaspoons sea salt
¼ cup sake
1 tablespoon sesame oil
2 tablespoons sugar
2 tablespoons soy sauce
1½ tablespoons apple-cider vinegar
1 tablespoon cornstarch
salt and cayenne pepper to taste*
FOR GARNISH:
Minced scallions and gingerroot

TROUT HEMINGWAY

Makes 8 servings.

INSTRUCTIONS:
Pour ¾ cup of the lemon juice into a pie plate, add ¼ cup water. Place the flour in another pie plate and the sesame seeds in a third one. Dip the trout fillets in the lemon-water mix, dredge them with flour, dip them in the lemon water again. Roll them in the sesame seeds until well coated, pressing gently to cover completely. Melt the butter on a cast-iron

INGREDIENTS:
*8 trout fillets
1 cup fresh lemon juice; takes 4 to 6 lemons; they could be squeezed at home and transported in a plastic bottle
1½ cups whole-wheat flour
1½ cups sesame seeds*

griddle or in a couple of skillets. Fry the coated fillets until golden, about 6 minutes on each side. Transfer the fish to the serving plates. Deglaze the pans or griddle with the reserved lemon juice, pour the juices over the fish. Season with salt and cayenne pepper.

4 tablespoons unsalted butter
Sea salt and cayenne pepper to season
Lemon wedges for garnish

ORANGE TROUT WITH WILD RICE

Makes 8 servings.

INSTRUCTIONS:
Combine the wild rice and the vegetable-stock powder with 6 cups cold water. Bring to a boil. Lower the heat, cover the pot, and simmer for 45 minutes until the rice is tender. Drain and toss with half the butter and the chopped scallions, except the reserved green part.

Stuff each trout with a slice of the remaining butter and a lemon slice. Sprinkle the inside of the fish with salt and cayenne pepper to taste. Spread the rice mixture inside a large Dutch oven; lay the trout on top. Combine the orange juice, lemon juice, and cardamom. Pour the liquid on the trout and rice. Cover the Dutch oven with the lid. Place it inside the campfire with some hot coals on top of the lid. Let the trout and rice "bake" for 30 minutes. Remove the pot from the fire. The trout should be just flaky when touched with a fork.

Place one trout on each serving plate with a serving of rice. Sprinkle the rice with the reserved scallion greens. Garnish each trout with the grated orange peel.

INGREDIENTS:
*2 cups wild rice
2 tablespoons instant vegetable-stock powder
1/2 cup unsalted butter, 4 ounces
6 scallions, chopped fine; reserve 1/4 cup of the green part for garnish
1/4 cup chopped fresh mint leaves, wild mint if possible
8 small trout, boned, but with the 2 fillets still attached together along the back edge
Sea salt and cayenne pepper to taste
1 lemon sliced thinly into 8 slices
1 cup orange juice, made from concentrate
1/2 cup lemon juice, about 2 lemons
1/2 teaspoon cardamom
Freshly grated orange peel*

DINNER SIDE DISHES

YOGURT RICE

This is a rice salad to make at home. It will marinate during transportation.

Makes 8 servings.

INSTRUCTIONS:

Heat the olive oil in a small frying pan. Add the gingerroot, mustard seeds, coriander seeds, and cayenne pepper. Cook, stirring over medium heat, until the seeds begin to pop. Cool.

In a large bowl, stir together the cooked rice, yogurt, and peas. Mix the lemon juice and the salt with the seasoned oil and pour the dressing over the rice mixture. Stir until the dressing is evenly blended with the mixture.

Store the salad in an airtight plastic box. Seal with duct tape and refrigerate until departure.

INGREDIENTS:

- *2 tablespoons olive oil*
- *1 tablespoon minced fresh gingerroot*
- *1 teaspoon mustard seeds*
- *1 teaspoon coriander seeds*
- *¼ teaspoon cayenne pepper*
- *4 cups cooked brown rice*
- *1 cup unflavored low-fat yogurt*
- *1 cup cooked but still firm green peas*
- *1 tablespoon fresh lemon juice*
- *1 teaspoon sea salt*
- *¼ cup chopped coriander leaves*
- *A few coriander sprigs for garnish*

WILDERNESS TEMPURA

Makes 8 servings.

Special equipment: For this dish you will need a large deep skillet for deep frying. Each person will need chopsticks to hold the vegetable morsels. You may prefer to use long fondue forks or simply to cut long thin branches from the bushes and use them as for toasting marshmallows.

INGREDIENTS:

- *A selection of dehydrated vegetables of your preference: whole mushrooms, sliced celery heart, zucchini, bell pepper, beetroot, artichoke, broccoli*

INSTRUCTIONS:

Pour some hot water on the vegetables to rehydrate them. If you have beets, keep them separate or they will tint all the other vegetables pink. It is not necessary to bring the vegetables back to their fresh state. Just like dried fruit, they are very good still chewy and parched. You just want to soften them.

Mix all the batter ingredients together; add 2 cups cold water to make a very thick batter. Stir to blend it well. If it is still too thick add a little more water, up to ⅔ cup. Pour the sesame oil in a deep skillet and heat it until a drop of water, thrown into it, sizzles; but the oil should not be smoky. Using chopsticks, forks, or sticks, let each guest dip a vegetable morsel into the batter until well coated, then into the hot oil until browned all over.

The Angel Lake trout sauce makes a delicious accompaniment.

flowerets, etc. If you can find some wild mushrooms—and you're certain they're not poisonous—add them too.

THE BATTER:
- *2 cups whole-wheat flour*
- *¼ cup whole bran*
- *½ cup freeze-dried eggs, 2 ounces*
- *1 teaspoon instant vegetable-stock powder*
- *½ teaspoon ground cumin*

- *1 pinch cayenne pepper*

FOR DIPPING:
- *1 quart sesame seed oil*

BREAKFASTS

OATMEAL BISCUITS

Makes 16 biscuits.

INSTRUCTIONS:

Stir the flour, baking powder, and salt together. Cut the butter into very small pieces and, using your fingers, rub it into the flour mixture until it resembles coarse sand. Stir in the oats. Combine the eggs, soy milk, and honey together. Add the wet ingredients all at once to the dry ingredients. Stir just to moisten.

Drop the batter by spoonfuls onto the greased griddle. Flatten the biscuits with the palm of your hand and cook them

INGREDIENTS:
- *1½ cups whole-wheat flour*
- *1½ tablespoons baking powder*
- *½ teaspoon salt*
- *5 tablespoons unsalted butter*
- *1½ cups quick-cooking oats*
- *1 egg plus 1 yolk beaten together to blend*

4 to 5 minutes on each side, turning them over once.

Note: Cook the biscuits before you cook the fish on the griddle. Keep them warm, wrapped in a piece of foil, while you cook the fish.

2 tablespoons soy-milk
   powder mixed with
   ½ cup water
3 tablespoons honey

MOROCCAN APPLE-DATE BUTTER

I would recommend that the butter be prepared before the trip, and carried in a plastic container.

Makes 2 cups butter.

INSTRUCTIONS:
Mix together the apple, lemon juice, cinnamon, honey, and chopped dates. Blend into the butter until well combined. Transfer to a plastic box and refrigerate.

INGREDIENTS:
½ cup finely chopped,
   peeled, tart apple
1 tablespoon lemon juice
¼ teaspoon ground
   cinnamon
2 tablespoons honey
½ cup finely chopped pitted
   dates
1 cup soft unsalted butter

THIN CORNMEAL HOTCAKES

Makes 40 3-inch hotcakes.

INSTRUCTIONS
Combine the cornmeal, sugar, and salt together. Add the boiling water all at once. Stir rapidly to obtain a smooth batter. Let stand 2 minutes.

   In the meantime, stir the soy-milk powder with 1 cup warm water. Beat the eggs and soy milk together. Stir into the cornmeal mixture.

   Heat a little oil on the griddle. Pour small amounts of batter on the griddle, which should be quite hot. The cakes will form a lace pattern and cook very fast. Turn them over

INGREDIENTS:
2 cups yellow cornmeal
2 teaspoons turbinado
   sugar
1 teaspoon sea salt
2 cups boiling water
2 eggs
2 tablespoons soy-milk
   powder
Vegetable oil for frying

once, brown the other side, and transfer to a pie plate near the fire to keep them warm. Repeat until all the batter is used. Serve the hotcakes topped with rice-bran syrup.

DESSERTS, FOOD BARS

BAKLAVA

Makes 8 servings.

PREPARATION:

The baklava is baked at home and sliced as instructed below. Lift 16 whole pieces out of the pan and place them on a clean cooking sheet to quick-freeze them. A few hours later, or the next day, when they are hard and therefore easy to handle, layer them in a stiff cardboard or plastic box with waxed paper between the layers. It is important to have a box of the right size, so that the baklava pieces are not crushed together but no gap is left between the top layer and the top of the box. Seal it with duct tape and put it back into the freezer until departure time.

Note: Take a 1-pound box of phyllo dough, thawed to room temperature; unfold the stack of pastry sheets and cut through the whole stack crosswise to make 2 equal halves. Refold 1 half, wrap it in plastic, and refreeze it. Cover the remaining stack with a piece of waxed paper first and a damp dishcloth second to keep the sheets moist and pliable.

INSTRUCTIONS:

Combine the ground nuts, sugar, and cinnamon in a bowl and blend evenly.

INGREDIENTS:
½ pound ground shelled
  pistachio nuts
½ pound ground walnuts
¼ cup turbinado sugar
1 teaspoon ground
  cinnamon
½ pound phyllo pastry (see
  note below)
½ pound unsalted butter
30 whole cloves

FOR THE SYRUP:
1 cup apricot preserves
¼ cup diced unsulfured
  dried apricots
2 tablespoons honey
1 tablespoon fresh lemon
  juice

Melt the butter and preheat the oven to 375°F.

Uncover the phyllo dough, lift one sheet of pastry and lay it in a 9-by-13-inch baking pan. Re-cover the stack as before. Brush the phyllo sheet with a little melted butter and sprinkle it evenly with 2 tablespoons of the nut mixture. Repeat until 12 sheets have been used. Top the 12th sheet with 1 cup of the nut mixture. Continue as before until all the phyllo dough and all the nut filling have been used. Mark 4 points equally spaced on each side of the dish and from these points cut the baklava just through the top sheets diagonally. Stick a whole clove in the center of each diamond. Bake in the preheated oven 40 to 45 minutes until well browned and crisp.

While the baklava is baking, prepare the syrup: Heat the apricot preserves in a small saucepan. When it is liquid enough, strain it and reserve the fruit pieces. Return the preserves to the saucepan. Chop the fruit pieces and return them to the pan with the chopped dried apricot, honey, and lemon juice. Let it simmer gently until the baklava is ready. Pour half the syrup on the hot baklava, wait 15 minutes, and pour the rest evenly.

Let it cool completely. Cut the diamond-shaped pieces all the way through. Quick-freeze and package 16 whole pieces as instructed above. Keep the rest for snacking.

DATE BONBONS

Makes 24 bonbons.

PREPARATION:

The bonbons are very soft, and if you try to make them ahead of time and keep them in a bag, they will turn to a mushy mess. The fun about this dessert or snack is that it can be done anywhere, and each adventurer can participate and make his or her own bonbons if the group wishes. Just have all the ingredients ready, in separate bags. No cooking is required, just clean hands!

INGREDIENTS:
1 cup chopped dates
½ cup ground almonds
½ cup ground pistachios
2 teaspoons dry lemon peel
Enough shredded unsweetened coconut in which to roll the bonbons.

INSTRUCTIONS:
Mix thoroughly all the ingredients except the coconut. Taking about one heaping tablespoon mixture at a time, roll it with your hands to form a ball. Roll each ball in the coconut to coat completely.

ANISE BISCOTTI

Makes about 36 biscotti.

INSTRUCTIONS:
Cream the butter; beat in the sugar a little at a time until light and fluffy. Beat in the eggs, one at a time, until the mixture is thick and pale. Beat in the anise extract.

Combine the white flour, whole-wheat flour, baking powder, salt, and ground almonds. Beat the dry ingredients into the butter mixture. You should have a sticky dough. Chill it one hour.

Preheat the oven to 375°F. Halve the dough. Pat each half into a 14-by-4-inch loaf. Brush it with an egg wash made with 1 egg mixed with 2 tablespoons water. Sprinkle the anise seeds evenly and pat them gently to stick to the dough.

Transfer the loaves to a greased baking sheet. Bake in the upper third of the oven for 20 to 25 minutes, until golden brown. Let cool until you can touch the loaves. With a serrated bread knife, cut into ¾-inch slices. Place them on 2 baking sheets, on their sides, and bake them for 5 minutes. Turn them over and bake for 5 more minutes. Cool on racks. Store in an airtight container.

INGREDIENTS:
- ½ cup unsalted butter, at room temperature
- ¾ cup raw turbinado sugar, ground to granulated-sugar consistency in a blender
- 3 large eggs
- 1 tablespoon pure anise extract
- 2 cups unbleached white flour
- 1 cup whole-wheat flour
- 2 teaspoons baking powder
- ½ teaspoon salt
- ¼ cup ground blanched almonds
- 2 tablespoons anise seeds

ZUCCHINI-CAROB BARS

Makes 8 large cake bars.

PREPARATION:
Make these zucchini-carob bars at home. Freeze them

INGREDIENTS:
- 2 cups whole-wheat flour
- 1 tablespoon cinnamon

and wrap them in waxed paper for transportation inside a cardboard or plastic box.

INSTRUCTIONS:

Preheat the oven to 350°F.

Sift together the flour, cinnamon, baking soda, salt, and baking powder.

In the large bowl of the electric mixer, beat the eggs until frothy. Beat in the sugar, oil, and vanilla until thick and pale. Stir in the zucchini and flour mixture until well combined. Fold in the walnuts and carob chips.

Pour the batter into a greased and floured 9-by-13-inch baking pan. Bake 25 to 30 minutes until a wooden pick inserted in the center of the cake comes out clean. Let cool completely. Cut the cake into 8 large bars and place them on a clean baking sheet to quick-freeze them. Several hours later, or the next day, wrap each one individually in a plastic film. Store them in a box and keep them in the freezer until departure.

2 teaspoons baking soda
½ teaspoon sea salt
¼ teaspoon baking powder
3 large eggs
2 cups turbinado sugar ground to the consistency of granulated sugar in the blender
1 cup pure vegetable oil, safflower or sesame
1 tablespoon vanilla powder
2 cups loosely packed, grated zucchini
1 cup lightly toasted chopped walnuts
1 cup unsweetened carob chips

TAHINI-GRANOLA BARS

Makes 32 bars.

INSTRUCTIONS:

Place all the ingredients in the food processor and process until well combined. Do not process too much or the mixture will become stiff.

Oil the bottom of a 9-by-9-inch pan. Press the mixture into the pan and refrigerate.

Several hours later, or the next day, cut into 32 bars. Wrap each one in a plastic film. Store the bars inside a box and refrigerate or freeze until departure.

INGREDIENTS:

2 cups raw tahini
1 cup granola
½ cup soy-milk powder
½ cup brown sugar
2 tablespoons honey
½ cup raisins
½ cup shredded coconut

7

New Year's Eve in a Yurt

I sink one ski and then the other into nine inches of fresh powder, leaving a double scar of progress on the immaculate landscape of a perfectly still winter day. Even though I cannot see our guests behind me on the trail, I hear their laughter echo up the narrow Fishhook Valley. I look back, balancing myself under a thirty-five-pound pack, and smile. The humor is good. No matter what, people always enjoy the trail to our backcountry ski shelter, a Mongolian yurt. It is such an easy trail: two and a half miles from Redfish Lake, in the spectacular Sawtooth Mountains, winding through the forest with hardly any altitude gain.

As I resume my strange dance step, stomping down the snow, my mind wanders. I imagine how those faces are going to light up as they enter the yurt. They always do. No one ever anticipates what the yurt will look like, even though they may have seen pictures of it half buried in the snow among the trees or glowing like a mysterious spaceship at night. They are always struck by the cozy interior, the reassuring wood stove, the bright tablecloth, the sleeping pads, the pine trees from the forest turned as if by magic into the floor, the bunk beds, the table, and stools.

They are going to be even more impressed tonight because, on the day before Christmas, Bob, Nina, and I made a special trip to the yurt. We brought a little fir tree inside and decorated it with garlands and candles. But the greatest joy will be mine, when I see their astonished looks—their wide eyes and open mouths—as I begin to display the food on the table. Suddenly it all makes sense: the long hours of preparation, the hard pull on the trail.

Tonight is New Year's Eve, and I have planned the greatest display of flavors and colors I can conceive. I hope I have not forgotten anything! Behind me, Bob effortlessly pulls the 175-pound sled, which is linked to his waist by two aluminum poles. There is no going back home or to the market from here. This fact allows me to completely relax the minute we are on the road. No one except Bob knows the tension and the fatigue that go with the preparation of a feast. But right now, as I press this new powder under my skis and watch the hint of a rosy mist caressing the jagged skyline, I am certain there is nothing else I would rather do!

I rehearse the show in my mind. Tonight, as the wood stove warms up the yurt for the evening, I will warm up the guests' bodies with a hot and spicy golden punch. Then I will prepare the hors d'oeuvres: a red-pepper dip for poached scallops and shrimp, sun-dried tomatoes and zucchini slices, followed by a deep-fried brie cheese with an almond crust served with slices of red and green apples and black pumpernickel cocktail bread. Red and green, for the holiday season!

Then everyone will sit around the table and we will start dinner with a cream of chestnut soup. In France, chestnuts are a must for the holidays. The accompaniment to the soup, delicate tiny cheese puffs, must be packed in a box with bunches of waxed paper for safe transportation.

After that, I will present the "pièce de resistance": a boned shoulder of lamb. I never take the bones into the backcountry; there is a limit to the weight we allow ourselves to carry! This shoulder is stuffed with an herb mixture, then rolled and baked. It is easy to warm up at the yurt. I serve it with a mint sauce—made the English way—and apple chutney. The vegetables are French-style green peas and lemon-braised baby carrots. The bread is also a product of our land, made with Idaho organic flours and potatoes.

The dessert should create the top surprise of the evening: a bûche de Noël. I will decorate the cake just before dinner, when everyone is outside. I made the yard-long chocolate roll ahead of time and froze it. It is easier to carry this way. As it comes back to yurt temperature in my wilderness kitchen, I will pipe the chocolate frosting onto the cake to make it look just like the bark of a tree. Then I will create knots on the log here and there and assemble the "mushrooms." Made of meringue, they are also very fragile and have to be packed with a lot of waxed paper. They are placed in clusters along the bûche de Noël, and voilà! They appear so real that some people don't think of eating them for dessert!

The guests will come back to the yurt and, in the dim light of the Coleman lanterns, they will think the log is an interesting centerpiece. Wait until they eat it! I know how good it is—I have tested and tasted it too much while making it—and that's why it is so good to be working hard on the trail now!

We are getting very close to the yurt. Ah, here are some tracks in the snow. I recognize them—they belong to Remy Martin! I gave this name to the pine marten who has adopted the space under the yurt as his home. He feeds on the food scraps we throw into a hole behind the woodshed. He is one of the few creatures that spend the winter here in the forest instead of moving to the lower valleys, or flying southward on wings, or finding a big cozy hole in which to hibernate. But Remy Martin, the smartest of all, won't go hungry all winter!

Happy New Year, Remy Martin! Happy New Year everyone, and welcome to the yurt!

NEW YEAR'S EVE DINNER MENU

Golden punch

*Poached scallops and shrimp with
sun-dried tomato and zucchini slices
and red pepper dip*

*Almond-crusted deep-fried brie cheese with
red and green apple slices and black bread*

Cream of chestnut soup with cheese puffs

*Herbed stuffed rolled shoulder of lamb
with mint sauce and apple chutney*

*French-style green peas
Lemon-braised baby carrots*

Idaho potato rye bread, sweet butter

Traditional French "bûche de Noël"

GOLDEN PUNCH

Makes 8 servings.

PREPARATION:

For this recipe, I use fruit juice concentrate, not much to carry, and add the water at the campsite. The spices are measured ahead of time and gathered inside a piece of cheesecloth, tied with a string. The whole spice bag is thrown into the punch. It keeps the spices away from the guests' glasses, and when the punch is gone, the spice bag is thrown into the fire.

INSTRUCTIONS:

At the campsite, pour the juice concentrates into a 2-quart pot. Add 6 cups of water, the honey, and the spices. Bring to a boil; reduce the heat, cover the pot, and let the punch simmer for at least 10 minutes. Ladle into heatproof serving glasses.

INGREDIENTS:

12 ounces apple juice concentrate
4 ounces orange juice concentrate
¼ cup honey
1 teaspoon whole allspice
1 teaspoon whole clove
1 3-to-4-inch cinnamon stick, broken into small pieces
Ground coriander, cardamom, and nutmeg, to taste
1 square of cheesecloth and a string to tie the whole spices together

RED PEPPER DIP

Makes 2 cups.

PREPARATION:

Make the dip at home, and carry it in a well-sealed plastic container. Be sure to seal the whole length around the lid with duct tape.

INSTRUCTIONS:

Broil the peppers in the oven, about 4 inches from the heat, until they are charred on all sides. Wrap the peppers inside a brown paper bag and let them "sweat" for 20 minutes. Peel and seed the peppers and purée them in a food processor. Add the remaining ingredients and process the mixture to a smooth cream. Transfer to a plastic container and refrigerate.

INGREDIENTS:

1½ pounds red bell peppers
1 cup plain yogurt
¼ cup cream cheese
1 tablespoon lemon juice
1 tablespoon finely chopped parsley
1 tablespoon finely chopped thyme
1 tablespoon finely chopped chives
1 tablespoon finely chopped basil

2 cloves of garlic, minced
Salt and cayenne pepper to
taste

ALMOND-CRUSTED DEEP-FRIED BRIE CHEESE

Serves 6 to 8 as an appetizer.

PREPARATION:

Nothing needs to be done ahead of time. The whole recipe can be assembled and cooked at the campsite.

INSTRUCTIONS:

Just before preparing the cheese, cut the apples into wedges, cutting the core away. Cover them tightly with a plastic film and reserve them in a cool place.

Shake the egg in the bottle to blend and pour it into a deep plate. Mix together, in another deep plate, the ground almonds, rosemary, cayenne, and cardamom; stir to blend.

Brush the mustard over the brie cheese to cover evenly. Dip the whole cheese first into the egg, then into the almond mixture, then into the egg again and into the almond mixture again. Make sure it is well coated.

Pour the peanut oil into an 8-inch skillet. Heat it over high heat until a little bit of almond mixture dropped into the oil sizzles, but the oil is not smoking. Lower the heat and fry the cheese 2 to 3 minutes on 1 side; turn it over with tongs and let the other side brown, another 2 minutes. The cheese should be evenly browned with a firm crust. Remove it to paper towels to drain the oil; place it on a platter surrounded with the apple wedges. Let each guest cut a wedge of cheese and place it on a piece of apple. Slices of black pumpernickel cocktail bread, cut in half diagonally, may be used as an alternative to the apple wedges.

INGREDIENTS:

1 eight-ounce brie cheese
1 tablespoon Dijon
mustard
1 large egg broken into a
small plastic bottle
2 ounces ground blanched
almonds
¼ teaspoon rosemary
leaves, finely chopped
1 pinch cayenne pepper
¼ teaspoon ground
cardamom
2 cups pure peanut oil

ACCOMPANIMENTS:

1 or 2 each, red and green
apples
Black pumpernickel
cocktail bread

CREAM OF CHESTNUT SOUP

Makes 8 servings.

PREPARATION:

The soup is cooked at home with half the amount of water needed. This results in less weight and less volume to transport on the trail.

INSTRUCTIONS:

Bring a large quantity of salty water to a boil. In the meantime, with a sharp knife cut a slit around each chestnut through the two skin layers. Throw the chestnuts into the boiling water and let them simmer for 25 minutes.

Peel and quarter the onions; slice them very thin. Melt the butter in a large casserole, add the onions, and stir to coat them with the butter. Lower the heat; press a buttered foil—buttered side down—against the onions, cover the pot, and let the onions "sweat" for 10 minutes. Uncover the pot, remove and discard the foil. Add four cups of cold water to the onions with the thyme, bay leaves, salt, and cayenne pepper. Bring the bouillon to a boil, lower the heat, and let it simmer 30 minutes.

When the chestnuts are done—they should be tender—drain them. Let them cool a little and remove the peel with the thin skin under the coarse shell. Purée them in a food mill or a food processor.

When the onion bouillon is ready, puree it too in the processor and mix in the chestnut purée, with the cardamom. Pour the mixture into a plastic container equipped with a well-fitted lid. Seal the entire length of the lid edge with duct tape. Refrigerate until departure time.

At the campsite, pour the onion-chestnut purée into a soup pot with 4 cups of cold water. Bring it to a boil, stirring occasionally. Add the crème fraiche, stir, and let the soup simmer over low heat until ready to serve.

TO MAKE CRÈME FRAICHE:

One or two days before you want to use it, heat 3½ cups of heavy cream to the point of scalding. Let it cool to 100°F.

INGREDIENTS:

2 pounds fresh chestnuts
2 pounds onions
2 ounces unsalted butter
1 teaspoon ground thyme
1 teaspoon sea salt
4 bay leaves
¼ teaspoon cayenne pepper
1 teaspoon ground cardamom
1 cup crème fraiche (Instructions to make crème fraiche follow.)

Add ½ cup buttermilk, mix well. Pour the mixture into an insulated bottle or a yogurt maker and let it stand at least 6 hours or up to 24 hours. You should have a very thick cream with a sweetish fermented flavor. Refrigerate until ready to use. It will keep up to 1 week when refrigerated.

CHEESE PUFFS

Makes 18 to 24 cheese puffs.

PREPARATION:
Bake the puffs at home and carry them to the campsite in a box padded with lots of waxed paper.

INSTRUCTIONS:
Have ready: a pastry bag with a plain round tube, size 6 or 7 for small puffs, 2 jelly roll pans or baking sheets.

Cut the butter into small pieces. Put it into a saucepan with the water and the salt. Set the pan over medium-low heat, stir with a wooden spoon until the mixture comes to a rolling boil. Throw the flour in, all at once, stir vigorously until it is blended with the liquid and the dough comes away from the sides of the pan. Transfer it to the bowl of the electric mixer, add the 3 eggs, 1 at a time, beating well after each addition. Beat the dough until it is very shiny. If the dough is still a bit stiff, add up to half the 4th egg, and beat again. Beat in the cheeses and refrigerate the dough for at least 30 minutes.

Preheat the oven to 400°F.

Put the dough into the pastry bag. Pipe little balls about ½ inch high on the baking sheets. Try not to leave any point on the top. You can smooth the top with a wet finger. Brush the top of each ball with the remaining beaten egg. Do not let any of the egg touch the baking sheet or the puffs will not rise as well.

Bake the puffs in the preheated oven for 20 minutes. They

INGREDIENTS:
1 cup water
⅛ teaspoon salt
4 ounces unsalted butter
1 cup unbleached or whole-wheat flour
3 large eggs, plus 1 broken into a small dish and beaten to blend
½ cup shredded Gruyère cheese
2 tablespoons grated fresh Parmesan cheese

should be golden all over. If not, lower the oven temperature to 350°F. and bake them a little longer; the time depends on the size of the puffs. Five minutes before they are ready, take them out of the oven and cut a slit in the side of each puff to release the steam; then return them to the oven to finish baking.

Let them cool on a wire rack completely and refrigerate them in a box or a bag.

HERBED STUFFED ROLLED SHOULDER OF LAMB

Makes 8 servings.

PREPARATION:

Prepare the stuffing at home. Stuff the shoulders and wrap them in butcher paper first and then in a plastic bag. Refrigerate no more than overnight or freeze them if they have to be kept longer before departure. Proceed with the recipe at the campsite.

INSTRUCTIONS:

To prepare the stuffing, heat the oil in a frying pan. Add the onion and cook it, stirring occasionally until soft. Transfer it to a large bowl, add the ground meats, the parsley, the garlic, herbs, Cognac, and salt and cayenne pepper to taste. Knead thoroughly with both hands until well blended.

Form two equal rolls with the mixture.

Lay each lamb shoulder flat on a working surface, place a roll of stuffing on each, and roll the shoulder around the stuffing. Fasten each shoulder with a string. Wrap the meat as instructed above and refrigerate or freeze until ready to use. If the rolls have been frozen, place them in the refrigerator the night before the trip to start the thawing process.

At the campsite, take the meat out, but keep it in its wrappings to allow it to thaw completely. Three hours before

INGREDIENTS:
THE LAMB:
- 2 small shoulders of lamb, boned
- 2 tablespoons olive oil
- 2 onions, sliced thin
- 4 celery stalks peeled, cut into 1-inch lengths
- 4 carrots, scrubbed and sliced
- 2 turnips, peeled and sliced
- 1 or 2 teaspoons chicken-stock powder
- 2 tablespoons each butter and flour

STUFFING:
- 2 tablespoons olive oil
- 1 large onion, finely chopped
- 1/2 pound pork sausage meat
- 1/2 pound ground veal
- 1/2 cup chopped parsley

dinner, brown the rolled shoulders in the two tablespoons of oil in a large pot that can contain the two side by side. When the meat is browned on all sides, remove it and brown the sliced onions, carrots, celery, and turnips. Put the meat back into the pot, cover it tightly. Let the meat and vegetables cook very slowly on top of the stove for 2½ hours. Turn the meat over occasionally. If the food looks too dry, pour a little hot water into the pot. Turning the lid upside down and keeping its cavity filled with cold water prevents the food inside the pot from drying out.

Take the meat out, place it on a platter, remove the strings, and cover it with foil to keep it warm. Strain the pan juices into a small saucepan, skim off the fat, and add ½ cup of hot water with the chicken-stock powder, if necessary, to obtain about 2 cups of sauce. Bring it to a boil while you mix the butter and flour together in a bowl. Add the kneaded butter bit by bit to the sauce as you stir constantly to thicken the sauce. Slice the meat rolls, and serve with the sauce.

2 cloves of garlic, minced
½ cup mixed fresh herbs, chopped (thyme, marjoram, basil, oregano...)
2 tablespoons Cognac
salt and cayenne pepper

ENGLISH-STYLE MINT SAUCE

Makes about one cup sauce.

PREPARATION:

Make the sauce at home and pour it into a small bottle for transportation. Serve it at "yurt temperature" in a bowl.

INSTRUCTIONS:

Strip stems from the mint leaves, chop the leaves fine, and pound with the sugar until smooth. Add the boiling water to improve the color and melt the sugar. Add the wine vinegar and the salt to taste.

Mint sauce should be bright green, smooth and pulpy, not liquid.

INGREDIENTS:
1 cup fresh mint leaves, tightly packed
¾ cup raw sugar
½ cup boiling water
¼ cup wine vinegar, or more to taste
Pinch of salt or more to taste

APPLE CHUTNEY

Makes 4 cups.

PREPARATION:

Chutneys can be made at any time. They will keep three to four weeks refrigerated and can be frozen for longer storage.

INSTRUCTIONS:

Wash and cut the apples in wedges. Cut the core away and peel. Put the apples into a saucepan with the water and cook until soft, 10 to 15 minutes.

In the meantime, mix the spices together. Heat the butter in a deep skillet, add the spices; cook them, stirring, for 1 minute. Add the apples and cook them over high heat until the water evaporates. Add the sugar, stir, and cook the mixture over medium-low heat until it becomes jamlike, about 15 minutes. Remove from heat and let it cool completely. Store in airtight containers.

INGREDIENTS:

2½ pounds apples (I prefer green tart apples)
¼ cup water
2 tablespoons butter
1 teaspoon ground cumin
2 teaspoons crushed red pepper, or more for very hot chutney
½ teaspoon nutmeg
¼ teaspoon clove
½ teaspoon turmeric
½ teaspoon ginger
½ teaspoon cinnamon
2 cups brown sugar, firmly packed

FRENCH-STYLE GREEN PEAS

Makes 8 servings.

PREPARATION:

Clean, cut, and measure all ingredients before the trip. Pack them in separate plastic bags and assemble the recipe at the campsite.

INSTRUCTIONS:

Put the peas into a large saucepan with the lettuce, scallions, sugar, bouquet garni, 4 tablespoons of the butter, and the water. Cook for 20 to 25 minutes, until the peas are tender. Keep a large plate with cold water on top of the pan to keep the peas moist.

INGREDIENTS:

8 cups shelled fresh or frozen peas
1 head romaine lettuce, shredded
16 to 20 scallions, cut in 2" pieces
1 tablespoon raw sugar
1 large bouquet garni: thyme, parsley, bay leaf, and mint tied together with a string

Before serving, remove the bouquet garni. Add the remaining butter and the salt, stirring until the butter is melted. You may press one tablespoon butter into one tablespoon flour and add it to the peas, stirring until a creamy sauce coats them.

½ cup unsalted butter
1 cup cold water
Salt to taste
Optional: 1 tablespoon
butter, 1 tablespoon flour

LEMON-BRAISED BABY CARROTS

Makes 8 servings.

PREPARATION:

Clean and scrub the carrots before the trip. If you are using regular carrots instead of baby ones, cut them into oblong lengths. This recipe is very easily assembled at the campsite and requires a very short time to prepare. To save water, fuel, and a saucepan at the campsite, boil the carrots ahead of time.

INSTRUCTIONS:

Cook the carrots in 6 cups of salty boiling water for 12 minutes. Drain them; if you are doing this ahead of time, let them cool completely and pack them in a plastic bag.

A few minutes before serving, heat the butter in a skillet. Add the sugar and the carrots. Cook over low heat for 5 minutes. Add the lemon juice and cook 1 more minute. Sprinkle the parsley on top and serve.

INGREDIENTS:
2 pounds baby or regular
carrots
4 tablespoons unsalted
butter
2 tablespoons raw sugar
¼ cup lemon juice
2 tablespoons chopped
parsley

IDAHO POTATO RYE BREAD

Makes two one-pound loaves.

PREPARATION:

Make the bread any time before using it. Wrap airtight in foil, freeze, and store for a few days to a month.

INGREDIENTS:
1 or 2 Idaho potatoes
2 tablespoons raw sugar
2 tablespoons active dry
yeast

INSTRUCTIONS:

Peel, wash, and cube the potatoes. Put them into salty cold water in a saucepan. Cook them until tender, 15 to 20 minutes. Drain them and reserve 1½ cups of the cooking water. Mash the potato and measure 1 cup. Reserve the rest for another use. Let the potato water cool to 110°F. Pour it into the electric blender bowl. Add the sugar and stir. Sprinkle the yeast on top of the water. Set it aside for 10 minutes.

Blend the mashed potato, egg, and molasses into the yeast. Beat in 2 cups of the unbleached flour. Add the rye flour, walnuts, salt, and fennel seeds. Beat thoroughly with the wire whisk. Change to the dough hook, and knead in the remaining unbleached flour. The dough should be a little sticky but workable. Knead it 10 minutes. Transfer it to an oiled bowl; cover it with a plastic film and let it rise in a warm place 1 hour.

Punch the dough down; form 2 loaves, round or oblong. If you choose to use baking tiles, soak the tiles in water during the bread's first rising. Drain them out of the water and line a baking sheet with them. Sprinkle the tiles with the cornmeal and set the 2 loaves on them for the second rise. If you do not use tiles, place the loaves on greased baking sheets. Let them rise again for 50 to 60 minutes.

Preheat the oven to 375°F., unless you are using the tiles (tiles have to go into a cold oven).

When the loaves are doubled in bulk, slash the tops with a razor blade. Place them in the oven. Turn the thermostat to 375°F. if using the tiles. Bake the loaves about 35 minutes, until they sound hollow when tapped. Cool them on wire racks.

1 large egg
2 tablespoons molasses
3 to 4 cups unbleached flour
3 cups rye flour
¾ cup chopped walnuts
(3 ounces)
1 tablespoon salt
1 teaspoon fennel seeds
1 teaspoon cornmeal

BÛCHE DE NOËL

Makes 1 14-inch-long cake.

PREPARATION:

Some traditions just never die, especially when they taste as good as the French "bûche de Noël," literally, "Christmas log." I don't know how or when the tradition started; all I know is that no family in France can celebrate Christmas without it. For one week before Christmas, numerous log-like cakes adorn every pastry shop window, with various flavors—chocolate, coffee, chestnut—and various decorations—meringue mushrooms, almond paste, holly, fruit, gnomes... After the holidays they disappear like magic, never to be seen again for one year! So go traditions—they let themselves be ignored for a while, but always pop up at the right time, totally predictable and imperishable. For me at home in Idaho, but so far from my native country, one strong tradition like this one is enough to bridge the separation. I have never failed to make my own "bûche" every year. Why not, when it tastes so good? Once a year I become French and decadent with the butter, the sugar, the chocolate... just once a year!

And who said traditions make life easy? Not this one! But if you are really willing and organized, you can enjoy it in a yurt, in the heart of the American national forests. Actually, a log is quite appropriate there. The easiest way to make the bûche is to prepare ahead of time the chocolate roll, the frosting, and the meringue caps and stems for the mushrooms. For the travel on the sled, the chocolate roll is frozen hard, the frosting is stored in a plastic box, and the meringues are in a box, too, well padded with waxed paper. Make sure not to forget the pastry bag with a star tube, size 4.

INGREDIENTS:

THE CHOCOLATE ROLL:

1 tablespoon dry cocoa
6 tablespoons unbleached flour
Pinch of salt
4 large eggs, separated
¼ teaspoon cream of tartar
¾ cup granulated sugar
½ teaspoon vanilla

THE CHOCOLATE BUTTER-CREAM FROSTING:

4 large egg yolks
½ cup granulated sugar
2 cups (16 ounces) unsalted butter
¼ cup very strong coffee
6 ounces semisweet chocolate

THE MERINGUE MUSHROOMS:

2 large egg whites
½ cup granulated sugar
A little cocoa powder

INSTRUCTIONS:

MAKE THE CHOCOLATE ROLL: .
Preheat the oven to 325°F. Grease and flour a 15-by-10-inch

jelly-roll pan. Sift the flour several times with the cocoa and the salt. Beat the egg whites until foamy. Add the cream of tartar and continue beating until stiff peaks form. Gradually beat in half the sugar until the mixture is very glossy and stiff.

In another bowl, beat the yolks until thick. Beat the remaining sugar and the vanilla into the yolks until thick and pale. With a metal spoon, fold the flour mixture into the yolk mixture alternately with the whites until well blended.

Pour the batter into the prepared pan, spreading it evenly. Bake 20 to 25 minutes, until the edges begin to brown. Run a metal spatula around the edges to loosen the cake and turn it over onto a dishcloth or a piece of waxed paper. The dishcloth or waxed paper should be sprinkled with flour to prevent sticking.

Trim the stiff edges of the cake away and roll the cake with the cloth or paper, lengthwise, while still warm. Let it cool completely.

MAKE THE FROSTING:

Cream the butter and reserve. Dissolve the sugar in ½ cup water; bring it to a boil and let it boil until the syrup reaches 230°F. to 234°F. on a candy thermometer.

In the meantime, beat the yolks until thick. As soon as the syrup reaches the proper temperature, pour it gradually on the yolks, beating at high speed; continue beating until the mixture is cool, thick, and light.

Beat the creamed butter into the yolk mixture with the coffee flavoring.

Melt the semisweet chocolate in a double boiler. Beat the cool but liquid chocolate into the butter frosting.

TO FINISH THE CHOCOLATE ROLL:

Unroll the cake and remove the cloth or paper. Spread half the chocolate frosting on the cake, one inch from the edges. Roll the cake again without the cloth or paper. Transfer the rolled cake to a jelly-roll pan and quick-freeze it. When it is hard enough to handle, wrap it in clean waxed paper and then in foil. Seal the ends and place it back in the freezer.

TO MAKE THE MERINGUE MUSHROOMS:

Preheat the oven to 250°F.

Beat the whites until stiff peaks form. Gradually add half

the sugar, continue beating until very stiff and glossy. Fold in the remaining sugar with a metal spoon.

Fit the pastry bag with a plain tube, size 5. Line 2 baking sheets with waxed paper. Fill the pastry bag with the meringue and pipe out "mushroom caps and stems" onto the prepared baking sheets. Vary the sizes. Sprinkle the caps and stems lightly with cocoa powder. Bake them 30 to 40 minutes, until the stems and the cap tops are crisp. Remove the stems from the sheet and let them cool. Turn the caps over and press an indent underneath. Bake them 15 minutes longer until crisp. If the meringues begin to brown, turn the heat down. When the stems and caps are cooled, store them in a box and refrigerate.

TO ASSEMBLE THE CAKE:

At the campsite, unwrap the roll and let it warm up. Keep the frosting in a warm place to soften. Fill with the frosting the pastry bag fitted with a star tube, size 4. Pipe it lengthwise onto the chocolate roll, unevenly, like the bark of a tree. Trim the ends of the cake diagonally. Use the scraps to form stumps along the log.

Assemble the mushrooms. Spread the bottom of the caps with a little chocolate frosting, and gently press a stem into the indent. Place the mushrooms in several clumps on and along the log. Sprinkle some powdered sugar over the log and mushrooms to resemble a fresh sprinkle of snow.

Note: The dehydrated expedition food described in this book is available packaged in portions of 2 or 4 servings, as are many other trail foods and beverages. Please write for a free catalog to THE TREKKING CHEF, P.O. Box 1686, Sun Valley, ID 83353; tel: 208/788-2761.

INDEX

almond(s)
-apricot spread, 64
butter bars, 151
mandel bread, 119
-pistachio couscous, 78
-roasted garlic-cheese spread, 129
soup, 15
Angel Lake trout, 173
anise biscotti, 180
antipasto salad, 96
appetizers and first courses. *See also*
    Dip; Sandwiches; Snacks; Spread
almond-crusted deep-fried Brie
    cheese, 186
cheese puffs, 189
litchi nuts, stuffed, 11
olives, marinated, 52
roquefort-walnut loaf, 160
spinach, leek, tofu, and cheese pie,
    51
vegetable patties
    felafel with nut and garlic sauce,
        75
    potato galettes with herb butter,
        144
    spinach, with tomato sauce, 77
    zucchini, with vegetable sauce,
        76
Apple(s)
-apricot bars, 122
chutney, 192
chutney with tahini spread, 131
-date butter, Moroccan, 177
-date granola, 146
-pear leather, 120
sauce, potato cakes with, 112
apricot(s)
-almond spread, 64
-apple bars, 122
bars, 42
-lentil spread, 130
Moroccan lamb tagine with, 17
-nut bars, 152

baby food, Heinz instant, xvi
backcountry minestrone, 16
baklava, 178
banana-granola bars, 121
barley
-lemon pudding, 150
pressed, xvii
pudding, 79
and turkey casserole, 71
bars
almond butter, 151

apricot, 42
apricot-apple, 122
apricot-nut, 152
banana-granola, 121
buzz, 151
fig, 117
molasses pecan, 152
nutty-rye, 44
protein, 43
rice-bran syrup, 83
tahini-granola, 181
tofu cream, 44
trek, 82
zucchini-carob, 180
basil
pesto, 24
sun-dried salad with fresh, 53
beach greens, 97
bean(s)
chips, 134
garbanzo
    felafel with nut and garlic sauce,
        75
    sopa da panela, 70
    -tahini spread, 66
and tomato soup, Green's, 138
berry(-ies)
-cheese spread, 65
sauce, couscous in, 149
beverages
golden punch, 186
hut-to-hut skiing, 6
biscotti, anise, 180
biscuits, oatmeal, 176
blackberry-cheese spread, 65
blinchiki with blueberry filling, 148
blueberry(-ies)
-buttermilk pancakes, 33
-cheese spread, 65
filling, blinchiki with, 148
-honey sauce, 34
bonbons, date, 179
boreks, chicken, in shredded phyllo
    dough, 18
bread
Finland country, 37
Idaho potato rye, 193
Italian country, 34
miller's, 115
oatmeal panbread, 114
pita, toasted, 38
potato, Idaho braided, 36
sugarless gingerbread, 38
breakfast dishes
almond-pistachio couscous, 78

barley-lemon pudding, 150
barley pudding, 79
blinchiki with blueberry filling,
    148
blueberry-buttermilk pancakes, 33
cornmeal hotcakes, thin, 177
couscous in fruit sauce, 149
cream of wheat pudding, 81
crêpes with gooseberry sauce, 29
egg and cheese puff, 31
granola, 11
    apple date, 146
guryevskaya, 113
kasha pudding, 80
millet porridge with raisins, 147
Moroccan apple-date butter, 177
oatmeal biscuits, 176
oatmeal cream with fruit sauce, 32
oatmeal panbread, 114
oats pudding, 79
pancakes
    about, 126
    blinchiki with blueberry filling,
        148
    blueberry-buttermilk, 33
    buckwheat, 82
    quick, with honey butter, 150
    tofu-lemon, 113
porridge with fruit and nuts, 114
potato cakes with apple sauce, 112
sesame-coconut bulgur, 78
tofu-lemon pancakes, 113
zapekanka with strawberry soup,
    147
Brie cheese, almond-crusted deep-
    fried, 186
broccoli soup, 137
brownies, carob-orange, 116
Bûche de Noël, 195
buckwheat. *See also* Kasha
pancakes, 82
bulgar wheat (cracked wheat), xv
with lamb sauce, 73
pilaf, 110
sesame-coconut, 78
-spinach salad, 167
butter
apple-date, Moroccan, 177
clarified, about, xv
coriander-lime, grilled chicken
    breasts with, 21
herb, potato galettes with, 144
honey, quick pancakes with, 150
buttermilk
-blueberry pancakes, 33

-carrot soup, 98
buzz bars, 151

cabbage slaw, Oriental, 168
cake
  Bûche de Noël, 195
  date-walnut, with rice-bran syrup
    glaze, 39
  orange raisin, 45
  potato hash, 95
  St. James carob, 40
campfire pie, 117
capers, tofu-feta spread with, 131
carob
  cake, St. James, 40
  -orange brownies, 116
  -zucchini bars, 180
carrot(s)
  baby, lemon-braised, 193
  -buttermilk soup, 98
  pickled, 10
casserole
  lentil-rice, 142
  potato-smoked fish, 74
  turkey and barley, 71
cauliflower Stilton soup, 14
cheese
  about, xvii
  berry spread, 65
  Brie, almond-crusted deep-fried,
    186
  cream cheese-Parmesan spread, 8
  and egg puff, 31
  and egg soup (stracciatella), 98
  feta
    -red pepper spread, 10
    -tofu spread with capers, 131
  and fruit sandwiches, grilled, 163
  puffs, 189
  -roasted garlic-almond spread, 129
  and spinach, leek, and tofu pie, 51
cherba: Arabic tomato-mint soup, 69
chestnut soup, cream of, 188
chicken
  boreks in shredded phyllo dough,
    18
  breasts, grilled, with coriander-lime
    butter, 21
  sweet spicy rice pilaf with (zarda),
    72
chips
  bean, 134
  earlier recipes, 133
  shrimp, 133
chocolate cake, Bûche de Noël, 195
chowder, salmon, 101
chutney
  apple, 192
  apple, and tahini spread, 131
  peach, 165

-tofu spread, 66
cinnamon
  fried tortillas with honey and, 118
  milk soup with rice, 140
clarified butter, about, xv
coconut
  rochers congolais, 54
  -sesame bulgur, 78
  winter squash with, 144
cookies
  anise biscotti, 180
  mandel bread, 119
  rochers congolais, 54
coriander
  -curry soup, 136
  green bean soup with, 170
  -lime butter, grilled chicken
    breasts with, 21
corn(meal)
  hotcakes, thin, 177
  patties with red pepper sauce, 145
couscous
  about, xv
  almond-pistachio, 78
  basic method for steaming, 23
  fish baked in foil stuffed with, 104
  in fruit sauce, 149
  guryevskaya, 113
  salad sandwiches, 162
  shrimp curry with, 140
crab
  cakes with horseradish herb sauce,
    93
  poached, with horseradish herb
    sauce, 106
cracked wheat. See Bulgur wheat
cranberry turkey chips, 67
cream cheese-Parmesan spread, 8
cream of rice zapekanka with
  strawberry soup, 147
cream of wheat pudding, 81
crème fraiche, 188
crêpes with gooseberry sauce, 29
croûtes, French onion soup with, 100
croutons, 71
cucumber, wild, 97
curry
  -coriander soup, 136
  shrimp, with couscous, 140

Dahl, sour, with tadka, 136
date
  -apple butter, Moroccan, 177
  -apple granola, 146
  bonbons, 179
  -walnut cake with rice-bran syrup
    glaze, 39
dehydration, xi–xii
dehydrator, xiii

desserts and sweets. See also Bars;
  Cake; Cookies; Pie
  baklava, 178
  date bonbons, 179
  Turkish birds' nests, 41
dill-buttermilk soup, 137
dip
  red pepper, 186
  zucchini-tofu, 166
dressing, lime, fresh fruit salad with,
  167
drying food, xi–xii
duck sandwiches, broiled, 159
duct tape, xiii–xiv

egg(s)
  and cheese puff, 31
  and cheese soup (stracciatella), 98
  freeze-dried, xv
energy spread, 132
English muffins, fish cakes on, 91
English-style mint sauce, 191
equipment, xiii–xiv

felafel with nut and garlic sauce, 75
feta cheese
  -red pepper spread, 10
  -tofu spread with capers, 131
fig bars, 117
Finland Country bread, 37
fish
  à la sétoise, poached, 105
  baked, with lemon sauce, 106
  baked in oil, couscous stuffing, 104
  broiled marinated, 104
  cakes on English muffins, 91
  Navarre, poached, 102
  smoked
    -potato casserole, 74
    spread, 9
    spread, sandwiches, 9
  steaks with tahini sauce on rye, 94
  trout. See Trout
food bars. See Bars
freeze-dried food, about, 125–26
French lemon pie, 53
French onion soup with croûtes, 100
French-style green peas, 192
fruit(s)
  and cheese sandwiches, grilled,
    163
  dried
    salad, stewed, 169
  leather, apple-pear, 120
  porridge with nuts and, 114
  salad, fresh, with lime dressing,
    167
sauce
  couscous in, 149

for grilled fruit and cheese
sandwiches, 163
oatmeal cream with, 32

galettes, potato, with herb butter,
144
garbanzo bean(s)
felafel with nut and garlic sauce,
75
sopa da panela, 70
-tahini spread, 66
garlic
jam, 164
roasted, almond-cheese spread,
129
gingerbread, sugarless, 38
golden punch, 186
gooseberry sauce, crêpes with, 29
granola, 111
apple date, 146
-banana bars, 121
tahini bars, 181
green bean soup with coriander, 170
Green's beans and tomato soup, 138
green pea(s)
French-style, 192
soup, with mint, 12
guryevskaya, 113

halibut steaks with tahini sauce on
rye, 94
ham and onion and mustard spread,
65
harira, 50
herb(s, -ed)
brown rice with, 25
butter, potato galettes with, 144
horseradish sauce
crab cakes with, 93
poached crab with, 106
-lentil soup, 100
stuffed rolled shoulder of lamb,
190
tomato soup, 13
turkey chips, 67
honey
-blueberry sauce, 34
butter, quick pancakes with, 150
flakes, xvi
fried tortillas with cinnamon and,
118
horseradish herb sauce
crab cakes with, 93
poached crab with, 106
hotcakes, cornmeal, thin, 177

Idaho potato braided bread, 36
Indian poached trout, 172
Italian country bread, 34

jam, garlic, 164
jerky, turkey, 68

kasha, xvi
pudding, 80
as side dish, 108
with wild mushrooms, 143
Korean soup, xvi

lamb
herbed stuffed rolled shoulder of,
190
and lentil soup, Moroccan (harira),
50
sauce, bulgur wheat with, 73
tagine with apricots, Moroccan, 17
leather
apple-pear, 120
pumpkin, 121
leek, spinach, tofu, and cheese pie,
51
lemon
-barley pudding, 150
-braised baby carrots, 193
pie, French, 53
sauce, baked fish with, 106
-tarragon veal, 19
-tofu pancakes, 113
lentil(s)
-apricot spread, 130
-herb soup, 100
and lamb soup, Moroccan (harira),
50
red, orange salad, 26
-rice casserole, 142
soup, sour dahl with tadka, 136
lime
-coriander butter, grilled chicken
breasts with, 21
dressing, fresh fruit salad with, 167
linguini
primavera, 141
with vegetables, 110
litchi nuts, stuffed, 11

mandel bread, 119
miller's bread, 115
millet porridge with raisins, 147
minestrone, backcountry, 16
mint
green pea soup with, 12
sauce, English-style, 191
-tomato soup, Arabic (cherba), 69
molasses pecan bars, 152
Moroccan apple-date butter, 177
Moroccan lamb tagine with apricots,
17
mountain sorrel (sourgrass), 97
mushroom(s)

soup, 99
wild, buckwheat kasha with, 143
mustard, ham and onion spread with,
65

nut(s, -ty)
-apricot bars, 152
and garlic sauce, felafel with, 75
litchi, stuffed, 11
porridge with fruit and, 114
-rye bars, 44
Turkish birds' nests, 41
nutrition, xi

oat(meal)
biscuits, 176
cream with fruit sauce, 32
granola, 111
apple date, 146
-banana bars, 121
tahini bars, 181
panbread, 114
porridge with fruit and nuts, 114
pudding, 79
-tomato soup, 69
olive(s)
marinated, 52
spread, green, 166
onion(s)
ham and mustard spread with, 65
soup, French, with croûtes, 100
orange(s)
-carob brownies, 116
raisin cake, 45
red lentil salad, 26
trout, with wild rice, 174
oriental cabbage slaw, 168

pancakes
about, 126
blinchiki with blueberry filling,
148
blueberry-buttermilk, 33
buckwheat, 82
quick, with honey butter, 150
tofu-lemon, 113
parmesan cheese-cream cheese
spread, 8
parsley sauce
for Green's beans and tomato soup,
139
potatoes in, 108
pasta
linguini primavera, 141
linguini with vegetables, 110
spaghetti and zucchini with pesto,
24
pâtè, spinach, 7
sandwiches, 8

patties
  cornmeal, with red pepper sauce, 145
  vegetable
    felafel with nut and garlic sauce, 75
    potato galettes with herb butter, 144
    spinach, with tomato sauce, 77
    zucchini, with vegetable sauce, 76
peach chutney, 165
pear-apple leather, 120
pecan molasses bars, 152
pepper(s), red bell
  dip, 186
  -feta cheese spread, 10
  sauce
    cornmeal patties with, 145
    tofuburgers with, 27
  soup, tomato-, 135
pesto, zucchini and spaghetti with, 24
phyllo dough, chicken boreks in shredded, 18
pickle carrots, 10
pie
  campfire, 117
  lemon, French, 53
  spinach, leek, tofu, and cheese, 51
pilaf
  cracked wheat, 110
  rice, sweet spicy, with chicken (zarda), 72
pistachio-almond couscous, 78
pita bread, toasted, 38
plastic bags with hermetic closures, xiii
porridge
  with fruit and nuts, 114
  millet, with raisins, 147
potato(es)
  braided bread, Idaho, 36
  cakes with apple sauce, 112
  flakes, xvi
  galettes with herb butter, 144
  hash cake, 95
  in parsley sauce, 108
  rye bread, Idaho, 193
  -smoked fish casserole, 74
protein bars, 43
protein powder, instant, xvi
protein spread, 130
pudding
  barley-lemon, 150
  cream of wheat, 81
  kasha, 80
  oats, 79
puffs, cheese, 189

pumpkin leather, 121
punch, golden, 186

raisin(s)
  millet porridge with, 147
  orange cake, 45
raspberry-cheese spread, 65
relishes and condiments
  fresh tomato relish, 164
  garlic jam, 164
  green olive spread, 166
  peach chutney, 165
  pickled carrots, 10
  zucchini-tofu dip, 166
rice
  brown, with herbs, 25
  cinnamon milk soup with, 140
  lentil casserole, 142
  pilaf, sweet spicy, with chicken (zarda), 72
  saffron, 109
  yogurt, 175
rice-bran syrup, xvii
  bars, 83
  glaze, date-walnut cake with, 39
rilletes de saumon, 49
rochers congolais, 54
rolls, shrimp, 20
roquefort-walnut loaf, 160
rye
  bread, Idaho potato, 193
  fish steaks, tahini sauce on, 94
  -nutty bars, 44

saffron rice, 109
St. James carob cake, 40
salad
  antipasto, 96
  cabbage slaw, Oriental, 168
  couscous, sandwiches, 162
  fresh fruit, with lime dressing, 167
  orange red lentil, 26
  seashore, 97
  spinach-bulgur, 167
  stewed dried-fruit, 169
  sun-dried tomato, with fresh basil, 53
salad greens, about, 97
salmon
  chowder, 101
  rillettes de saumon, 49
  sandwiches, 93
  smoked
    -potato casserole, 74
    spread, 132
sandwiches. See also Spread
  broiled duck, 159
  couscous salad, 162

crab cakes with horseradish herb sauce, 93
fish cakes on English muffins, 91
fish steaks, tahini sauce on rye, 94
fruit and cheese, grilled, 163
roquefort-walnut loaf, 160
salmon, 93
shrimp-paste ribbon, 161
smoked fish spread, 9
spinach pâtè, 8
sauce
  blueberry-honey, 34
  fruit
    couscous in, 149
    for grilled fruit and cheese sandwiches, 163
    oatmeal cream with, 32
  gooseberry, crêpes with, 29
  horseradish herb
    crab cakes with, 93
    poached crab with, 106
  lamb, bulgur wheat with, 73
  lemon, baked fish with, 106
  mint, English-style, 191
  nut and garlic, felafel with, 75
  parsley
    for Green's beans and tomato soup, 139
    potatoes in, 108
  red pepper
    cornmeal patties with, 145
    tofuburgers with, 27
  tomato, spinach patties with, 77
  vegetable, zucchini patties with, 76
scurvygrass, about, 97
seal-a-meal machine, xiii
seashore plantain, about, 97
seashore salad, 97
sesame (seed)
  -coconut bulgur, 78
  tahini. See Tahini
shrimp
  chips, 133
  curry with couscous, 140
  -paste ribbon sandwiches, 161
  rolls, 20
smoked salmon spread, 132
snacks. See also Appetizers and first courses
  shrimp chips, 133
  soybeans, toasted, 12
  spiced walnuts, 133
  turkey chips, cranberry, 67
  turkey chips, herbal, 67
  turkey jerky, 68
  typical daily snack allowance, 60–61
sopa da panela, 70

soup
  almond, 15
  beans and tomato, Green's, 138
  broccoli, 137
  buttermilk, -dill
  carrot-buttermilk, 98
  cinnamon milk, with rice, 140
  cream of chestnut, 188
  curry-coriander, 136
  French onion, with croûtes, 100
  green bean, with coriander, 170
  green pea, with mint, 12
  harira (Moroccan lamb and lentil),
      50
  lentil-herb, 100
  minestrone, backcountry, 16
  mushroom, 99
  red pepper-tomato, 135
  salmon chowder, 101
  sopa da panela (garbanzo bean),
      70
  sour dahl with tadka, 136
  Stilton cauliflower, 14
  stracciatella (egg and cheese), 98
  strawberry, zapekanka with, 147
  tomato, herbed, 13
  vegetable, with wild sorrel, 171
sour dahl with todka, 136
sourgrass (mountain sorrel), about,
    97
soybeans, toasted, 12
soy-milk powder, xvii
spaghetti and zucchini with pesto, 24
spiced walnuts, 133
spinach
  -bulgar salad, 167
  and leek, tofu, and cheese pie, 51
  pâté, 7
    sandwiches, 8
  patties with tomato sauce, 77
spread
  apricot-almond, 64
  berry-cheese, 65
  cream cheese-Parmesan, 8
  energy, 132
  feta cheese-red pepper, 10
  green olive, 166
  ham, onion, mustard, 65
  lentil-apricot, 130
  protein, 130
  roasted garlic-almond-cheese, 129
  salmon, rillettes de saumon, 49
  smoked fish, 9
    sandwiches, 9
  smoked salmon, 132
  tahini, with apple chutney, 131
  tahini-garbanzo, 66
  tofu-chutney, 66
  tofu-feta, with capers, 131
squash, winter, with coconut, 144

stevia, xvii
Stilton cauliflower soup, 14
stock, vegetable, instant powder, xvi
stove, xiv
stracciatella: egg and cheese soup, 98
strawberry soup, zapekanka with, 147
sugar, turbinado, xvii
sugarless gingerbread, 38
sun-dried tomato salad with fresh
    basil, 53
syrup. See Rice-bran syrup

tadka, sour dahl with, 136
tahini
  -garbanzo spread, 66
  granola bars, 181
  sauce, fish steaks on rye with, 94
  spread
    with apple chutney, 131
    energy, 132
    protein, 130
tarragon-lemon veal, 19
tempura, wilderness, 175
tofu
  -chutney spread, 66
  cream bars, 44
  -feta spread with capers, 131
  -lemon pancakes, 113
  and spinach, leek, and cheese pie,
    51
  -zucchini dip, 166
tofuburgers with red pepper sauce,
    27
tomato(es)
  relish, fresh, 164
  sauce, spinach patties with, 77
  sun-dried, salad with fresh basil, 53
  soup
    beans and, Green's, 138
    herbed, 13
    mint-, Arabic (cherba), 69
    oats-, 69
    red pepper, 135
tortillas, fried, with honey and
    cinnamon, 118
trek bars, 82
trout
  Angel Lake, 173
  Hemingway, 173
  Indian poached, 172
  orange, with wild rice, 174
  smoked
    -potato casserole, 74
    spread, 9
    spread, sandwiches, 9
turkey
  and barley casserole, 71
  chips
    cranberry, 67
    herbal, 67

jerky, 68
turkish birds' nests, 41

veal, lemon-tarragon, 19
vegetable(s)
  linguini primavera, 141
  linguini with, 110
  patties
    felafel with nut and garlic sauce,
      75
    potato galettes with herb butter,
      144
    spinach, with tomato sauce, 77
    zucchini, with vegetable sauce,
      76
  sauce, zucchini patties with, 76
  soup
    minestrone, backcountry, 16
    with wild sorrel, 171
vegetable-stock powder, instant, xvi

walnut(s)
  -date cake with rice-bran syrup
    glaze, 39
  -roquefort loaf, 160
  spiced, 133
wild rice, orange trout with, 174
wild sorrel, vegetable soup with, 171
wilderness tempura, 175
wintercress, 97

yogurt rice, 175

zapekanka with strawberry soup, 147
Zarda: sweet spicy rice pilaf with
    chicken, 72
zucchini
  -carob bars, 180
  patties with vegetable sauce, 76
  and spaghetti with pesto, 24
  -tofu dip, 166